BREAKTHROUGH TEAMWORK

Outstanding Results Using Structured Teamwork®

DENNIS A. ROMIG, PH.D.
President, Performance Resources, Inc.

Professional Publishing®
Chicago • London • Singapore

◥▛ Times Mirror
M Higher Education Group

Library of Congress Cataloging-in-Publication Data

Romig, Dennis A.
    Breakthrough teamwork : outstanding results using structured
teamwork / Dennis A. Romig.
        p. cm.
    Includes bibliographical references and index.
    ISBN 0-7863-0427-8
    1. Work groups. I. Title.
HD66.R645 1996
658.4′02--dc20   95-49786

Printed in the United States of America
1 2 3 4 5 6 7 8 9 0 QF 3 2 1 0 9 8 7 6

PREFACE

As unbelievable as it may sound, it is possible today for every work group and team to achieve ongoing breakthroughs in performance.

Starting 20 years ago with a summary of 200 teamwork research studies from around the world, I began a quest to find or create a step-by-step methodology that would develop teams to achieve continuous breakthroughs. What I learned from those early studies was both helpful and surprising. Annually I added new studies to the database, which now includes over 1,200 studies. My associates and I applied them in training and consulting with over 400 teams, including teams from Motorola, Texas Instruments, Westinghouse, Amoco, Johnson & Johnson, and other world-class organizations. The major conclusion is: Ordinary people can achieve superhuman feats repeatedly when formed into structured teams.

> **Ordinary people can achieve superhuman feats repeatedly when formed into structured teams.**

As the results from the new studies were built into the training, the teams that received the training and coaching achieved outstanding results—at a faster pace! Along the way, my colleagues and I have had more fun and success than is imaginable. The organizations made tons of money as their teams continually surpassed their own performance records. Five of the organizations—including Texas Instruments, Portugal, and Texas Instruments, Singapore—won national quality awards.

WHY WRITE A BOOK?

Currently there is a huge need in organizations for the breakthroughs that the effective use of teams can provide. Most organizationwide strategic programs such as total quality management and work process reengineering require a foundation of teamwork to be successful. Chapter 1 describes how every management expert agrees on the

need for teamwork to enable the organization to successfully implement any major change. The obstacle until now has been that there
was no clear definition or methodology for how to succeed with teamwork.

The second reason for this book is that many executives and
managers continue to raise fundamental questions about the actual
efficacy of teamwork programs. The questions I am asked most often
are highlighted below.

*Can you prove that teamwork programs directly improve work-group
performance?* Executives and managers ask for research to prove the
business value of teamwork programs because they have personally
experienced so many poor programs. They went to the off-site resort
hotels and played team games and simulations. They did the "trust
fall" and participated in other nonverbal activities they refer to as
"touchy-feely." Managers left these programs shaking their heads,
wondering whether this was the best way there was to improve team
functioning.

Executives and managers may be surprised when they read the
conclusions of teamwork research in Chapters 2 and 3. The concise
summaries of the 1,200 articles in my database reveal both "what
works" and "what does not work." For example, the unstructured
"touchy-feely" activities described above do not lead to better work
performance. On the other hand, team goal setting can help any team
achieve breakthrough results. The summary of the research will also
show that group brainstorming as normally practiced in most organizations today is not very effective. Chapter 6 will present a new type
of brainstorming, supported by research, that increases team creativity and subsequent work results.

*Does any teamwork program consistently achieve significant business
results?* Many executives and managers are skeptical about the usefulness of teamwork programs. They remember being promised that if
they implemented quality circles, a form of team problem solving,
untold improvements would occur. There were similar high hopes for
results from employee involvement, participative management, and
total quality management programs, hopes that were never fully realized. Chapter 4 will present examples of breakthrough teamwork
successes from the most competitive industries in the world: semiconductor, aerospace, oil and gas, and high-technology assembly manufacturing.

You will learn about a team of operators from ABB (Asea Brown
Boveri) that increased its manufacturing productivity from $1 million
of product shipped per month to $2 million; a knowledge team of

petroleum engineers from Amoco that cut its time to forecast remaining oil and gas reserves from 119 person-days to 29 person-days; a test and assembly team from Texas Instruments that reduced its manufacturing cycle time 42 percent on one of the company's major products; and four teams at E-Systems (now a division of Raytheon) that saved their company $2 million in a single year.

What does the word teamwork really mean? Many executives and managers say they have good teamwork now. When I probe and ask them what they mean, they reply to the effect that everyone gets along with one another. The company may be losing millions of dollars due to poor performance, but the people get along with one another. A comprehensive definition and model of breakthrough teamwork are presented in Chapter 5. The definition reveals the potential capability of teams to achieve continuous breakthroughs in performance, not just to get along.

It is easy for a few teams in any organization to achieve creative breakthrough. But how can all of the teams achieve outstanding and ongoing results, all of the time? Part Two of this book describes how you can implement the 10 research-based components of Structured Teamwork® to improve your team's communication, cooperation, coordination, and creative breakthroughs. Chapters 6 through 15 will provide team leaders, members, and facilitators with a constant reference of the key ingredients in developing and sustaining breakthrough teamwork. If you are starting up a new team, read about team mission and goals. If most meetings you attend are a waste of time, learn the latest research and methods for how to have effective and energizing meetings in Chapter 8. If you are on a team that is experiencing conflict, you will benefit from the use of the skills and steps described in Chapter 9. You will see how the 10 teamwork components are interconnected so that as a team increases its proficiency in a new component, there will be greater success with the other components.

How does an executive or manager lead his or her organization to breakthrough? Many executives and managers have a glimpse of the vision of where their organization needs to go to win in the global marketplace. Part Three describes how to link empowerment with Structured Teamwork as the engine to power an organization to reach any strategic goal. Many leaders find themselves at the top of disconnected organizations. Systematic empowerment programs can help an executive bridge the gaps in what currently may be a disconnected organization.

Worldwide, in every industry, there are a few companies that have traveled 5 to 10 years ahead of everyone else on the breakthrough teamwork journey. How can other companies catch up when the leaders show no signs of slowing down? Many companies need to do more than start or revitalize their teamwork program. They need to implement an accelerated methodology that enables their organization to catch up to the leaders swiftly and run with them. The research, results, and methods of Structured Teamwork will assist you and your organization to race with the leaders.

Note to the busy executive: To help you absorb this material more quickly, I have summarized the key elements of this book at the end of each chapter. You will see these elements listed under the heading Breakthrough Points.

Dennis Romig
Austin, Texas
September 1995

ACKNOWLEDGMENTS

I appreciate and gratefully acknowledge the following individuals who assisted me in both creating and describing the breakthroughs presented in this book.

The executives:

Gary Heerssen
José Morais

T. Don Stacy
Bob Watt

The managers:

Ray Gumpert
Jim Oates
Scott Ross

Terry Ross
Stan Wenger
David Willis

The change agents:

Sheri Brainard
Bill Easter
Mike Greig
Mary Frances Henry

Harlan Oelklaus
Dave Olski
Matt Rollins

The researchers:

Deb Acevedo
Steve Beebe
Randy Hirokawa

Carl Larsen
Edwin Locke
Carol Wilson

The editors and reviewers:

Patricia Aguilar
Mark Henry
Keith McGowan
Kathy Olson

Hillary Roberts
Cindy Zigmund
Carrie Sestak
Janet Renard

And thanks to Laurie J. Romig, vice president, consultant, curriculum developer, wife, and sidekick.

CONTENTS

PART ONE

THE QUEST FOR
BREAKTHROUGH
TEAMWORK

1
CHAPTER

All of the Experts Agree: Teamwork Is Necessary

Teamwork is no longer an option. It is essential for growth, even survival. Corporations can't just *say* they're doing teamwork; they must actively use it and promote it to improve performance. But teamwork as we commonly practice it today is not enough. Companies need an organizationwide vehicle that ensures ever-improving, even spectacular, business results.

This book describes how your organization can take teamwork to a new level by using a research-based methodology that promotes spectacular business results on a continuous basis. Many managers and executives think of teamwork as applicable only to short-term projects for small, isolated groups that need a high degree of coordination and close communication. Or even worse, they think of teamwork programs as simply employee relations programs. Skepticism among managers about teamwork and even misunderstanding about the meaning of the word *teamwork* are high.

Recently, I was enjoying the spicy dishes of India at a business lunch with the president of a large organization, whom I will call J.D. He informed me that he did not think his management team needed a teamwork program because everyone got along well. In fact, the group was the best set of individuals who had ever worked for him.

Despite the fact that everyone "got along," J.D. and I were meeting because his organization was losing millions of dollars every month! One of J.D.'s subordinates, who had improved performance 25 percent by taking his division through the Structured Teamwork program, wanted me to persuade J.D. to take his management team through the program. During lunch, J.D. made it clear that he had little interest in teamwork. He was interested, however, in leading his company in either a total quality management or a work reengineering initiative. During a pause in the conversation, I reflected on my experience with total quality management (TQM) and work reengineering efforts.

It has always seemed to me that the TQM movement is not just about quality. Work reengineering initiatives, likewise, are not just about improving business and work processes. Their real objective is to achieve a type of organizational breakthrough where every employee is involved in a coordinated effort to achieve great business results.

Organizational breakthrough is when spectacular business results occur by improving the utilization of the people and resources already in the company. It is taking what is already present—the individuals, the work groups, and the organization—to new heights of accomplishment.

Organizational breakthrough is when spectacular business results occur by improving the utilization of the people and resources already in the company.

Throughout the 1980s and 1990s, company after company initiated one or more management innovations. The most frequently implemented are presented in Figure 1–1. The programs were initiated with high hopes and an almost religious fervor. Executives made the speeches they were told to make. They kicked off the innovation's requisite training programs—all with a sense of hope. Everyone went through overview training and participated on committees, spending inordinate amounts of time on these activities. All too frequently, as the months turned into years and there were little or no improved business results, the committees gradually stopped meeting. Slogans and posters were taken off the walls. No one officially declared the program dead, it just sort of faded away.

F I G U R E 1–1

Management Innovations[1]

Management Innovation	Proponents	Approximate Date the Innovation Became Widespread
Japanese management techniques	William Ouchi Richard Tanner Pascale Anthony Athos Richard Schonberger	1981
Excellent companies	Tom Peters Robert Waterman, Jr.	1983
Total quality management (TQM)	W. Edwards Deming Joseph Juran Phillip Crosby	1986
Customer satisfaction	Tom Peters Nancy Austin Karl Albrecht	1987
Continuous improvement (kaizen)	Kaoru Ishikawa Masaaki Imai Jerry Bowles Joshua Hammond	1988
World class manufacturing	Richard Schonberger	1989
The learning organization	Peter Senge	1991
Work reengineering	Michael Hammer James Champy	1993
Visionary companies	John Kotter James Collins Jerry Porras	1995
?	?	1996 and beyond

The missing ingredient in virtually every unsuccessful case was a comprehensive methodology for rapidly involving the minds and hearts of every employee in the goals and techniques of the management innovation.

The management innovators have stated both in their speeches and writings the absolute necessity of teamwork for the approach to succeed. Figure 1–2 lists some relevant quotes.

FIGURE 1–2

What the Experts Say about Teamwork[2]

Richard Pascale and Anthony G. Athos, *The Art of Japanese Management: Applications for American Executives*	"Matsushita . . . believes that a great many little people, paying attention each day to *how to improve their jobs,* can accomplish more than a whole headquarters full of production engineers and planners."*
Tom Peters and Robert Waterman, Jr., *In Search of Excellence*	"It's also remarkable how effective *team use* in the excellent companies meets, to a tee, the best academic findings about the makeup of effective small groups."*
W. Edwards Deming, quality consultant	"This is a road map here to follow to make the pie bigger. And you can do it! . . . Did you ever stop to think of the power of *teamwork?*"*
Karl Albrecht in *The Only Thing That Matters*	"A spirit of *collective teamwork,* caring about one another, and pride in their contribution will translate into genuine interest in and concern for the needs of the customers."*
Jerry Bowles and Joshua Hammond, *Beyond Quality*	"The new strategy is to *build teams that design and continually improve* the functioning of organizational processes, producing customer satisfaction."*
Richard Schonberger, *World Class Manufacturing*	"World-class manufacturing requires that *everyone help manage* the enterprise, that all employees be involved up to their ears in the pursuit of continual and rapid improvement."*
Peter M. Senge, *The Fifth Discipline*	"Team learning is vital because *teams,* not individuals, are the fundamental learning unit in modern organizations. This is where 'the rubber meets the road'; unless teams can learn, the organization cannot learn."*
Michael Hammer and James Champy, *Reengineering the Corporation*	"People working in a reengineered process are of necessity *empowered.* As process team workers they are both permitted and required to think, interact, use judgment, and make decisions."*
James Collins and Jerry Porras, *Built to Last*	"People . . . have a fundamental need for *connection* with other people, sharing with them the common beliefs and aspirations. More than any time in the past people will demand opearing *autonomy . . .*"*

*Italics added.

The experts know that teamwork is a prerequisite for their innovation to have a pervasive impact. It is clear that teamwork is a powerful factor in each innovation's equation for success, but exactly what type of teamwork is needed? Teamwork has gone through several generations of development since the end of World War II, when management researchers began directing the study of teams and groups to more peaceful objectives.

The knowledge about how people in the workplace apply teamwork can be viewed as five successive waves of thinking and research, as seen in Figure 1–3.

Wave 1   The first wave, prevalent in the 1950s and 1960s, was characterized by the use of teamwork to improve *communication* between people, primarily among the bosses and between the bosses and their subordinates. The goal was to have the communication become more open, honest, and two-way. During Wave 1, companies would typically kick off their teamwork programs by holding training sessions away from work at a luxury hotel or resort. Favorite locations included ocean or lake vistas and offered access to golf or tennis. The assumption was that managers and workers might be more open in their communication if they played together away from the pressure-cooker work environment. This approach to team building was often called sensitivity training because one key goal of the event was to have participants become more aware of their own feelings as well as those of the people they worked with. To get people to be more open, teamwork facilitators asked them at the start of a workshop to talk about hobbies and nonwork interests. Gradually the topics became

FIGURE 1–3

Five Waves of Teamwork Approaches

Wave 1:	Openness in communication is promoted.	1950s–1960s
Wave 2:	Cooperation and group dynamics are studied.	1960s
Wave 3:	Quality circles and participative management are implemented.	1980s
Wave 4:	Self-managed work teams proliferate.	1990s
Wave 5:	Continuous breakthrough is the ultimate aim.	1996 and beyond

more focused on the relationships and communication between the individuals at the workshop.

The Wave 1 programs increased openness and sensitivity in communication. There was, however, no significant improvement in the teams' work performance. Open communication, while useful, is not enough by itself to achieve breakthrough teamwork.

Wave 2   Teamwork programs in Wave 2, for the most part, concentrated on improving group dynamics through improved *cooperation* among people who worked together. Group cohesion, support, and esprit de corps were the primary attributes investigated and proposed in the 1960s and 1970s. The emphasis was on improving individuals' willingness to help one another. If one worker had too much to do or had a problem, other workers came to the rescue.

> **It is easier for people to learn how to play together than for people to learn how to work together to achieve breakthrough results.**

In Wave 2, researchers studied groups seeking to understand the skills that promote group cohesion and cooperation. Once again, the teamwork programs were conducted off-site in resort locations. Work simulations and recreation were emphasized, resulting in the creation of improved and more positive group dynamics. Unfortunately, the improvements did not transfer back to improve work performance. The major conclusion from the results of the first two waves is this: It is easier for people to learn how to play together than for people to learn how to work together to achieve breakthrough results.

Wave 3   The third wave of teamwork approaches emerged in the 1980s with a focus on quality circles and participative management. Quality circles as a teamwork method came from successful Japanese companies that had significantly improved the quality of their products and services, resulting in dominant positions in the automobile and electronics industries. American executives and managers who traveled to Japan learned about quality circles and wanted to apply them in their U.S. companies.

During their visits, the Americans asked the Japanese industrial leaders how they had thought of putting their workers into teams to solve what were normally considered management issues. The Japanese described how, when they came over to the United States after World War II to study American industrial productivity, they were surprised by something they saw in the corporate boardrooms. During executive and management committee meetings, the president of the company would ask the viewpoints of the other executives around the conference table before a decision was made. Initially, the Japanese observers were incredulous. In their companies, the top man always made the decision and everyone was expected to obey.

The Japanese managers took the idea of participative management in the boardroom and applied it to the shop floor. That is how quality circles were born. Following the participative management and quality improvement methods of W. Edwards Deming and Joseph Juran, the Japanese executives and managers began the economic miracle.

The quality circle and participative management movement was a major shift to driving the study and use of group dynamics into the heart of the work system itself. No longer was the emphasis only on teamwork as a "feel-good" program for employees. It became not only legitimate but also desirable to discover how to channel group dynamics into achieving improved work results. But quality circles achieved mixed results almost from the beginning of their use in the United States. A major obstacle to their success was the managers' and workers' perception that being pulled away from work to go to a meeting room to solve a problem was a waste of time because it was not related to getting the real work done. The reasons for this perception are valid. How to overcome this obstacle will be presented in the following chapters on empowerment.

None of the first three waves of teamwork approaches, either alone or combined, have been sufficient to carry teams and organizations where they want and need to go—to breakthrough. Many managers are frustrated and confused about teamwork because of the unfulfilled promises of the first three waves. They hear rumors and read isolated reports of spectacular business results from teams and wonder how it can be.

Wave 4 The teams that are achieving great business results are a part of the fourth wave, self-managed or self-directed work teams. This approach has the greatest potential for business impact because the team and group dynamics are structured around the work and work systems. However, some businesses are not achieving the anticipated business and work-performance improvements. From the research, I have summarized success factors of teams over the last 20 years. I know why teams are failing, and I have developed a step-by-step process that allows teams to succeed consistently. The process is called Structured Teamwork.

Working on the frontiers of Wave 4 with some of the best executives, managers, and organizational development consultants, I see teams already operating at the Wave 5 level. While Wave 4 teams achieve breakthroughs in work improvement, they usually only sustain that performance for a year or two. The Wave 4 teams are the ones that occur in isolated fashion, with one or two teams within an organization, or one manufacturing site or product-line division. These teams are unfortunately limited in their sustainability. Consequently, most experts concur that the usefulness of teams is limited to small groups working together for short periods of time.

Wave 5   Wave 5 teams produce *continuous breakthroughs*. An analogy is Chuck Yeager's breaking through the sound barrier in the X-1 plane. After Yeager and his plane exceeded the speed of sound, he and other pilots pushed the limits, continually beating previous speed records. Continuous breakthrough teamwork transcends the limitations of Wave 4. Wave 5 teams can achieve breakthroughs year after year.

You will discover how continuous breakthrough teams sustain and increase the competitive advantage of their companies. The creation of new and superior products and services was once sufficient to maintain a competitive advantage. In the emerging global business environment, characterized by nearly instantaneous communication, companies can quickly lose the normal competitive advantages that the creation of new products and services used to confer. Wave 5 teamwork will be absolutely essential for the business conditions of the 21st century.

STRUCTURED TEAMWORK: THE CORE OPERATING SYSTEM FOR ANY ORGANIZATIONAL BREAKTHROUGH INITIATIVE

Back at the Indian restaurant with J.D., my challenge was to determine how to merge his vision of what he wanted through a work reengineering or total quality initiative with the required teamwork infrastructure to enable results to occur. J.D. had said his own team of subordinates was a good team because they got along with one another. I decided to walk him through the five waves of teamwork and have him evaluate his own management team against the five waves. I first asked him to assess the *communication* of his subordinates with him and with one another. He replied that the communication was OK. I then asked him to rate how well they *cooperated* with one another—did they share money and people across their divisions to help each other? He laughed as he said, "No way!" How about their coordination when there was a companywide strategic goal? Did the vice presidents work together to have each of their divisions implement key strategies and actions in a coordinated fashion? He answered that there was coordination among some but clearly not all of them.

Next, what creative breakthroughs had his subordinates come up with to enhance the overall performance of the organization? At this, the president leaned forward and asked me to describe what I meant. He wanted to know how to achieve the type of teamwork that results in creative breakthroughs. After I explained the fifth wave of teamwork, *continuous breakthroughs*, the president asked me to come and present this model of teamwork to his staff and work with them to achieve it. J.D. and his management team used Structured Teamwork with work reengineering to achieve profitable results.

Implementing Wave 5 teamwork is not easy; it requires behavioral change and organizational development. As we all know, changing human behavior is a challenge, whether we are trying to start a physical exercise program or maintain a diet. This book combines the knowledge gained from years of research and hands-on experience with over 400 teams. Engineers and scientists who are the core of the high-technology companies appreciate the research-based teamwork model. Leaders are looking for the best approach to sustaining the growth and health of their organizations.

The Structured Teamwork methodology presented in this book systematically and consistently develops work groups and individuals into breakthrough teams by providing training in key team skills. Bob Watt, managing director of Phycom, a managed care software firm in Seattle, views Structured Teamwork as the core operating system for any company hoping to achieve organizational breakthrough with any strategic initiative. The various initiatives, like work reengineering and total quality management, are like the application software running on a personal computer. They require the "operating system" of Structured Teamwork to provide the internal infrastructure

FIGURE 1–4

Structured Teamwork: The Core Operating System for Organizational Breakthrough

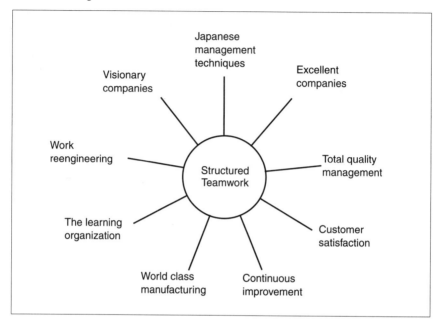

of employee involvement, creativity, team skills, and rapid implementation (see Fig. 1–4).

Too many executives have spent their careers climbing to the tops of their organizations only to look down from the lofty heights and see the pyramid below crumbling to pieces. The pace of business today is so fast that all managers must constantly justify their license to operate. Leaders of companies at all levels are seeking organizational breakthrough. There is no real choice; today's competitive levels force leaders either to pursue organizational breakthrough or to face organizational breakdown and breakup.

BREAKTHROUGH POINTS

- Managers at all levels want organizational breakthrough.
- Leaders of management innovations emphasize the importance of teamwork in achieving organizational breakthrough.

- Since 1950, five waves of teamwork approaches have swept through management development: openness in communication, cooperation and group dynamics, quality circles and participative management, self-managed work teams, and continuous breakthrough.
- Structured Teamwork is the core operating system for successful management innovations.

2

CHAPTER

Teamwork Research and Other Exciting Topics

WHEN WE START TALKING ABOUT RESEARCH I MUST GET PERSONAL

"Teamwork programs are a waste of time." You'll never guess who made that statement. Several years ago, one of my consulting clients was a brilliant training director responsible for many organizations across the state of Washington. She was responsible for one organization that had so much conflict between the different managers and their functions that organizational performance was decreasing. My client stated that she wanted a teamwork program first for the managers and then for the employees. My instant reply was, "Teamwork programs are a waste of time."

The client said that she knew I base all of my firm's training and consulting on research summaries of "what works." Her organization would pay my firm to find and summarize the existing research on teamwork. If the research showed that teamwork was not effective, as I thought it would, I would not have to do the project. On the other hand, if teamwork was found to be effective in improving organizational results, I had to agree to develop and conduct a teamwork training program for her organization.

In the time available, I located 200 studies on teamwork. Their results, however, were contradictory. Some studies proved that teamwork was effective. Others said it was a waste of time. Discouraged, I told myself, "This is why business professionals do not like management research. It's impossible to prove anything!"

I then took a step I had found useful in previous summaries of management research. I examined the quality of the research methodology itself. Practically anything can be proved by a management study that uses paper-and-pencil attitude survey changes as the major outcome variable to indicate success. Most new management methods that obtain success as measured by paper-and-pencil attitude survey results do *not* always obtain corresponding improvements in actual work performance. For example, studies have indicated that piping music into a work area improves employee attitudes as measured by paper-and-pencil tests. However, the research on music in the workplace and work performance as measured by actual work results shows that piping in music causes no overall significant improvement in worker performance.[1]

Studies that measure actual performance improvements can usually be repeated in new settings, and the same conclusions can be drawn. Consequently, the first characteristic of good research in the workplace is that it measures behavior and performance, not just attitudes. This point is very important to a research-oriented person like me, but it is even more important to the average business leader who is trying to improve his or her bottom line!

The second characteristic of well-executed research is the presence of a control group or comparison group. In control-group research, an organization or work group similar to the one receiving the experimental approach is selected and does not receive the method being studied. The purpose of the control group comparison is to ensure that the improved work results are actually due to the new management method and not to changes in the economy or business conditions. After completion of the study, the control group's work results are compared to those of the group receiving the teamwork program. If we find a statistically significant difference between the results of the two groups, then we know the program or method is effective. Many management innovations *fail* to achieve positive results when measured against control groups.

One last characteristic of good applied research is that it is conducted within business organizations using managers and employees versus university settings using only college students. Although college-student studies can be useful, they offer only brief simulations of work compared to the pressure-packed workplace where one's paycheck is always at risk.

The most powerful research meets all three criteria: it is conducted in a real business organization with a matched comparison group using improved work behaviors and performance as the outcome measures. I call such research a *hard-data study*. When I used these criteria to cull the hard-data teamwork studies from the 200 conflicting research studies for my Washington client, I was startled by the results.

TEAMWORK IN BUSINESS AND INDUSTRY GETS GREAT RESULTS! SOMETIMES

The word *sometimes* tells the whole story. In the studies involving teamwork programs, positive business results occurred based on the specific ingredients and methods used in the program. Some teamwork programs, like sensitivity training, almost always had no business impact. If the teamwork program was directed only toward helping employees or managers get along, or toward improving communication, or toward reducing conflict, there was usually no improvement in business results. If, on the other hand, the program emphasized ways the team could structure how work goals would be reached or how work problems would be solved, business results improved. *When the teamwork approach promoted employee participation in work-goal setting, goal measurement, work methods improvement, or problem solving, there were successful business results!* There was increased productivity. Group and individual work performance increased. In some cases, the costs of doing business were significantly reduced.

One of the early control-group studies I found examined whether involving employees in setting their own work goals would improve productivity.[2] The goal-setting experiment was conducted at a large midwestern U.S. clothing factory. One work group in the factory was given one hour of goal-setting training, which included the group setting its first week's work goals. The group had a half-hour weekly team meeting to review the past week's performance and to set the next week's goals. Productivity improved an average of 11 percent per week. The control group was from a similar work area. To ensure that the results were due to team goal setting and not just to getting management attention and time to meet as a group, the control group participated in planned weekly discussions. The control group's productivity increased only 1 percent. The difference of 11 percent versus 1 percent was statistically significant.

Another series of studies was done on the attribute of group or team cohesiveness. Group cohesiveness was defined as team members supporting one another and the team itself. That sounds like a good attribute for a team to have. Unfortunately, the studies found conflicting results in the relationship between group cohesiveness and team productivity and performance. Group cohesiveness did not always make a positive difference. *Group cohesiveness made a difference in performance only when the cohesiveness was focused on work production.*

> **Teamwork programs that focused solely on improving how people got along with one another at work did not significantly improve work performance.**

In addition, several hard-data studies found that workshops that focused primarily on interpersonal experiences and resembled group counseling did not consistently increase productivity in the workplace.[3] These findings lead to the second major conclusion of the research summary: Teamwork programs that focused solely on improving how people got along with one another at work did not significantly improve work performance.

I was amazed. My personal prejudices against teamwork were based on my perception that teamwork was primarily an employee "feel-good" program of interpersonal rah-rah cheerleader pep talks. Here the research showed that my prejudices were well founded. However, while "feel-good" programs didn't work, significant business improvements could be had if the teamwork program drove right into the heart of how the work is planned, managed, and performed.

Since many of the teamwork success stories reported in business publications are from manufacturing, there is a belief that implementing teams makes sense only in factories. However, the clothing-factory study reported above also examined the value of team goal setting with office workers. The programs for the office goal-setting work group and office control group were exactly the same as those for the factory groups. While the control group obtained approximately a 4 percent improvement in productivity just from the weekly discussion groups, the team goal-setting group had about a 24 percent increase! Goal-setting training and weekly use of goal setting and goal performance review improved the productivity of office workers as well as factory workers. Teamwork programs are just as relevant for office and white-collar workers as for shop and manufacturing workers.

By incorporating the conclusions of the hard-data research studies, my associates and I developed a teamwork training program for our Washington client that improved the cooperation and, more important, actual work performance in her organization.

HARD-DATA STUDIES: WHO CARES ANYWAY?

There is a lot that can be written about teams, teamwork, and the breakthrough organization, but what is vitally important is knowing how teams do real work to obtain great results. What can be learned that will guide team development and the development of the organization so that every team gets great results every time? Teamwork is composed of two words: *team* and *work*. To examine the work part, I reviewed research on business, quality, and industrial engineering. To consider the team aspect, I decided to learn from studies drawn from a broad array of disciplines:

- Management.
- Social psychology.
- Communication.
- Organizational development.
- Sociology.
- Education and adult learning.

Taking the best teamwork and breakthrough teamwork research from around the world and combining the findings into a systematic methodology produced an incredible resource any organization can use to achieve rapid breakthrough teamwork.

Visionary leaders believe in teamwork and participative leadership as ways to get increased employee commitment. However, adding a research-based road map to the visionary leader's commitment shortens the journey between the leader's passionate beliefs and actual breakthrough teamwork.

Skeptical managers are encouraged as they discover the research base of teamwork because it confirms commonsense beliefs about teamwork. Managers are relieved to discover that research does not support emphasizing extensive explorations of personal feelings about co-workers. They are pleasantly surprised to discover that work teams can achieve positive and sometimes dramatic improvements by properly using team goal setting and team problem solving.

HOW BREAKTHROUGH TEAMWORK RESEARCH HELPED COMPANIES AND WHAT I LEARNED ALONG THE WAY

I have successfully used summaries of research to resolve conflicts between leaders, managers, and workers at Johnson & Johnson, Monsanto, Rolm Corporation, Hayworth Manufacturing, Amoco, Advanced Micro Devices, Texas Instruments, and others. The following examples show how breakthrough teamwork research helped companies and what I learned along the way.

Motorola

In 1981, Motorola's management trainers were in trouble. Motorola's visionary leader, CEO Bob Galvin, had mandated a new strategic program, the Participative Management Program (PMP), which emphasized improving teamwork between the workers and the managers. The first training course, called PMP Perspectives, was an introduction of the new program to all of Motorola's managers and supervisors. In the course, Galvin communicated on videotape why he thought the program was necessary for Motorola's future.

Unfortunately, most of the managers and supervisors in the training classes were skeptical and even angry about embarking on a program that would give workers a bigger role in the areas they managed. They took out their antagonism on the management trainers, demanding some proof that the new approach would be good for business and that it was not just a warm-and-fuzzy, feel-good activity. The management trainers were caught in the middle. They were loyal to Bob Galvin and his new approach, but they did not know how to answer the questions of the supervisors and managers, most of whom were engineers and scientists.

Dave Olski, the manager of training at Motorola's Austin, Texas, site, and Dave Willis, a lead trainer, were especially concerned because instead of the PMP Perspectives course winning support from the managers, it was creating opposition. They found out about my hard-data research summary of teamwork and participative management. They convinced the PMP course managers in Motorola's headquarters to contract with me to update the research and build it into the Motorola PMP courses. The research summary that was produced predicted that PMP would succeed if the following conditions were met:

1. Employees helped set the business and work goals they were responsible for achieving.
2. Work goals were strategic, reach-out (challenging but not impossible), specific, time based, and measurable.
3. Employees helped develop how the goals would be measured and were involved in collecting and communicating goal measurement data.
4. Employees who actually achieved measurable, significant business improvements were recognized and rewarded.
5. Employees and their manager or supervisor had regularly scheduled and well-executed team meetings.

How did the teamwork research help Motorola? In Phoenix, the Corporate PMP Planning Committee, made up of top managers from throughout Motorola, held a major planning meeting. The first few agenda items dealt with identifying the desired organizational and behavior changes in Motorola that PMP should attempt to achieve. Total chaos and conflict emerged as the managers discussed their different opinions. Strong feelings were expressed and, in the heat of the battle, the committee's own teamwork was severely strained. They were going nowhere. The desired breakthrough teamwork seemed unlikely.

The group was sufficiently aroused when my agenda item was reached. I began simply: "If it is improved business results that you want, here is a summary of what several hundred research studies say. . . " The conclusions listed above, plus others, were presented. The level of positive enthusiasm jumped off the scale as committee members reacted and asked follow-up questions right and left. The committee began to quickly identify what PMP's priorities should be and how to implement them. As a result, the managers felt powerful, confident, and united in their direction. The research conclusions helped to create consensus where there had been conflict. Factual data provided a foundation for resolving differences.

As the new PMP courses that incorporated the research were taught, there was increased support from the participants. Sometimes it was reluctant support until the manager actually tried the new teamwork and participative management skills. Then the positive business results of his or her team sold the manager. Motorola's management trainers loved it! The training was more fun. People acquired new skills and attitudes. The trainers formed many valuable friendships as the managers took the new skills to heart and sincerely tried to improve the working culture and how everyone was treated. Of course there were still problems, but the trainers, as concerned change agents, were now viewed as credible resources to coach the change.

Westinghouse

A vice president of the Westinghouse Defense Company, Ed Silcott, had a vision for the new electronic defense plant in College Station, Texas. He wanted it to be state of the art in the use of computers and robotics. He also wanted it to be state of the art in terms of organizational culture. A committee of four that included Scott Ross as the human resources representative visited model manufacturing plants all over the United States. The vice president and the committee decided that the new organization's culture would be centered on the use of self-managed teams and sociotechnical job design. Sociotechnical job design is based on observations of highly productive coal-mining operations in England where workers' social needs for involvement in planning the work, communicating results, and solving problems are allowed to overlap with the technical requirements of the work. Sociotechnical job design methods are necessary to achieve self-managed work teams. As this major element of the organization's vision was put in place, the plant was constructed, and managers from Westinghouse's major division in Baltimore were relocated to Texas.

The management team of the new Electronics Component Plant hired and trained the initial group of employees. Although the start-up was proceeding smoothly, there were many conflicts and questions in the management team about whether the team's vision of self-managed teamwork would truly lead to good business results. About this time, reports that did not look favorable were coming in from numerous companies that had tried some form of self-managed teamwork. Some locations, after achieving initial success, were having negative results, while other locations were spending three to four years in designing and planning activities and not getting any of the desired business results. The Westinghouse management team felt that it was spinning its wheels and likewise did not know what the goals of self-managed teams were or how to get them.

I was invited to present the teamwork research summary to the managers. Initially, it was like being the focus of a press conference surrounded by hostile reporters. The questions they asked were, however, challenging and thoughtful. Gradually, the tension eased as my research-based answers confirmed their personal experiences so far. The new conclusions I shared, based on my research updates, included the following:

- Team members must receive training in interpersonal skills and conflict management training for team meetings to be productive.
- In a team-based organization, there is more, not less, conflict.
- Team meetings must have desired outcomes, agendas, structured participation, and meeting minutes.

The managers were frustrated, partly because teams were allowed to have team meetings but little was accomplished in them. They shared with me the way their teams were organized. The Westinghouse self-managed work teams were coordinated by team advisors, who did a few of the functions that supervisors do in traditional organizations. But for the most part, the team advisors were supposed to facilitate the team as it managed many of the supervisory tasks. One team meeting I observed was totally dysfunctional. Various problems were discussed, but at the end of each discussion the team always delegated the work and action items to the team advisor. Members of the team took no ownership of their team problems or solutions. The team members expected their team advisor to do all of the work. This situation was a clear example of "reverse empowerment" or reverse delegation. The team meetings weren't producing great business results, and the team members were becoming less responsible for their work, not more!

Another major problem was dealing with the high amount of conflict among the team members themselves and between the teams and their team advisors. The management team had anticipated less conflict in their more empowered culture. They were shocked to find the opposite. When employees bring their "hearts and minds" to work, they naturally have strong feelings about their ideas. When their ideas clash with those of others, and with the way work processes have always been done, conflict results. The conflict itself is not the real problem. The real problem is that most organizations that implement self-managed work teams do not explicitly teach managers and team members conflict management skills. The healthy new conflict is therefore poorly managed, and not only are the results hard on the people involved, but the business also suffers, sometimes dramatically. At Westinghouse, where methods of dealing with conflict were not incorporated into the training program, the conflict was destructive rather than creative.

The research gave direction to the management team on how to use self-managed teams and how to solve major implementation problems. Research-based training programs were developed and provided to the managers, team advisors, and team members. The Westinghouse Electronics Component Plant went on to be a model plant in terms of performance and teamwork. The organization documented $30 million in hard-dollar cost savings in its first two years due to a combination of its flexible team-based manufacturing system, integrated computer systems, and material distribution system. Managers and key contributors were frequently invited to present the Westinghouse success story at major self-managed teamwork and organizational development national conferences.

Scott Ross went on to become the human resources manager at another Westinghouse manufacturing facility that initiated innovative teamwork approaches. The research-based teamwork has allowed the Westinghouse Electronics Components Plant to continue to experience productivity and performance improvements even after the promotions of numerous plant managers and the exit of other key managers. Some organizational development theorists write that major cultural changes disintegrate when the charismatic leader who initiated the cultural change leaves the organization. This experience, however, exemplifies how a research-based cultural change can sustain itself, even with the loss of the visionary leader.

An Industrial Glass Manufacturer

It's not only managers who create the opportunity to achieve breakthrough performance. Sometimes it's the workers themselves. Increasingly, union leaders are helping to push for real changes. That was the case at a large industrial manufacturer of glass for skyscrapers and other large buildings in New York. Employees of industrial companies in New York are represented by active labor unions. Labor unions at different companies sometimes actively resist teamwork and other participative management programs, often for the valid reason that management has not appropriately involved the local union leadership.

The union committee at the industrial glass manufacturer, however, was flat-out scared. They saw plant after plant going out of business in New York. The committee members then began reading about and hearing of the organizational and business breakthroughs of companies that were using self-managed teams. They thought that if something like self-managed teamwork was implemented, the ensuing improvement in business results would save their plant. The union leaders had heard of the success that my colleague Bill Easter and I had achieved at Westinghouse and at a Johnson & Johnson plant in Round Rock, Texas. At the first dinner meeting with the union and management, some of the key managers expressed their opposition to self-managed teams at their company. The agenda for the next day was revised to allow me to present research on how an effective teamwork project could be implemented that would achieve improvements in two areas in which the plant desperately needed to improve: (1) reducing scrap and rework and (2) increasing productivity.

My presentation of the research created a lively but thoughtful debate. At the conclusion, not only was there an agreement to begin teamwork, but the managers enthusiastically supported the change effort from that point on. The research summary included all of the key conclusions presented earlier in this chapter, plus some new research about breakthrough teamwork. These conclusions resulted from a special review I did of all the hard-data studies that could be found in the areas of organizational development and organizational consulting. The three most important findings applied to the industrial glass manufacturer were the following:

1. Employee participation in job redesign and work process improvement significantly improves performance.
2. Successful organizational change begins with significant results in one or two pilot areas.
3. Frequent communication across all levels of the organization accelerates effective change.

Much research had been done worldwide on job redesign, job enrichment, and quality of work life. Most of the research examined the effects of changing what work was done, how the work was done, the facilities, and other conditions under which the work was performed. The bottom-line finding: When workers themselves are involved in the job redesign, there will be significant and consistent improvements in both business results and work performance.

Some managers do not like using pilots or small test cases for major changes. They want to change the whole organization at once on the assumption that implementing the change in one or two areas only slows down breakthrough teamwork. Actually, using small test cases speeds up change because most people will agree to and start pilots in $1/2$ to $1/12$ the time it takes to plan and get approval for a major organizational change! Organizations often spend 12 to 18 months planning a major organizational change, because managers want to overplan to prevent any possible problem from occurring. Pilot teams can start in Month 3, and a major organizational change can be implemented in Month 6. Quickly moving to pilots allows everyone to identify and resolve any real problems while they are small and isolated.

At the industrial glass manufacturer, the two work areas most in need of business improvements were selected as pilot areas. A job redesign team that included workers from the job area itself was established for each pilot. The combined commitment of the managers and the labor leaders helped the teams achieve major reductions in scrap and the cost of production within the first 12 months. Whereas the company's survival had previously been in jeopardy, the teams' achievements built a foundation for financial success.

Management research, especially summaries of hard-data studies, can provide direction for successful implementation of employee involvement, teamwork, and self-managed teams. Chapter 3 reveals how the Structured Teamwork methodology was developed and what key research-based findings serve as its foundation.

BREAKTHROUGH POINTS

- In order to evaluate what does and does not work in teamwork, good research must (1) measure behavior and performance, not just attitudes; (2) use a control group; and (3) be conducted within business organizations using managers and employees.

- Research indicates that teamwork generates great results, *sometimes*.

- Teamwork programs that focus solely on improving interpersonal relations fail to significantly improve work performance.

- Successful business results have been generated by teamwork approaches that promote employee participation in work goal setting, goal measurement, work process improvement, or problem solving.

- For team meetings to be productive, team members must receive training in interpersonal skills and conflict management.
- Team-based organizations have more, not less, conflict.
- Employee participation in job redesign and work process improvement significantly improves performance.
- Successful organizational change begins with significant results in one or two pilot programs.

3

CHAPTER

Discovering a Methodology for Consistent Breakthrough

As research on teamwork and organizational development was synthesized, a key conclusion emerged: Goal setting and goal measurement are the foundation of successful teamwork. Team goal setting and goal measurement consistently improve work-group performance. Other teamwork components are much more likely to produce good results when combined with team goal setting and goal measuring than when they are used alone.

> **Goal setting and goal measurement are the foundation of successful teamwork.**

Team goal setting creates the context and purpose for improving team communication, team meetings, team conflict management, and all of the other aspects of teamwork. My colleague Terry Ross observed, "There can be no team unless they have goals." Without the group members establishing their own work goals, team participants can legitimately ask, "Teamwork for what purpose?" Having the team learn how to set and measure important work goals drives teamwork into the heart of the work system.

Goal setting by itself, however, is not as powerful as when it is combined with other teamwork components. One study found that when goal setting was used along with other teamwork components, there was a 40 percent improvement in work performance beyond what was achieved with goal setting alone![1]

My review of the hard-data studies on breakthrough teamwork indicated that, in addition to team goal setting and goal measurement, the following nine components significantly improved the performance of teams:[2]

- Team creativity skills.
- Effective team communication.
- Effective team meetings.
- High-quality conflict management skills.
- Team mission setting.
- Clear team roles and responsibilities.
- Effective team problem-solving skills.
- Effective team decision-making skills.
- Continuous work process improvement skills.

Each of the above components, when combined with one or two of the other components, especially goal setting and goal measurement, achieved significant business results.

Often, after I had presented this research summary, clients who were implementing teamwork reported that their teams took too long to make decisions. I would ask them if the team had received explicit training on how to make decisions. The answer was uniformly *no*. The same result occurred with problem solving and conflict management. Teams were trying to solve problems, but were wasting a lot of time. The organizations were seldom, if ever, providing explicit team training and development in the team components that research said would help.

In the absence of explicit training, teams were developing mission statements but were taking 8 to 12 hours to do it. Contrast this with the two to three hours it takes teams that have been trained in how to develop mission statements. Once again, organizations were not providing teams with any specific process to develop the mission nor with any information on how that team mission fit in with the other aspects of being a good team. The results they were achieving were sometimes solid, but there were gross inconsistencies. I was alarmed at the amount of time and money I saw being wasted. It didn't take much thought to figure out that if these widespread gaps in team competencies were filled, great results would happen.

The obvious answer was to combine all 10 teamwork components, including team goal setting, into a systematic but flexible road map for training and developing a breakthrough team in a collapsed or reduced time interval. Research indicated that when teams used three or four of the components, there were significant positive results. Adding more weight to the combined approach was J. M. Nicholas's excellent review of 65 organizational development studies.[3] Nicholas concluded that the most effective organizational development approach included a team-building program that provided training in goal setting, decision making, and job redesign. Team building was defined as improving team problem solving and group effectiveness in the workplace. Using a combination package to develop breakthrough teams was clearly the most powerful way to put organizations in a position to achieve breakthrough results.

The following important conclusion should, from this point forward, guide team development programs: Team development for breakthrough teamwork is a methodology, not an event! Up to this time, the majority of teamwork programs were one-shot team-building events. Usually a work group was taken off-site, to a hotel or a resort. The event was kicked off with a few introductory games or activities. The top-ranking manager gave a short speech on the importance of teamwork. There was a little focused work on one or two of the teamwork components listed earlier. The content usually had no explicit connection back to the workplace. The afternoon and evening were filled with recreational activities. The program ended and everyone went home. Any improvement in productivity would last only a short time.

Team development for breakthrough teamwork is a methodology, not an event!

The research indicated that a different approach—one that was systematic and comprehensive—would be more effective and long lasting. Since the studies showed that individual teamwork components could achieve some improvements with some work groups, why not combine the best of all of the components so that *great* improvements could occur with *all* work groups?

Over the years, I have learned that this process works best when it begins with a full and careful assessment of a team's current level of functioning in each of the 10 major teamwork components. The assessment not only helps the leader develop a plan for helping the team members learn the skills they need but also provides a baseline for the team to measure its own progress.

Each of the elements of the process should be introduced gradually so that team members internalize them by daily use as they perform their work tasks. Generally, teams benefit the most from receiving training in all 10 elements, since teams need all 10 skills to maximize their potential for achieving breakthrough results. Figure 3-1 summarizes the benefits of each component.

I was enthusiastic about the potential that these 10 components, linked together, could have in team development. However, the research review also revealed a disturbing pattern. Just spending time on, for example, team communication did not in and of itself improve a team's work results. The situation was similar to the problem the Westinghouse plant had with team meetings: Just having team meetings did not improve work performance. Research began to reveal that there was a right way and a wrong way to do each of the 10 components of teamwork. Figure 3–2, in very simple terms, uses the research conclusions to contrast successful methods with unsuccessful methods for achieving breakthrough results.

Looking at the second component, team communication, research has consistently indicated that group sharing of feelings and conflicts about work, co-workers, and bosses does not improve the group's work performance. This approach to team building is sometimes called human relations laboratory or sensitivity training (see p. 7). Paul Buchanan reviewed 68 studies of interpersonal and personal skills development in human relations laboratories and found that such programs improved only individual functioning as measured by various paper-and-pencil tests.[4] Buchanan concluded, "The value of the laboratory experience for job performance, however, is less convincing . . ." None of the studies showed a strong cause-and-effect link between increasing interpersonal sensitivity and improving work performance. Other hard-data studies have shown that teamwork programs that focus on having people share their honest feelings about one another do not improve work results.[5]

Human relations laboratory–type team-building programs are usually not done in the context of work goals or team mission. They do sometimes pull out people's honest feelings, and people do share

FIGURE 3–1

The Benefits of the 10 Components of Structured Teamwork

Component	Benefit of Component
1. Team creativity	Having groups do planning and problem solving promotes breakthrough performance only if the team uses creativity. Without creativity, a lot of time and effort can be expended with no payoff.
2. Team communication	Team communication skills and ground rules and norms create a supportive work climate that promotes creativity, breakthrough thinking, risk taking, and team member commitment.
3. Team meetings	Team meeting skills and structures harness the incredible energy available in group dynamics and produce high achievement in meeting goals. The team meeting is a mini-replication of the team's culture. Establish high-performance/high-commitment team meetings and there will be a high-performance/high-commitment culture. The energy of a highly participative and effective team meeting is contagious.
4. Conflict management	When employees are asked to bring their hearts and minds to work to care and think about quality, productivity, cycle time reduction, and other workplace problems, there are conflicts. The conflicts can be healthy and result in breakthrough solutions when team members have effective and powerful conflict management skills.
5. Team mission	The team mission statement establishes work priorities, unleashes the power of idealism, and aligns the team with the organization's mission.
6. Team goal setting	Effective team goal setting and action planning promote team member involvement and increase success and commitment.
7. Team roles and responsibilities	Roles and responsibilities are established and clarified regarding how each team member supports the other team members and the team's internal and external customers.
8. Team problem solving	Team members enthusiastically assume the role of solving problems together in and out of team meetings instead of bumping problems up to management and then griping. Using basic and easy-to-implement problem-solving steps, team members solve problems on the fly as they do daily work.

(continued)

The Benefits of the 10 Components of Structured Teamwork (concluded)

Component	Benefit of Component
9. Team decision making	The most difficult of all team participative management tasks is team decision making. Without decision-making skills, teams flounder, waste time, get in arguments, and end up requiring the manager to make the decision. With these skills, teams make superior decisions and experience high commitment and rapid implementation of the decision.
10. Work process improvement	Team members learn how to improve work processes. Work in all organizations tends to suffer from bureaucratic creep, with process steps losing the value they had at one time. Team members aggressively look for ways to improve work processes and eliminate waste and cycle time.

themselves and what is within them at that time and place. The problem is that such sharing occurs outside of the work context and can be destructive, both to the people involved and to the work environment. Breakthrough teams, on the other hand, pull out the very best from their members. Team members "play above their heads." Instead of sharing the emotional garbage that comes out in human relations laboratory–type experiences, they share the best that is within them— their hopes, their important values, their desire to do the best work. Other team members and the manager or leader are seen as valuable collaborators helping the team achieve its highest work goals.

One study showed that there is a more direct approach to improving team communication for increased work performance.[6] That approach is to teach a specific set of interpersonal skills to the team members, preferably together as a team. For example, most employees do not know or use good listening skills. Poor listening skills often cause delegated work assignments to be performed incorrectly because the listener does not hear some important part of the assignment. Poor interpersonal listening skills are major contributors to conflict between team members both in and out of meetings. How many times have you heard two people arguing at work and you said to yourself, or to them, "Wait a minute, you are both saying the same thing!" The study mentioned above revealed that when team members

FIGURE 3–2

The 10 Components of Teamwork: Research Conclusions

	Component	Successful	Unsuccessful
1.	Team creativity	Structured brainstorming and nominal group technique.	Unstructured brainstorming.
2.	Team communication	Interpersonal communication skills training.	Group sharing of feelings and conflicts.
3.	Team meetings	Structure including agenda, meeting minutes, specific roles, and meeting format.	No agenda. No clearly defined roles.
4.	Conflict management	Specific skills organized in five-step model.	Confrontation or avoidance.
5.	Team mission	Idealistic and externally focused.	Internally focused. Financial results only.
6.	Team goal setting	Specifically worked goals with measurements and time target.	Do-your-best goals with no specific target.
7.	Team roles and responsibilities	Developed in relation to how to achieve team goals. Future-oriented roles to make more decisions.	Roles and responsibilities narrowly defined and static.
8.	Team problem solving	Systematic problem-solving model with a defined target objective.	No model, trial and error, or only tools and techniques.
9.	Team decision making	Systematic evaluation of pros and cons of alternatives, with defined target objectives.	Just talking about alternatives.
10.	Work process improvement	Work process improvement and specific goals and focus.	Work improvement without specific goal setting.

were given systematic interpersonal communication training with modeling, practice, and performance feedback, there was a direct, positive impact on individual and team work performance.

Team creativity is a component that showed a dramatic contrast between unstructured techniques and research-based methods. When groups engaged in the usual free-flowing, anyone-can-talk form of creativity called brainstorming, there was no significant difference compared to individuals working alone. However, performance improvements in creativity and work results did occur when groups used more structured forms of brainstorming and creativity enhancement such as writing down ideas before sharing them and allowing one idea per person at each sharing opportunity.[7] The ineffectiveness and inefficiency of unstructured brainstorming are among the major criticisms some managers and engineers use to argue that teamwork as a whole is not valuable.

Another study showed that team problem solving promoted improved work results when a structured, step-by-step approach was used.[8] When groups are confronted with problems in the absence of a systematic approach, they often use trial-and-error tactics that do not always solve the problem. The most successful structured approaches include clearly defining the problem and identifying and addressing its causes. By systematically defining the causes of the problem, the team can be sure that, once the solution is put into action, that particular problem will not recur.

Decision making is an area of management and group performance that cries out for a successful approach. A major activity of management teams as well as work teams is to generate alternative courses of action and then select the best one. Much time is spent in and out of meetings as people argue for their favorite option. Randy Hirokawa, who has spent a lifetime researching how teams can make effective decisions, discovered that if a team can systematically list and compare all of the potentially positive and negative consequences of each alternative, the ensuing decisions will be significantly better.[9] As teams make better decisions, some of those decisions will directly benefit goal achievement.

As I continued reviewing the research, what became obvious was that the more systematic or structured the teamwork component was, the better the team's performance. As teams were developed, the structure of the 10 components effectively replaced direct supervisor control of the work team. Team members internalized the new skills and created self-management and control, full of effective teamwork shaped by the structured skills and processes they had learned. The success of structured approaches in developing breakthrough teams provided the rationale for calling the research-based methodology Structured Teamwork.

As yet another research conclusion, the following finding can make the difference between success and failure of the whole team development program: The focus of team training and development should be the natural work group.

A whole group of studies revealed that the natural work group should be the focus of team training and development.[10] The natural work group includes all of the individuals who must coordinate their activities to get work done. For example, a natural work group from the factory floor includes the equipment operators, the maintenance technician who keeps the equipment running, the engineer who helps plan the work flow and work methods, and the supervisor or team leader. As the team members learn the team skills together, they immediately implement the skills outside the training to improve the work itself. Natural work group team members have daily opportunities to use the new skills immediately.

> **The focus of team training and development should be the natural work group.**

Developing the natural work group team as a unit that learns each structured skill and step of the process together can be contrasted with the usual teamwork training approach, in which employees attend team classes with people with whom they do not normally work. Companies that take on major training initiatives simply to expose everyone to certain skills often form large classes composed of an assortment of employees. The training manager of a Texas-based oil company called this the "sheep-dip" approach to training. Organizations are often tempted to use this approach to teach team skills. It may be convenient and fast, but it does not work. With sheep-dip training for teams, there are no gains and no breakthrough improvements.

> **Teams should be trained and developed with their leader.**

Remember that the natural work group includes the supervisor or team leader. Therefore, to improve the coordination and increase the creative breakthroughs of the whole team, the supervisor or team leader must learn the same skills as the other members of the team. Thus, teams should be trained and developed with their leader.

Research especially supports having the supervisor or team leader go through the training and development with his or her team.[11] A major goal of team development is to increase the team's authority to solve problems and make decisions without the supervisor's required involvement. For this to occur feasibly, the supervisor must participate with the team to decide which decisions will be relinquished and how fast.

In one organization, the structured team development was conducted in a top-down manner. From the president down, each level of managers went through the training twice. The president went through the team development training with vice presidents. When the vice presidents saw the dramatic improvements in communication, coordination, and creativity that were achieved with the president's team, they wanted the same degree of improvement with their own teams. So they arranged to go through the training a second time with their subordinates. This pattern was repeated all the way through the organization, with favorable results.

For most organizations, people's time is more important than money. One reason is that time is worth a lot of money. A manufacturing worker's hourly wage, including benefits and other company expenses, for example, may be between $15 and $40 an hour. The time value of that hour, when applied to the products being manufactured, is between $75 and $150 an hour per employee. Using less than the best training program when employees are taken off-line for team development is a money-losing proposition.

Research does make a difference. There are more exciting conclusions! They will be presented to describe how to do each of the 10 components of Structured Teamwork.

BREAKTHROUGH POINTS

- Goal setting and goal measurement are the foundation of successful teamwork.

- The 10 components of Structured Teamwork are goal setting and goal measurement, team creativity skills, effective team communication, effective team meetings, high-quality conflict management skills, team mission setting, clear team roles and responsibilities, effective team problem-solving skills, effective team decision-making skills, and continuous work process improvement skills.

- Team development for organizational breakthrough is a methodology, not an event.

- A systematic and comprehensive approach to teamwork that addresses each of the 10 areas is more effective and long lasting.
- There are successful and unsuccessful ways to address the 10 areas of teamwork.
- The focus of team training and development should be the natural work group.
- Teams should be developed and trained with their leader.

4

CHAPTER

Breakthrough Teamwork and the Bottom Line

Breakthrough teamwork unlocks a company's potential for great business results. Increased productivity, lowered costs, time savings, and improved quality—all can be achieved using Structured Teamwork.

And the results occur quickly. Some teams have dramatically increased productivity levels *at the same time that workers were spending part of their day in the Structured Teamwork classes.* Because Structured Teamwork is based on goal setting and goal reaching, the entire methodology is results oriented. The results, like the goals, are not vague or warm and fuzzy; rather, they are specific, bottom-line-oriented, *quantifiable* business results. Consider the remarkable results that teams have enjoyed after implementing Structured Teamwork to address improvements needed in the following areas:

Productivity

- One team doubled shipments from $1 million per month to $2 million. (Asea Brown Boveri [ABB], Coral Springs)
- Engineering design time was slashed from 26 weeks to 14 weeks, allowing another team to handle 40 percent more business. (ABB, Coral Springs)

- One team improved its productivity 20 percent per machine through cross-training, improved coordination, and creative work process improvement breakthroughs. (Advanced Micro Devices)

- One work team developed standardized tooling for all its processes, reducing changeover time from three days to 15 minutes. (E-Systems Montek, Salt Lake City)

Quality

- One team reduced defects on microchip wafers by 30 percent. (Advanced Micro Devices)

- Another team reduced quality defects by 50 percent within nine months. (ABB, Coral Springs)

Time Savings

- A computer chip assembly and test team decreased its cycle time 42 percent while still in training. (Texas Instruments, Portugal)

- An ABB team reduced the manufacturing cycle time of a complex electronic product from 14 days to 2 days. (ABB, Coral Springs)

- On-time shipments jumped from a pretty good 80 percent to a near perfect 99.9 percent for another team. (ABB, Coral Springs)

- The division expanded to 14 work teams in the operations department, and these teams (now operating without outside consultants) have saved the division over 41,000 labor hours in a little over two and a half years. (E-Systems Montek, Salt Lake City)

Cost Savings

- Three "test case" manufacturing work teams reduced their production labor costs by an average of 18.9 percent while still undergoing Structured Teamwork training. (E-Systems Montek, Salt Lake City)

- While saving labor hours, the work teams simultaneously reduced scrap and rework rates. One team reduced scrap from 9.4 percent to less than 1 percent. (E-Systems Montek, Salt Lake City)

- Four teams saved their company a total of $1.5 million cash in six months. (E-Systems, Garland)

- One newly formed purchasing team saved over $550,000 in direct materials in the first six months of its existence. (E-Systems Montek, Salt Lake City)

- Work teams helped initiate a short-term "reduced work week" so the company could weather a major customer's "inventory reduction" without resorting to layoffs. (E-Systems Montek, Salt Lake City)

Executive Decision Making

- During the team decision-making training, an executive team decided not to build a new office building, a decision that saved the company several million dollars! (Amoco Canada Petroleum Company Ltd.)

- Another team reduced management committee meeting time by 50 percent while increasing meeting effectiveness. (Amoco Canada Petroleum Company Ltd.)

Too good to believe? Read the following descriptions to see how they did it. Then learn in later chapters how you can achieve similar breakthroughs that produce quantifiable business results.

PRODUCTIVITY AT E-SYSTEMS

One of the high-technology companies experiencing success with Structured Teamwork is the Garland Division of E-Systems, in a suburb of Dallas, Texas. The company produces electronic systems for commercial and government applications. The operations group at Garland faced a tremendous challenge to reduce costs, and needed dramatic improvement from four key product teams composed of engineers, operators, and testers.

The company decided to rapidly implement Structured Teamwork in order to achieve its goals. At the start of the initiative, almost all of the team members were skeptical. Their preconceived definition of good teamwork was "Everyone gets along with one another." Since they thought they all got along with one another, they assumed they had good teamwork and wondered, "Why the big fuss?" Before long, however, their enthusiasm for teamwork training began to build as they saw the improved work results arising out of improved communication and coordination.

The training itself began in February for three of the teams. Another team was soon added. By June, less than four months later, the four teams combined had saved the company $1.5 million actual on-the-books cash dollars! This rapid team development reduced rework, cut labor hours, and lowered material costs. The teams went on after their training and saved an additional $500,000. This success brought real-world results and also a very nice write-up in the company magazine, *The Printed Circuit*. Some of the results of the four teams are summarized in Figure 4–1.

One engineer, who was initially the most skeptical and antagonistic, later surprised everyone by volunteering to be trained as one of E-Systems' internal Structured Teamwork facilitators.

FIGURE 4–1

E-Systems Garland, Texas, Team Results

Team	Results
Log Amp	▪ 32% improvement in productivity (5,300 hours). ▪ Reduced cycle time from 13 weeks to 6 weeks.
Band 1 Team	▪ Raised first-time yield of subassemblies to 98%. ▪ Substantially reduced rework. ▪ Reduced cycle time.
Inter-frequency Team	▪ 30% reduction in rework. ▪ Improved productivity.
Hybrid	▪ 40% reduction in manufacturing inspection. ▪ 25% reduction in hybrid process cleaning time. ▪ 44% reduction in time to attach components.
All 4 teams	▪ Saved $2 million in labor and material costs for the year.

Permission obtained from E-Systems to share these results.

BREAKTHROUGH TEAMWORK AT ABB CORAL SPRINGS

Asea Brown Boveri (ABB) in Coral Springs, Florida, designs, markets, and manufactures electrical relays and relay systems, which are used to manage the distribution of electricity. Most of us have personal experience with electrical relays when lightning strikes and we see our lights flicker off and on. The relays help reestablish the integrity of that portion of the power distribution system that was disrupted by the lightning strike. In short, they help keep the lights on during thunderstorms.

Although ABB's management had established over 20 quality improvement teams to work on high-leverage customer-focus projects, ABB Coral Springs customers were dissatisfied. They had informed ABB managers that they required improvements in the following areas if ABB was going to continue to be their supplier:

- On-time delivery.
- Near perfect quality.
- Reduced lead times and cycle times.
- Reduced cost.

Better, faster, and cheaper was the challenge for ABB, as it is the challenge today for every business. Unfortunately, many of the teams ABB had established to effect the required improvements were teams in name only. The team leaders would schedule meetings, but no one would show up. Action items would be delegated to team members but never get done. Project deadlines would be set and then totally ignored. Week after week, managers would sit listening to reports of slow or no progress toward the customer-focused goals. Frustration grew within the ranks of management and the team leaders.

ABB had already adopted a business strategy designed to reduce costs, cycle time, and quality defects using a manufacturing innovation known as just-in-time (JIT). Just-in-time involves ordering parts just before they are needed in order to reduce the costs associated with keeping a large inventory. JIT has the potential to reduce cycle time and improve quality. At ABB Coral Springs, however, JIT had not yielded the desired improvements. Manufacturing workers resisted the JIT system the engineers and managers had designed.

Jim Oates, the manager spearheading JIT, decided that Structured Teamwork might be the solution for overcoming the organizational conflict that had arisen over the new approach. A cross-functional and cross-level steering team, which included Jim, was developed to do the detailed measurements and planning. The Line 5 natural work group, which included the supervisor, the assemblers, the testers, and the manufacturing engineer, would decide how JIT would actually work in their area. Both groups went through the Structured Teamwork development program.

After implementing Structured Teamwork, the steering team and Line 5 achieved the following results:

- The average cycle time dropped from 14 days to 2.3 days.
- There was a 50 percent improvement in quality as measured by reduced defects.

- Overdue orders were reduced from 15 per month to zero.
- Productivity increased 21 percent even though the team was averaging between six and eight hours a month in team meetings and the training itself.

These results were possible because the workers, the managers, and the engineers *worked together* to adopt JIT, implementing it in the way that would work best for the company. Structured Teamwork allowed ABB to break through the resistance to change that had initially stalled the JIT program.

The Team Engineers, the second ABB Coral Springs team to go through Structured Teamwork, presented an early discouraging picture. The members of the team were assemblers and testers from three different assembly lines who initially thought there was no need to interact with or help each other. In fact, the team members stated that there were certain people they did not like and if teamwork meant liking each other, they wanted no part of it! Additionally, their profit center manager, Russ Frame, was skeptical at first about the value of the program because all of the so-called team-building sessions he had experienced were "loosey-goosey," nonsubstantive affairs with no real results.

It was decided to delay starting the teams until after Russ went through some of the Structured Teamwork program himself. To Russ's credit, after he went through the first session he became convinced of the value of the methodology. He was especially impressed with the session-by-session flow of the installation process where skills and structures like interpersonal communication were covered and then immediately applied by the team to get real work improvements.

The first team from Russ's area, the Team Engineers, began shipping every order on time, and the overall success of on-time deliveries grew to 99 percent. What is remarkable about this result is that the team achieved it *while reducing its lead time*, that is, the amount of turnaround time required after a customer places an order. Anyone in scheduling knows that it is possible to show an improvement in on-time delivery by allowing a longer lead time and promising a later delivery date at the beginning. The Team Engineers did just the opposite. At the same time they were improving on-time shipping performance, they reduced their lead times 60.6 percent for in-stock relays and 44.3 percent for nonstock relays. Figure 4–2 summarizes the characteristics and business results of the ABB Team Engineers before and after Structured Teamwork training.

FIGURE 4–2

ABB Team Engineers Results

Team Characteristics before Structured Teamwork	Team Characteristics after Structured Teamwork	Results of Structured Teamwork
■ The supervisor was the only person in the department who felt responsible for on-time shipments.	■ Individual team members volunteer to be responsible for customer order follow-up.	■ 99% of all orders are shipped to the customer on time.
■ Team members were concerned only with the requirements of their own jobs.	■ Team members look before and after their operation to see what is required to get the order out on time.	■ Overdue shipments to customers were reduced by 81% from the previous year.
■ Employees ignored details such as following proper Kanban procedures and just-in-time practices.	■ Attention to detail happens every day.	
■ There were no visible measurements of on-time delivery.	■ Meaningful measurements were developed and are displayed throughout the department.	
■ There was no customer-service orientation.	■ There is a very high customer-service orientation among all team members.	

Due to these results and the successes of a number of the teams, Russ Frame decided to expand Structured Teamwork to other work areas where JIT and Kanban, another productivity improvement program, had been previously implemented with less than optimal results. The Achievers team was one of the next to receive training in Structured Teamwork.

The Achievers team members were enthusiastic about the training from the very beginning. As a group, they already treated each other in a supportive way. The natural leaders in their ranks saw the Structured Teamwork initiative as something they endorsed. They quickly began to work on improvement projects during the team training and team meetings.

The Achievers' results were spectacular! They reduced cycle time on their Kanban cylinder units by over 64 percent. Cycle time on the e-elements, a component of electrical relays, was reduced from 3.3 days to 1.2 days. The team developed a multicard Kanban system, which ensured a continuous supply of parts. Personnel costs of the team were reduced 10 percent by maintaining their required productivity when one team member retired. The work-in-process inventory was reduced by $21,653 at the same time that material availability was increased. A measure of material availability and how well Kanban is being implemented is the number of empty parts bins or pans. The team decreased empty pans from 17.6 per day to 1 per day. They reduced quality defects 50 percent from previous years' levels. The team was able to provide 100 percent availability of defect-free subassemblies. They achieved a 99 percent on-time delivery to their internal customers, the Team Engineers, who used the parts to manufacture the relays.

Another team named itself the United Nations because its members came from all over the world. Six months after the team underwent Structured Teamwork training, its average cycle time dropped from 12 days to 3 1/2 days! The production rate increased 189 percent. Overdue orders decreased from an average of 25 relays per month to less than 1 relay per month. Other results are outlined in Figure 4–3.

Shan Shun, the division manager, told me excitedly, "The teams going through Structured Teamwork have doubled the shipments per month. A year ago they were averaging $1 million a month. They are now averaging $2 million a month! Last month, they shipped $3 million, so Jim Oates and I are taking all the team members and their spouses out to dinner at the country club." What pride they must have felt, and what power they must have recognized in themselves: "I did it." "We did it." "I can do more." Teamwork is a personal thing, since the team is made up of individuals, and personal growth can be a rewarding by-product of Structured Teamwork training.

Improved cycle time, reduced personnel and inventory costs, improved quality, and on-time delivery—these are the kinds of bottom-line results that Structured Teamwork makes possible. The results are not limited to the manufacturing environment, however. Engineers, negotiators, managers, and marketing and administrative personnel—all have obtained outstanding results from self-managed teamwork.

FIGURE 4-3

ABB United Nations Results

Team Characteristics before Structured Teamwork	Team Characteristics after Structured Teamwork	Results of Structured Teamwork
▪ Production scheduling done by a scheduler.	▪ Team members do production scheduling.	▪ Implemented a "pull system" that allows team members to react quickly to internal and external customer requirements.
▪ Consistently late orders.	▪ 22 straight weeks with no overdue orders.	▪ Reduced cycle time from 12 days per relay to 3 1/2 days per relay.
▪ Little or no team-member commitment to meeting delivery schedule.	▪ High team-member commitment to meeting schedule.	▪ Increased production rate 189%.
▪ Little or no looking forward or backward to anticipate customer requirements.	▪ Excellent visibility for team members to see and anticipate customer needs.	▪ Reduced overdue orders from an average of 25 per month to 0.8 per month.
▪ No teamwork practiced among team members.	▪ A high level of team-member support and communication.	

STRUCTURED TEAMWORK WITH KNOWLEDGE TEAMS

Amoco Canada

In the late 1980s, the chairman and president of Amoco Canada, T. Don Stacy, successfully guided a major merger of Amoco Canada with Dome Petroleum Ltd. Afterward, Don knew that the legal and financial merger was complete, but thought that the psychological merger had yet to be accomplished. Using the Structured Teamwork process, Amoco Canada began the implementation of a more participative and empowered culture, which helped individuals from the merged companies learn to work together to support the new alliance.

Structured Teamwork also solved a pressing business problem: costs and cycle time were dramatically reduced. The business results included cost savings of $13.7 million. Some of the specific cost savings were due to team-generated ideas about combining work functions, eliminating certain offices, and eliminating multiple approvals for decisions. The teams went after eliminating nonvalued work with the zeal of knights on the quest for the Holy Grail.

The drilling managers' team selected a project to reduce the amount of time and red tape that contractors had to go through to be on the master contractor list. Like most major oil companies, Amoco Canada often does not do its own drilling. Instead, it selects drillers from a pool of preapproved contractors. Prior to the team's process improvement, almost 20 separate steps per contractor were performed by Amoco to place a contractor in the pool. The process absorbed four hours of work time, but it was across a 12-week period. Exceptions and constant problems demanded additional time from the drilling managers. The structured team reduced the steps in the new process to eight and the time required to 95 minutes, a greater than 50 percent improvement in both areas. In addition to using the creative breakthrough ideas, a key strategy was to empower and give decision-making authority to the in-house Amoco Canada drilling experts who worked with the contractors every day.

Two other teams at Amoco Canada got fantastic results using Structured Teamwork. A team of petroleum engineers used Structured Teamwork to reduce the number of engineering workdays necessary to produce the annual forecast revenue and work-load plan. The team reduced the required days from 119 person-days per year to 29 person-days per year!

Another team, led by then-Vice President of Production Murray Todd, identified a major need to reduce time in weekly review meetings. Murray's team especially wanted to reduce the amount of time that meeting presenters had to wait in the lobby for their agenda item to come up. Presenters were sometimes waiting more than an hour beyond their scheduled time. Murray's team acknowledged that this wait did not promote empowerment and did not provide a good example of teamwork.

The team used process improvement and meeting structures to reduce the lag time presenters experienced. The production management committee meetings improved from consuming 150 percent of the allotted time to finishing on schedule, with no overrun time. The team members also shifted their meeting focus from immediate operational issues (which were usually already decided) to more strategic and high-leverage opportunities and problems.

T. Don Stacy is currently leading Amoco's exploration and production business in Europe and Asia. In a recent conference at the

Amoco Eurasia offices, Don excitedly told me, "Dennis, our meetings do not even resemble the old model. Instead of having our people make formal presentations and then I decide, I now go to their work area and we solve problems and make decisions together!"

ABB Coral Springs

Jim Oates, the manager who championed Structured Teamwork at ABB Coral Springs, was promoted to manage the Engineered Relay Systems group at ABB. The group designs and manufactures a system of electrical relays that fit into six-foot-tall gray metal cabinets. Relay systems represent a significant business opportunity for ABB, and a major challenge to successful teamwork. Because each relay system is designed individually for each customer, successful production requires the coordination of the customer's design requirements with marketing, system engineering, drafting, purchasing, parts inventory, assembly, and testing.

Jim knew that it took six to eight months just to complete the engineering and drafting of new relay systems. When that was completed, manufacturing activities could begin. Jim saw the opportunity to decrease the engineering and drafting cycle time. Once again, the Structured Teamwork training was the core methodology for both the steering team and the functional relay system teams to initiate major improvements.

The relay system teams tried an exciting innovation. They invited their customers to be members of the teams. As Jim related this aspect of their design process improvement, he acknowledged that he was worried about whether it would succeed. As he said, "We were opening ourselves wide open for the customer to see how we succeeded or failed to meet his requirements."

The gamble paid off. Engineering cycle time was reduced from six to eight months to three to four months. All systems began to be shipped on time, and the customers loved it! They liked being members of the ABB team, they liked the team approach that was being used to design their product, and they especially appreciated the results. ABB Relay Systems customers began to expressly request that the team approach be used with their relay systems. Once frustrated with delays, customers are now recommending ABB Relay Systems to their organizations. As Jim Oates shared with me, "We've finally got the customers on our side. The main thing is that they will be back!"

FIGURE 4–4

ABB Coral Springs Structured Teamwork Results
Marketing, Engineering, and Support Teams

Team	Results
Metropolitan Edison Customer Team	Completed relay systems in a record 18 weeks versus usual 23 weeks, despite customer-initiated design changes and material delays; created process that reduced time to collect accounts receivable from 64 days to 29 days.
Drafting Team	Reduced cycle time to produce printed circuit board layouts from 26 days to 9 days.
Hawaiian Electric Customer Team, Honolulu Airport Expansion Project	Shipped 14 relay panels in record 26 weeks instead of 32 weeks.
Providers Team (shipping and receiving department)	Reduced shipping errors to Puerto Rico by 69%; reduced transportation costs 55%; set up hardware Kanban market that saved $40,000; saved $110,000 by reducing order quantities of BOS parts.
Engineered Relay Systems Team (engineers and drafters)	Reduced engineering drafting cycle time by 34%.
COPS Team (information systems improvement team)	Decreased order entry and parts ordering cycle time from 6 weeks to 48 hours.
MDAR Team (engineering, manufacturing, and support)	Reduced cycle time by 75%; became a self-contained work group.

As the Structured Teamwork initiative was expanded to other management and administrative teams, almost every team obtained equally spectacular results. As shown in Figure 4–4, breakthrough is possible at every level and for every function within an organization.

COST REDUCTION, THE STRUCTURED TEAMWORK WAY

The results achieved at ABB Coral Springs show how Structured Teamwork can bring about widespread change and across-the-board improvement. At E-Systems Montek, the problem was more specific: cost reduction.

The Montek Division of E-Systems (a subsidiary of Raytheon) is located in Salt Lake City, Utah. The division is an international developer and producer of aircraft flight controls and navigation electronics, and a major supplier of Boeing aircraft components. Like many Boeing suppliers, Montek negotiates very competitive long-term contracts with Boeing. The price in these contracts is tightly scheduled for the life of the contract. Maintaining a reasonable profit for the life of the contract can be extremely difficult because inflation and regular pay increases tend to increase the cost of manufacturing.

Montek determined that the only workable option was to increase its manufacturing efficiency. To do this the company chose to implement structured work teams, which achieved significant and immediate results. While still undergoing Structured Teamwork training in the first half of 1993, the three "test case" teams (Montek simply named them A, B, and C) reduced their production labor costs by a weighted average of 18.9 percent. Since that time, while running on their own without continued outside consultant help, the teams have continued to improve and are now consistently operating an average of 23.87 percent more efficiently than they were in 1992.

These numbers reflect actual process hours saved, and it should be noted that all three teams managed to make these kinds of improvements while simultaneously reducing scrap and rework rates. The fact that these teams maintained the improved performance even after Harlan Oelklaus, the Structured Teamwork consultant, left means that the results were *not superficial*. The fact that they didn't increase performance at the expense of some other vital production area means that the gains were *not sacrificial*. The company is left with solid gains because the people are working smarter and better.

As part of the Structured Teamwork process, each team develops its own goals and measurements and creates its own charts for measuring the goals. This makes the entire team more closely involved in the process, and it also lets the teams have some fun. For example, the C Team's percent scrap hours chart is affectionately called the Pizza Party Chart to remind the members that each time they meet their reduced scrap goal, it's party time!

Montek is continuing to expand its use of Structured Teamwork. The division now has its own certified internal facilitators, who were trained and certified during the first 12 months of the project. The Structured Teamwork methodology has been implemented with 14 manufacturing teams, all of which are achieving significant results, and Montek is beginning to expand the use of the teaming concept into management areas. Here again, Montek is implementing the process in a practical and considered way, with four management "test teams" being implemented to start out. If these management teams achieve significant results, the concept will be expanded in the future.

EMPOWERMENT AND PRODUCTIVITY: THE AMD EXPERIENCE

One of the most competitive industries in the world is the semiconductor business. Semiconductor microchips are used in computers, printers, automobiles, appliances, and almost every other electronic device built today. One of the recent best players in this industry is Advanced Micro Devices, a company with sales totaling $2.1 billion in 1994.

The responsibility for manufacturing semiconductor products at AMD rests with the 2,000-person Wafer Fabrication (Fab) Division and its vice president, Gary Heerssen. Gary and 60 other key managers formulated a vision for a new, breakthrough manufacturing organization and laid out a road map to achieve that vision. Wisely, the managers decided that they could not achieve the enormous changes alone. The commitment and empowerment of the entire workforce were essential.

In addition, the managers recognized that they themselves had to change how they managed and treated people. The high-pressure world of semiconductors requires everyone to do a thousand little steps totally right every day. People could easily become angry and yell at each other when frustrations are at their worst. One of the first change principles Gary and his team embraced was an organization-wide ground rule: "Focus on the issue, not the person." There would be no personal attacks. This type of cultural change is essential in order to establish an organizational climate where employees think of and try creative work improvements.

A subsequent step in the road map was to begin Structured Teamwork training with line teams in order to promote the empowerment- and commitment-building processes. Most of the first wave of 30 teams achieved improved business results. One team set a goal to improve the productivity of its equipment by 7 percent in five months while going through the team training. It actually improved productivity by 12 percent in two months! It also reduced the cycle time for associated data entry and saved $30,800 per machine per year through other improvements.

A second team of operators went through the team skills training with the manufacturing engineer who was assigned to their area. As in all manufacturing areas, the equipment for making semiconductor wafers is expensive. In this case, a single Rainbow etcher costs $1 million. The team improved its productivity by 20 percent per machine through cross-training, improved coordination, and creative work process improvement breakthroughs. The manager of the work area was ecstatic. He had placed $1.2 million in his 1993 budget to buy a new Rainbow etcher. The improved productivity generated by the Structured Teamwork process made the purchase of the etcher unnecessary, so he turned the money back to the company.

Figure 4–5 summarizes the early business results that some of AMD's teams achieved while going through the team development process itself.

The Semiconductor Wafer Fabrication management teams also received Structured Teamwork training. One of AMD's breakthrough products is the advanced erasable programmable read only memory (EPROM) chip. Insiders refer to this chip as a flash memory chip. In the fall of 1992, the company was planning to move production of this chip to one of the fabrication areas. Gary and the Fab director, Preston Snuggs, agreed that as the Fab director's management team went through the Structured Teamwork training, they would immediately use the skills they were learning. They hoped to accelerate the technology transfer in order to produce more of the new flash memory chips faster than any Fab in the past. The Fab management team concurred with this priority and went through the team skills development in a very disciplined manner. The team completed the training

FIGURE 4–5

Results of Structured Teamwork in the AMD Wafer Fab Division

The following results were achieved by natural work group teams of operators without additional capital expenditures or project engineering attention:

- Reduced defect density on microchip wafers by 30 percent.
- Increased by 20 percent the number of moves on night shift by implementing cross-training and other solutions of the team.
- Reduced particle contamination in the work area contributing to improved product quality.
- Reduced cost of test wafers by $80,000 in one area.
- Solved a wafer boat problem that was causing misprocessing and scrap of otherwise good wafers; a $100,000 savings.
- Cut cycle time for required preventive maintenance that caused equipment downtime.
- Reduced to zero the rework caused by equipment misaligns and scan lines.
- Increased productivity by 15 percent by increasing coordination and reducing rework.
- Saw operators deemed "the worst shift" improve significantly to become "the best shift."

in January with total agreement that the program had significantly improved their teamwork. All of the managers began using the team-work methods throughout the Fab. In addition, the managers committed to training all of their natural work groups composed of operators, engineers, maintenance technicians, and supervisors in 1993. By the end of the second quarter of 1993, the business results were outstanding. The technology transfer of the flash memory chip was several months faster than the plan. Preston's organization produced millions of dollars worth of product more than the previous quarter. The Fab teams set performance records almost daily!

When employees are empowered through Structured Teamwork, they realize that it is their company, too, and that the performance of their company is up to them. An empowered team sets and achieves work goals and continually improves its work processes, with dramatic business results.

INTERNATIONAL VIABILITY OF STRUCTURED TEAMWORK

Structured Teamwork initiatives are viable in other countries and cultures besides those of North America. An example is a Texas Instruments microchip packaging plant in Porto, Portugal. José Morais, the plant manager, envisioned his organization on the forefront of empowerment in Europe. José and his team spent a number of months reading and studying how to implement empowerment. Interest and emotion were both high when Gene Marcum of TI's Semiconductor Training and Organizational Effectiveness group and I presented the research-based, structured approach to empowerment. After several hours of excited questions and answers, José remarked, "Dennis, you've taken all of the trauma out of implementing empowerment."

José and his management team went on to develop the corporate site values, vision, mission, and strategic goals, and to learn and apply the skills and tools of Structured Teamwork. Two pilot teams also received the training, and one team, the test team, reduced its cycle time by 42 percent while the training was being conducted! Cycle time reduction was a major team emphasis according to the team charter. The team goals and the problem the team chose to solve centered on improving cycle time while maintaining or increasing quality. The plant empowerment steering team has coordinated the implementation of three waves of training. The TI team members have produced leading-edge benchmark manufacturing results for a joint venture partner.

Currently, interest is high in Asia for how to do self-managed teams. For the past 15 years, quality circle teams have been highly successful. At the Texas Instruments Singapore plant, the two manufacturing product-line management teams wanted to pilot a team approach that was beyond quality circles. One of the product lines was able to start earlier than the other. The initial teams made significant improvements in quality and productivity; for example, one team improved its product quality by 25 percent. One of the Singapore site managers was so pleased with the overall business results in the first product line that he encouraged the implementation in the other product line.

CONCLUSION

Do you want to improve your quality by 50 percent or more? What would your boss say if you saved the company $1.5 million in cash? If you are about to embark on a major construction project, how would you like to eliminate the all-too-frequent delays caused by conflicts among all of the various engineers, managers, and users? If you have these or other goals to pursue, remember the results others have gained through breakthrough teamwork and Structured Teamwork methodology. Hang on to your seat as you learn how to get results like these yourself! But first we need to reach a new understanding of teamwork; that is the subject of Chapter 5.

BREAKTHROUGH POINTS

- Implementing Structured Teamwork results in increased productivity, improved quality, time savings, cost savings, and enhanced executive decision making.

- Improvements can occur even while teams are undergoing training.

- The principles of Structured Teamwork translate easily to other cultures because they are based on fundamental truths.

5

CHAPTER

Breakthrough Teamwork Leads the Way to Organizational Success

The most frequent definition of teamwork I hear from managers is "When people are pleasant and courteous to each other." When managers are courteous and do not personally attack anyone, a safe place where people speak up is often created. However, a safe, pleasant work environment does not, in and of itself, establish breakthrough teamwork. Courtesy and respect are necessary preconditions on the road to team breakthrough, but these terms do not define teamwork.

A NEW DEFINITION OF TEAMWORK

As teams are developed, they seem to progress through five levels of increased ability and performance. The five levels, presented in Figure 5–1, correspond to the five waves of teamwork approaches presented in Chapter 1. Because each of the levels begins with the letter C and has a multiplicative influence rather than simply an additive effect, the model is called C to the 5th, or C^5. C^5 provides a new definition of teamwork that anyone can assess their team against.

FIGURE 5–1

Levels of C^5 Teamwork

Level 1: Communication
- Communicate important information to each other.
- Share problems versus withhold problems.
- Listen and understand versus talk.

Level 2: Cooperation
- Help each other solve job-related problems.
- Assist fellow members with their work.

Level 3: Coordination
- Coordinate job duties and actions to achieve goals that the team helped set.
- Use coordination in both team meetings and on the job.
- Avoid uncontrolled duplication.

Level 4: Creative Breakthrough
- Achieve a major innovation in how to do the work or solve a problem.
- Use innovation to make or save a lot of money.

Level 5: Continuous Breakthrough
- Repeatedly achieve major work process improvements and job redesign improvements.
- Communicate improvements throughout the organization.

Level 1: Communication

The first level of performance improvement that happens as a work group goes through Structured Teamwork development is the increase in the frequency and quality of the *communication* among group members. Team members talk about work issues with an emphasis on improvements they can make immediately. They listen carefully to one another's problems or solutions. Until this time, two workers may have worked side by side for years and not spoken to each other the entire workday. If they did speak, they discussed their families and hobbies. Some workers may have been close personal friends for 20 years and attended each other's children's graduations and weddings, but never talked about work, or the difficulties of the machine they were running, or the products they produced.

A research study presented at the 1992 Positive Employee Practices Institute (PEPI) Associates Annual Conference indicated that 7 out of 10 employees will see problems at work and not tell anyone else. That is, 70 percent will withhold information on a potential problem from a co-worker, supervisor, or manager. The problems go unnoticed or unreported until they become crises. I recently heard that workers in one plant saw a potential manufacturing problem but were afraid to tell management. The problem cost $1 million before it was solved. When communication is open and encouraged, individuals feel free to share information about potential problems, which can then be prevented.

A good manager at one of our client companies was unsure about the value of teamwork for his subordinates, who worked four different shifts to provide seven-day, 24-hour coverage. After only two training sessions, during which team communication skills were taught, he was ecstatic! The cross-shift communication had improved dramatically. Employees were passing on accurate, specific, and complete status reports to the next shift, including information about problems. As a result of improved communication between shifts, all shifts increased their productivity.

Employees in every organization carry around ideas for how performance can be improved. When they see bureaucracy, waste, and inefficiency, ideas about better ways to do things pop into their heads. Many of the solutions for the biggest challenges already reside in the organization—inside the minds of workers, engineers, trainers, supervisors, and every other employee. All too typically, few employees share their insights because of the usual response of the manager or supervisor when the ideas are spontaneously imparted. The overwhelmed supervisor does not even listen to the idea. The verbal statements that managers hurriedly utter, after hearing a portion of what was actually said, include "We can't change that!" or "We already tried that!" or "That idea won't work!" The next time a good idea flits into that employee's brain, it stays there.

Granted, not all employee ideas work, but they must be listened to with respect so that the motivation that prompted the expression of the idea is protected and nourished. This motivation drives improvement and change. A primary rule of breakthrough is that for a team to create the breakthrough idea, the members must have a lot of ideas! Some ideas will not be useful. But the expression of the ideas must always be reinforced by good listening and communication. Good communication becomes the foundation for breakthrough teamwork.

Level 2: Cooperation

After communication has improved, teams experience a noticeable improvement in *cooperation*. Team members begin asking for and offering help as they work. When people have extra time, they check with co-workers or even the supervisor to offer their help because they want the team to achieve its goals. In how many places do you see workers regularly assisting fellow employees during slack time? Contrast this with stories about people who hide when they get their work done so no one can find them.

The 10 members of the Team Engineers team at Asea Brown Boveri (ABB) in Coral Springs worked two feet apart and initially did not help each other. The individual assemblers who put the different parts together and the testers who tested to make sure the parts functioned properly acted as if they worked in different cities. A tester would fail a part but would not tell the assembler standing only a few feet away the specific problem that caused the part to be failed. The isolation went even further. Individual assemblers who worked next to each other felt that they had nothing in common because they built different products, even though they used the exact same manufacturing tools, equipment, parts, and work processes. After beginning Structured Teamwork, the team members quickly discovered that they could help each other succeed. They realized that cross-training would allow assemblers on a product line that was not busy to help other team members who were swamped with orders. This level of cooperation has resulted in three consecutive years of almost perfect on-time delivery to customers!

At the management level, managers often compete with each other for the next promotion rather than cooperate in guiding the corporation. Many managers spend inordinate amounts of time calculating how to avoid problems and/or how to pass on problems to their peer managers. One organization conducted special meetings in which managers and their engineers wasted many hours a week trying to determine which manager was to blame for product quality problems and manufacturing scrap. The meeting was similar to a formal hearing or trial. As this same group of managers developed as a C^5 team, they concluded that identifying the person to take the cost hit was not as important as discovering and addressing the causes of the defects and scrap. The managers cooperated and reduced major quality problems, creating several million dollars of additional profit.

As mentioned in Chapter 4, in the semiconductor manufacturing industry, equipment utilization is a key measure of success because the machines are so expensive. A single machine can cost up to $5 million. The team members at Advanced Micro Devices took the initiative to conduct cross-training without being asked to do so by their supervisors. The initial team goals given to them by their managers were to improve quality and productivity. On their own, the teams realized that cross-training was a key ingredient to reaching the goals they had set for themselves. As the cross-training was implemented, cooperation increased between team members to the point that they were covering each other's machines during breaks and vacations. Productivity rose 15 percent to 35 percent just through increased cooperation.

Good communication can assist cooperation. Honest talking and accurate listening are key ingredients of communication that improve cooperation. A dramatically successful example is the way Jack Welch, CEO of General Electric, runs his quarterly division business meetings. Most major corporations have similar meetings where each vice president presents a hundred transparency slides in a darkened room. Everyone gets bleary eyed and their heads turn to mush from data overload. Welch allows three transparencies per division vice president. Each transparency answers one of the following questions: What did you do last quarter? What are your goals and strategies for next quarter? What problems or opportunities do you foresee? He closes the doors to encourage honest, direct sharing of problems. By encouraging conciseness and honesty, Welch is creating a meeting climate where his brightest executives can ask for and offer help to each other, all in the spirit of what is best for GE.

This willingness to ask for and give help produces geometric gains, which result in breakthrough teamwork. The challenge is to reduce cycle time in implementing cooperative solutions and actions.

Level 3: Coordination

As impressive as the results can be when team members begin to cooperate, the improvements are even more significant as teams develop to the third level of C^5 teamwork, *coordination*. Cooperation can occur informally throughout the workday as individual contributors communicate and give assistance to each other. Coordination, as the next level of teamwork, requires more structure and planning. Coordination is the "planful" fitting together of each person's work responsibilities and actions so that higher, more complex goals can be rapidly and fully achieved, and less complex goals can be achieved more easily. Coordination requires excellent team goal setting, work planning, team decision making, and conflict management. A team that has highly coordinated activities has no significant disconnects in work execution and no significant duplication, inefficiencies, or gaps in achieving its goals.

Most of us have an idea of how manufacturing works: small parts are assembled into bigger parts (cars, stereos, washing machines) or a series of chemical and mechanical processing steps leads to a final, sellable product (medicine, food, semiconductors, gasoline). Work must be coordinated both within each step of the manufacturing process and from one step to the next, and certain steps must be performed either simultaneously or consecutively to ensure efficient production of a quality product.

But where do the new products come from? They are conceived and proposed by product planning groups. Companies live or die based on how fast and how successfully they predict what their existing and new customers will want to buy next. In most companies, product planning can take from 18 to 24 months. One reason for the long lag time is the strong say that various representatives in sales, marketing, executive management, engineering, and research and development—not to mention key customers—have in the decisions. These stakeholders often have strong and emotional differences of opinion.

Ralph Katz has studied hundreds of research and development teams. His studies indicate that in the absence of formal team development, it can take a research and development team 24 months to achieve peak performance.[1] Most organizations cannot wait 24 months for their most important teams to evolve naturally! I worked with one organization that estimated that $50 million of potential sales were lost because of lack of teamwork and unmanaged conflict during two years of arguing back and forth over a controversial new product. Not only was coordination missing, but so were communication and cooperation.

This situation contrasts with that of another product planning group under incredible time pressure. The director of the group said, "Dennis, we need the mother of all teamwork programs for this project." The team completed the new product planning in only 4 months, versus 24 months. The teamwork skills and processes created great communication and cooperation, even though team members were spread across distant continents. But what really made the project succeed in an incredibly short amount of time was the close coordination of each team member's role and responsibility at each site and between the eight sites globally. Each action step in the jointly developed action plan had to be achieved on time: no delays, no excuses. Each team member was able to visualize the importance of his or her contribution for the team's/organization's success. Since the team members felt personally responsible to each other and supportive of the team mission and goals, each individual did his or her assigned tasks on time. That's team coordination!

Team coordination requires the team members to have developed a team mission and team goals and to understand their team's role in accomplishing the big picture. The mission establishes the idealistic purpose and central focus for the team's activities. The fact that improved business results can come simply from better coordination can confound experienced plant managers. John Caffall, a manager at Advanced Micro Devices Submicron Development Center in Sunnyvale, California, was familiar with the quality circle approach to teamwork. John had valiantly volunteered one of his work groups to be a pilot team in the organization's implementation of self-managed teamwork and empowerment. At the biweekly meeting of the organizational change steering committee, after hearing that the pilot team had significantly improved its daily productivity, he asked unbelievingly, "How could my pilot team be getting improved results? They haven't had enough time to even complete one project." John's pilot team had advanced due to developing its team mission and goals, and as a result experienced increased productivity through improved coordination. This immediate focusing of the team allows members to see how and where they must coordinate to achieve their goals.

Coordination is especially important in work that has many interdependencies. Most work and business tasks done by one individual are interconnected to tasks done by other individuals. To quote John Donne, in the world of work, "no man is an island," at least not without several bridges to other workers.

> **Highly interdependent work groups require coordination.**

Joseph Cheng conducted research on 127 work units in 33 Belgian organizations.[2] He found that the amount of coordination present in a work unit had a positive influence on both work productivity and quality. Effective coordination in interdependent work units had an even stronger influence on improved quality and productivity than in groups with low amounts of interconnectedness. The major conclusion is this: Highly interdependent work groups require coordination.

Aren't most organizations highly interdependent today? They will be more so in the 21st century as technology and communication become more linked. Additionally, global corporations are attempting to coordinate the production function of interdependent business entities through shared services.

Level 4: Creative Breakthrough

The first three Cs of great teamwork—communication, cooperation, and coordination—can result in significant improvements in business results. The next characteristic teams develop is *creative breakthrough*. When I walk executives through the first three levels of C^5, they usually nod politely until I get to creative breakthrough. Mentally, their organizational self-assessment got them through the first three levels, but their heads lift up in excitement at the thought of the potential existing in every team and in the organization as a whole to achieve creative breakthrough.

Team breakthroughs are no accident. Many employees think of breakthrough ideas. The problem is overcoming the inertia barrier to action. People have to do something different, including sometimes changing work routines. Teams will support breakthroughs when they participate in creating them and implementing them.

A team of operators in a computer chip fabrication facility came up with an idea to increase machine uptime. They worked with the engineer assigned to their work area. The engineer had some improvement ideas himself. He cooperated with the team members in fleshing out their idea, and they in turn developed a coordinated action plan to implement his improvements. Together the combined solutions resulted in over $1 million a year in increased productivity! As would be expected, management recognized and publicized the contribution. Creative breakthrough provides accelerated improvement.

Level 5: Continuous Breakthrough

Many teams hit a home run by achieving significant business results through one or two creative breakthroughs. Unfortunately, there are often no more home runs, no more $1 million improvements. In fact, typically there is no mechanism in place that encourages the team to repeat its spectacular performance. Part of the problem is the traditional approach to teamwork, which makes teamwork something different from part of the regular job. However, when the organization effectively increases the empowerment of the team, a framework for *continuous breakthrough* has been established.

One example of a team achieving continuous breakthrough is a team that works for Asea Brown Boveri's distribution relay manufacturing plant. The team had its first breakthrough by reducing late orders from over 5 percent to almost zero. Then it reduced the lead time it needed to manufacture its product by almost 35 percent using many creative breakthroughs developed over a year and a half. Members of the team then went to management and asked for engineering help to redesign the product in order to reduce the unit cost. The team members had a number of ideas, including eliminating parts they thought were redundant.

Management turned down their request, citing as the reason that all of the product engineers were needed to design new products requested by customers. Not wanting to back off, the team members asked if they could work on redesigning the product as a team project and have an engineer periodically check their work. Management had to agree since the team had achieved other breakthrough improvements.

The team went to work. The members grabbed spare time wherever they could. Each member of the team knew that the other manufacturing productivity and quality goals also had to be met. When engineering approved the redesigned part, the team discovered that it had reduced the unit cost by 33 percent. Anyone in manufacturing will tell you that even a 3 percent improvement in the cost of producing one unit of a product can add significantly to the bottom line, and here was a team that had a 33 percent reduction!

A breakthrough is different from an improvement, and continuous breakthroughs are different from continuous improvements. When the concept of continuous improvement was introduced to certain industries, the managers hollered. They felt they already had continuous improvement. I discovered in some cases they were right. In certain industries like computer chip manufacturing, the alternatives are to have continuous improvement or to go out of business. Typically, the managers and engineers are constantly modifying work procedures and specifications to reduce cycle time and improve quality. As I worked with these companies, I discovered that the magnitude of the improvements jumped dramatically when a fully trained team began to creatively utilize a continuous improvement attitude and tools.

Mike Webb described how his marketing department at Advanced Micro Devices utilized the one-on-one as a major form of interaction. In the one-on-one, a manager and a subordinate have time together to discuss goals, issues, or ideas that either party wishes to discuss. Open, two-way dialogue is encouraged. Mike described how, after being trained in Structured Teamwork, he started noticing that whenever he was in a one-on-one, he and his subordinate would come up with some brilliant ideas for improving their work and satisfying customer needs. The problem was that the people necessary to implement the ideas were not present. The ideas Mike and the other manager were excited about lacked a feasibility assessment and the critical mass of the rest of their management team. The ideas didn't go over well when they went into the next meeting and told the other managers, "Hey, John and I came up with these great ideas that we want all of you to start working on."

If the whole team is present and involved in generating ideas, it is easier for team members to commit their time and energies to rapidly implementing the ideas selected by the team. One key in business is not which company can come up with the most innovative ideas, but which one can get those ideas *into action* the fastest.

A team can achieve the first breakthrough with training and coaching. Teams experience what winning feels like. However, continuous breakthroughs by all of the work teams are required for breakthrough teamwork. Continuous breakthroughs require a supportive organization and a proven methodology of organizational change and development. The C^5 model is just such a methodology that injects this critical capability into the organization's culture.

Recall that my definition of teamwork consists of communication, cooperation, coordination, creative breakthrough, and continuous breakthrough (see Fig. 5–2). Each level requires the presence of the prior level. The C^5 model can be used to evaluate at what level any team or organization is functioning.

C^5 TEAMWORK RESULTS

Structured Teamwork is a process used to develop the C^5 teamwork model in work groups throughout an organization. Structured Teamwork is more than a one-shot, off-site project. It is a way to install team structures and skills to achieve all five levels of C^5 teamwork.

C^5 teams have an extra spark and energy! They have esprit de corps and an "all for one and one for all" attitude. Trust is high among all team members. Many people are confused and think that trust, enthusiasm, and cohesiveness are the causes of good teamwork. Esprit de corps and trust are, in fact, the effects of achieving the five

FIGURE 5–2

C^5 Teamwork Model

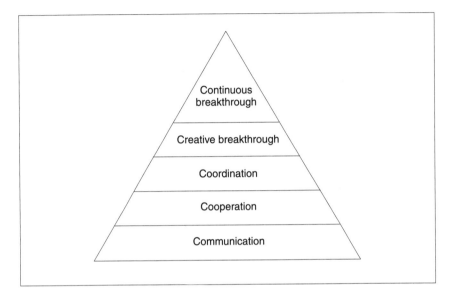

Cs. These desirable attributes occur only after a team experiences work performance successes over a period of time. It is a backward view of the cause-and-effect relationship that causes some team-building programs to focus on improving esprit de corps rather than improving the team's work performance. Simply stated, esprit de corps and trust are the effects, not the causes, of breakthrough teamwork. Specific results occur as a team moves through each level. Examples of some of the results are presented in Figure 5–3.

Esprit de corps and trust are the effects, not the causes, of breakthrough teamwork.

C^5 teamwork results in even more than just empowered, self-managed work teams that efficiently hum along doing whatever is asked of them. The achievable mission of every team is to be a world leader. C^5 is about teams and individuals getting so creative and innovative that they become world leaders in their own field of endeavor, whatever that may be.

FIGURE 5–3

C^5 Teamwork Results

Level	Business Results
Level 1: Communication	■ Problems are identified, defined, and communicated so that they can be solved. ■ True two-way communication results in better understanding and alignment on goals. ■ Clearer understanding of shared goals increases likelihood of their achievement.
Level 2: Cooperation	■ Productivity increases as employees help others when they have extra time. ■ Cycle time is reduced as employees structure the output of their work to reduce input barriers to the next workstation. ■ Work quality improves as employees ask for help when they are not sure how to do a task.
Level 3: Coordination	■ When work goals and team member roles are coordinated, goals are achieved on or ahead of schedule. ■ If a new opportunity or obstacle occurs, the team rapidly responds.
Level 4: Creative breakthrough	■ Significantly better solutions to problems and work process improvements are achieved.
Level 5: Continuous breakthrough	■ Faster and better ways to execute action plans are discovered all the time. ■ Opportunities for improving how all work is done are seized. ■ There is significant continuous improvement of all work processes and customer relationships.

BREAKTHROUGH POINTS

- Teamwork means more than just having a pleasant work environment.
- Groups of workers progress through five successively higher levels of teamwork as expressed in the C^5 model: from communication to cooperation to coordination to creative breakthrough to continuous breakthrough.
- Specific business results occur as a team moves through each level, leading to world leadership in its field of work.

THE 10 COMPONENTS OF STRUCTURED TEAMWORK

Preston Snuggs, a director at Advanced Micro Devices, remarked, "We've had blue-collar productivity programs for years. Until Structured Teamwork, we've never had a program for the white-collar employees, including managers. Now we have a productivity program for the whole organization."

The essential elements that make Structured Teamwork effective with both blue- and white-collar teams are its 10 key components:

The Core

■ Team creativity.

Communication and Cooperation

■ Team communication.

■ Team meetings.

■ Conflict management.

Coordination

- Team values, vision, and mission.
- Team goal setting.
- Roles and responsibilities and team organization.

Continuous Breakthrough Processes

- Team problem solving.
- Team decision making.
- Work process improvement.

In previous chapters, research conclusions supported these 10 components as the enablers to breakthrough teamwork.

As the accompanying figure shows, the foundation component of Structured Teamwork is team creativity. Breakthrough teamwork happens because team members creatively pursue new solutions to old problems. They develop innovative approaches to work pro-

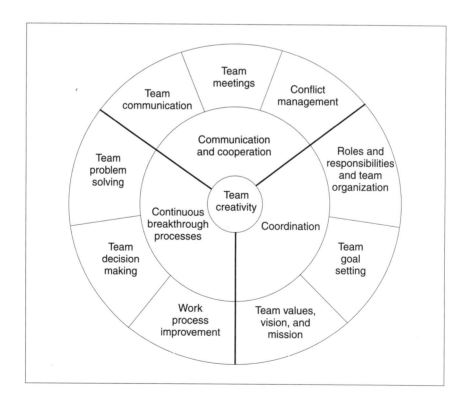

cesses, work layouts, and ways to work with customers and suppliers. Team creativity is utilized in each of the other components.

The other nine components cluster around three groupings of the C^5 model. The three groups are communication and cooperation, coordination, and continuous breakthrough processes.

The communication and cooperation cluster includes three teamwork components. Team communication ensures that team members use good communication skills both among themselves and with others with whom they must interface. Good team meetings guarantee the communication and cooperation of team members as they solve problems, make decisions, and improve work processes. Conflict management provides a way to resolve differences that occur in teams when people feel ownership for their work. Conflict is bound to result when people care. As these three components are mastered, teams are able to coordinate and create breakthroughs faster and more effectively.

Coordination includes three Structured Teamwork elements. The team identifies its values, and develops its own vision and mission statements. These activities ensure that team actions are coordinated and aligned. The team sets goals that are supported by real-time action plans and measurement indicators. Team members prioritize their time, actions, and decisions around the team goals. They coordinate their efforts to reach the goals. Finally, to assist the coordination efforts, team members clarify their roles and responsibilities and organize the team to achieve business results.

The final three elements of Structured Teamwork cluster around continuous breakthrough processes. The processes include team problem solving, team decision making, and work process improvement. The structured team processes enable teams to make breakthrough changes by depersonalizing team members' feelings about goals, roles, problems, and work processes. The processes provide objectivity and structure to allow teams to achieve great business results.

In the Structured Teamwork methodology, research not only helps select the 10 most important components of teamwork but also identifies the critical steps for how to achieve each component and how to link the components to each other. The most important research discovery was that the 10 components reinforce each other to achieve great business results. Team communication skills have their greatest impact on business results when team members use the skills to improve their problem solving, goal setting, and work process improvement activities.[1] Likewise, team goal setting, when combined with each of the other nine components, improves performance and results. Team creativity skills improve both the quantity and quality of team member ideas for their team mission and goals as well as for problem solving, decision making, process improvement, and even conflict management. Research findings show that, in addition to being mutually reinforcing, the 10 components have a multiplicative effect when properly used. The bottom line is that workplace teams trained in this method achieve breakthrough performances over and over.

Team development training and techniques must interweave the components as they are taught to and applied by the teams. For instance, communication skills training and practice in the Structured Teamwork methodology is introduced in the team communication training module, but the skills are practiced and applied in each of the other nine training modules. The accompanying Structured Teamwork Assessment offers a quick way to assess where your teams lie in their use of the 10 components of Structured Teamwork. Take a moment to rate your team.

Feel free to copy this assessment form if you would like to have your team members fill it out. Lower scores indicate components that might have high relevance for you and your team. The chapter references in the questionnaire are to chapters that deal specifically with that component.

Chapters 6 through 15 take a closer look at the research and methods for how to do each of the 10 components of Structured Teamwork. The order of Chapters 7 through 15 does not necessarily represent the sequence in which they should be presented in training. Training order should be based on the Structured Teamwork Assessment and pretraining interviews that discover which components a particular team is strong in and which need further work and development.

STRUCTURED TEAMWORK® ASSESSMENT

TEAM NAME_____

Using a 1–10 scale (10 = high; 1 = low), rate the following factors for your team. For example, if you feel your work climate is moderately supportive, write a 5 on the line in the Rating Today column. Put a 0 if the factor is *not* occurring today. Next, in the column entitled Rating in Six Months, write in the number that describes where you would like the team to be in six months.

	Rating Today	Rating in Six Months

The Core: Creativity

1. Our team regularly uses **creativity,** and each team member develops innovative ideas both during and outside team meetings. (Chapter 6)

Levels 1 and 2: Communication and Cooperation

2. Our team has a supportive work climate where we respect, understand, help, and compliment each other. We use good **communication skills.** (Chapter 7)

3. Our team has effective **meetings** that are frequent enough to maintain good coordination and support. (Chapter 8)

4. Our team **conflicts are effectively managed** instead of being ignored or allowed to disrupt the group. (Chapter 9)

Level 3: Coordination

5. Our team has a team vision, team values, and a clear, concise **mission statement** that establishes our priorities. (Chapter 10)

6. Our team has an understanding and commitment to our common **goals and work plans.** (Chapter 11)

7. Our team has a clear description and understanding of each member's **role and responsibilities.** (Chapter 12)

(continued)

Structured Teamwork® Assessment (concluded)

Levels 4 and 5: Continuous Breakthrough

8. Our team uses effective and timely **problem solving** during and between meetings. (Chapter 13) _____ _____

9. Our team makes important **decisions** in an effective and timely manner, and all members support the decisions. (Chapter 14) _____ _____

10. Our team continuously **improves its work processes,** including charting quality results and the use of work process flow diagrams. (Chapter 15) _____ _____

6
CHAPTER

Team Creativity: The Prerequisite for Breakthrough Teamwork

When I first began assembling teamwork success stories and read the remarkable 100 percent improvements in performance, I wondered. I tried to imagine how people could double their productivity. Do they walk and work twice as fast, as in an early black-and-white motion picture of Charlie Chaplin or the Keystone Cops? I was puzzled as I observed the teams I trained and saw their steady and significant improvement in business results. If anything, people walked more slowly and were more relaxed as their work results significantly improved. The improvement came not by working harder but by working smarter. And it was the teams' use of creativity skills that contributed to their working smarter.

Creativity is the booster rocket for teamwork. In the popular George Lucas film *Star Wars*®, the spaceship *Millennium Falcon*® is about to be captured. The ship accelerates into hyperspace to escape. The viewer experiences a sensation of incredible momentum; stars appear to rush by; the ship increases velocity to and then past the speed of light. Like the booster rocket, team creativity causes teams to accelerate and gives them the power to exceed their previous levels of best performance.

I have seen team after team achieve breakthrough performance as a result of creativity exhibited by team members in and outside of team meetings. Some ideas are low-tech solutions. A team member at a manufacturing plant used fingernail polish to mark where to line up cutting blades to manufacture components for automobile cooling systems. Another team member brought a hand scoop from home to load rivet joints into the automatic riveter so that the rivets wouldn't spill all over the floor.

Teams have also found success in applying creativity to high-technology problems. A team in a computer chip manufacturing facility wanted to reduce the amount of time it took to complete the chemical processes on the chips in their work area. During the brainstorming phase of the problem-solving process, the team members came up with 20 solutions. One of their wild ideas was to eliminate all of the quality inspection steps. That idea was impossible, but they did identify one inspection step they thought was not needed. They designed a sophisticated experiment and collected data to prove to management that there was no decrease in quality or other adverse effects when the inspection step was eliminated. Not only did they find that there were no detrimental effects, but they discovered that the quality inspection step had been contaminating the computer chips and causing rejects downstream in the manufacturing process! The elimination of the inspection step resulted in productivity and quality improvements adding up to $1 million of increased revenue per year from the work area.

Team creativity has been found to be necessary for the very survival of high-technology companies. Creativity is necessary for successful teamwork as well. Time for team training and team meetings is expensive. If teams attempt to communicate, plan, and problem-solve without creativity, they will barely return the investment made for their members' time away from production or normal work tasks. Look around at teams that show little improvement: these are the teams that neglect innovation and imagination.

Some say that synergy is a reason to have a team, that the whole (the team) is greater than the sum of its parts (individuals). Math examples have described synergy as $1 + 1 + 1 + 1 + 1 = 25$ or some similar amount higher than the arithmetic total. Synergy is supposedly the mystical force that creates the added value. But synergy need not be a mystery. I believe synergy can and must be explicitly developed. Creativity, when combined with team goal setting, builds synergy.

Kathleen Eisenhardt of Stanford University studied the decision making of executive teams at eight Silicon Valley microcomputer firms.[1] The speed of the top executive and his or her executive team's ability to make important decisions made the difference between profits and bankruptcy. A key difference between the successful companies and the losers was the executive teams' ability to consider many alternative solutions simultaneously. The creativity of the executive team that identified a variety of strategies for continuing to grow and survive made the difference in its success. The challenges facing all organizations require that many solutions be generated rapidly.

Every team can achieve performance breakthroughs using the team creativity skills and steps that have been discovered from research. Let's look now at the key principles of successful team creativity.

WHEN TO USE TEAM CREATIVITY

Team creativity and one of its major methods, brainstorming, are misunderstood. Most people think that the only time a team needs to be creative is in the solution development phase of problem solving. This is a very narrow utilization of team creativity. Teams can use team creativity skills in the following areas:

- Team goal setting.
- Goal and performance measurement.
- Development of creative action plans to achieve ambitious team goals.
- Team decision making.
- Problem identification.
- Quality improvement ideas.
- Work process improvement and reengineering.
- Conflict management.
- Job redesign.

In each of the above management areas, creativity by the team increases the subsequent impact of the task.

Countless teams are established every day to achieve important objectives, but they often fail to develop effective ways to measure their team objectives because such development is too difficult or time-consuming. It is especially hard for knowledge teams to develop relevant and easy-to-assess team goal measurements. For example, most goal and performance measurements focus on quantity or productivity because these standards are easy to measure. But other results, such as quality improvement and customer satisfaction, are just as important. Both research and experience indicate that having and using relevant and feasible measurements of team goals dramatically increases work and business breakthroughs. Teams must use creativity to generate effective measurements of their goals. Breakthrough teams must also use creativity in many of their other team activities: problem solving, conflict management, and work process improvement.

CREATIVITY TRAINING

Creativity, the ability to develop both a large quantity of ideas and highly imaginative ideas, is a skill. Some people are born with certain natural creative abilities in such areas as music, art, and inventiveness. But every person's creative thinking ability can be increased.

People at work can learn to be more creative.[2] When confronted with a problem requiring an innovative solution, most workers usually think of one or at most two potential solutions. Before creativity training, some managers complained that they were lucky to identify one or two good ideas after an hour-long discussion. After training, these same managers developed 20 good ideas in 15 minutes!

Significant work improvements occur when creativity training is combined with a team methodology like Structured Teamwork rather than implemented separately. Groups receiving both creativity training and problem-solving skills training increased their abilities in both areas.[3] In one study, trained teams were able to identify more complex underlying issues of major work and business problems than teams without specific training. This development in turn resulted in the generation of more relevant solutions. Increasing employee participation in decision making and goal setting also increased creativity in daily work activities.[4] An early research study of teamwork found that creativity training increased the development of unique solutions when there was a feeling of good teamwork and group cohesion in the team.[5] Creativity training by itself did not increase the quantity of solutions to work-related problems. This research explains why team creativity is most successful when implemented as part of the Structured Teamwork process: team creativity is reinforced and supported by the whole Structured Teamwork methodology.

STRUCTURED BRAINSTORMING VERSUS UNSTRUCTURED BRAINSTORMING

Most everyone has participated in the form of team creativity called brainstorming. A topic is thrown out to the group: "Cost reduction— how can we reduce our costs?" Immediately someone says, "Reduce the number of copies we make!" Someone else speaks up, "Yeah, and paper clips, too. Reduce the number of paper clips." People are free to contribute at any time. The only rule is that no one can criticize any- one else's ideas. This unstructured approach is the way most people have experienced brainstorming. It *is* like a storm: an uncontrolled storm, a tornado or hurricane. What if all of the group's storming energy could be captured and channeled?

Normally, proposing that a group use brainstorming causes a mixed reaction. Some individuals, usually creative people, get excited about the free flow of wild ideas. Most managers do not like brain- storming; they think it is a waste of time. The skeptics argue it is better to let people work alone. Guess what? The skeptics are right.

A whole series of research studies has found that pooling the ideas of individuals working alone results in more creative ideas than when the same number of people engage in unstructured brainstorm- ing.[6] The 3M Company conducted one of the early studies with groups of research scientists and advertising staff.[7] The individual approach generated 30 percent more ideas than group brainstorming, and the quality of the ideas was as good or better. The negative results of the traditional brainstorming approach have been used to discour- age the use of teams for creativity, and have discouraged some com- panies from attempting to use teamwork in the workplace at all.

There is a solution: *structured* brainstorming. Structured brain- storming methods have resulted in as much as a 100 percent improve- ment over unstructured brainstorming.[8] Edward De Bono, who has dedicated his life to improving individual and group creativity, stated that unstructured creativity "is a dead end. It appears to be attractive at first, but you really can't go very far. There are systematic struc- tured approaches to creativity that I believe have more substance."[9]

Structured brainstorming incorporates the best of a method called the nominal group technique with the best of interactive group brainstorming. The core element of the nominal group technique is to have individuals write down their ideas alone and send them to one person for consolidation. The missing ingredient in this technique is group interaction and the possible mutual stimulation of new ideas.

Another problem is establishing the momentum to propel the group to act on the best of the brainstormed ideas. When structured group interaction follows an opportunity for team members to initially generate ideas working alone, creativity takes off![10] The key principles of structured brainstorming are organized into the following four steps, which are discussed below:

1. Prepare.
2. Maximize participation.
3. Be positive.
4. Plan action.

Prepare

First, select a facilitator or someone to keep the team on track as it goes through the four steps of structured brainstorming. One study showed that teams using a facilitator generated almost 45 percent more unique ideas than teams not using a designated facilitator.[11] After receiving training in structured brainstorming, any member of the team can facilitate the team. When appropriate, have a perceived expert or a manager introduce the topic and ask the team for help in brainstorming solutions. This frees people to contribute ideas. I have seen team members work hard in a structured brainstorming session after someone they respected asked for their most creative ideas.

Challenging individuals within a group to think of as many ideas as possible increases the quantity of ideas. Also effective is setting a goal for a specific number of ideas and types of solutions. These goals and challenges increase the quantity and quality of the ideas that are generated.[12] Going for quantity is important because the number of ideas highly correlates with the quality of ideas. One study found that, in problem solving, a team can achieve an approximate ratio of one good idea for every 10 ideas generated.

Maximize Participation

The single most important step in maximizing participation is to have team members initially write down their ideas before anyone shares an idea. In approximately five minutes, each individual writes as many ideas as possible. This step ensures that each team member has at least one idea to share during the group interaction. Having individuals write alone first, before even one idea has been shared, increases the diversity and divergent thinking of the team. In unstructured brainstorming, the first individual who speaks sets, and therefore limits, the direction of thinking for the group. Recall that in the above example about a brainstorming session on ways to cut costs, the first person suggested reducing the number of copies made. That, in turn, stimulated the other group members to think of office-supply solutions. With this mindset established, it is doubtful that someone in the group would throw out a different cost reduction idea like reducing the amount of time it takes to win new customers.

Truly creative solutions often diverge from the "mainstream." Think for a moment about the points on a compass. In unstructured brainstorming, if the first person to speak has a "south" orientation, he or she will usually influence the group to think only of "south" ideas. If people are allowed to write their own ideas down first, the team will generally have "north," "south," "east," and "west" solutions, some of which will truly be breakthrough ideas. When team members take a few a minutes to write down their own uninfluenced ideas, there is greater participation as well as unique and diverse ideas.

One specific method to increase creativity is to encourage each team member to come up with one "wild idea" for whatever topic is being brainstormed. The great thing about wild ideas is there are no bad wild ideas. There was an Amoco Canada oil field that was using high-technology methods to recover oil. The cost of recovery, however, was $8.50 per barrel as compared to $3.00 per barrel at a comparable field. The oil field supervisor and his team argued that their costs were higher because there was a river running through the middle of their field. They also had a warehouse at the field that was loaded with $16 million of supplies and equipment.

The Amoco management shared with the supervisor and the team how their high costs were going to put them out of business. The team called for a brainstorming meeting. A variety of suggestions were proposed, but none of them would significantly reduce the costs. Finally, the supervisor proposed his wild idea, which was to get rid of the field's warehouse and transport the supplies in from a nearby location. The team quickly was able to reduce the costs to $6.00 per barrel and eventually approached the $4.00 per barrel cost. The wild idea made it possible for the team to achieve their cost reduction goal. The team brainstorming itself created the ownership for the ensuing implementation plan.

The next step for increasing team participation occurs during the kick-off phase of the group interaction of structured brainstorming.

Here, the facilitator asks that each individual share only one idea at a time. Going around the group and getting only one idea per person at a time is sometimes called round-robin participation. The opposite approach is when the most verbal team members present all of their ideas at once. This causes the more quiet individuals to not contribute, either because their ideas were already presented or because they feel intimidated. In contrast, round-robin participation increases the entire team's generation of creative solutions.[13]

Be Positive

Not criticizing another team member's idea is a valid principle in any kind of creativity. It is a critical part of unstructured brainstorming, and it applies equally well to structured brainstorming. There is a time when it is essential to nurture seedling ideas and not prematurely smother them with criticism. In fact, it is useful for the team and the facilitator to say encouraging words of support as people share their ideas with the rest of the group. This helps provide a "greenhouse effect" in which seedling ideas can grow and thrive, awaiting evaluation at the proper time.

Research has also found that outside observers or evaluators negatively affect a group's creativity.[14] Any type of judgmental or evaluative element reduces the quantity of solutions and therefore the number of potentially good solutions. People with negative attitudes, especially if they are facilitators or leaders, can kill team creativity and the likelihood of a team achieving any breakthroughs in business results. Therefore, it is important for team members to communicate positive attitudes toward the team, especially during team creativity activities.

Most of the rules about being positive are widely known. There is an equally important new aspect to being positive during structured brainstorming. Each team member must be positive in his or her self-talk. In creative situations, most of us, as we start to think of possible ideas, mentally criticize our ideas before even fully formulating the thought. We mentally say, "That won't work," "They won't like that idea," and similar critical statements. Edward De Bono discovered that if individuals would censor the negative self-talk and replace it by mentally making encouraging remarks, both the quantity and quality of creative ideas could be increased.[15] Mentally encouraging positive self-talk and mentally cutting off negative statements doubled idea production.[16]

Plan Action

Trained teams can implement the above steps and develop 20 to 30 ideas in 20 minutes. The advantage of collecting the ideas rapidly is that momentum and energy are generated, which can be transmitted to acting on the best ideas. The team identifies several ideas to start pursuing at the same time. Teams that simultaneously work on several solutions achieve rapid work and business improvements. The team transforms the selected creative ideas into an action plan, with specific team members identified by name and target due dates. Using the momentum that comes from any team creativity activity can break the implementation barrier.

This chapter began with a little funny musing about how fast teams might have to move to achieve 100 percent improvements in their work. The facts are clear: teams can achieve 100 percent–plus improvements in productivity if they will (among other things) put their creativity to work in a careful, structured way. If teams prepare, maximize participation, stay positive, and use their results to plan action, they will achieve impressive performance breakthroughs.

BREAKTHROUGH POINTS

- Creativity is the booster rocket for teamwork.
- Team creativity is not limited to problem solving but can be used in a wide variety of team tasks.
- Structured brainstorming produces superior results compared to unstructured brainstorming.
- The four steps in structured brainstorming are (1) prepare, (2) maximize participation, (3) be positive, and (4) plan action.

7

CHAPTER

Team Communication

COMMUNICATION AND COOPERATION

Chapters 7, 8, and 9 capture the three Structured Teamwork components that make communication and cooperation possible. This chapter provides the tools and skills necessary for team members to communicate effectively with one another and with others outside the team. Chapter 8 equips teams with meeting structures that help both communication and cooperation. It also identifies ways to promote participation in team meetings and methods to increase team member cooperation in meetings. Chapter 9, Conflict Management, gives reasons why handling conflicts as they occur is important and provides an effective approach to managing conflicts between team members. Often teams require development in team communication, meetings, and conflict management first, before the other teamwork structures can be established.

INTERPERSONAL COMMUNICATION

If teams need communication, what type of communication leads to breakthrough? One of the major complaints in every organization is the lack of communication. The results of almost every organizational attitude survey ever conducted indicate that there needs to be more communication. This finding seems contradictory because in most organizations, a huge quantity of information is disseminated. Information is shared downward to employees by management. Information is shared upward to supervisors and management by employees filling out data reports, preparing product reports, and completing all kinds of forms that process data. Why then do individuals in organizations always say that communication is a problem?

The answer to the question lies in the fact that often there is poor *interpersonal* communication; there is inadequate two-way communication between employees and their supervisors and managers, and often between managers and managers. There may be a lot of information sharing, but there is no interaction about the information and how it should be used on the job. Successful communication requires an interaction—a two-way interaction—regarding the information: talking about, discussing, and reviewing the information; analyzing its importance; and applying the information to assist in achieving goals and improving work.

Organizations that have strong interpersonal communication between employees, supervisors, and managers show good results on their communication surveys. An example is the Westinghouse Electronic Components Plant in Fort Payne, Alabama. The Westinghouse plant implemented team communication skills training that emphasized two-way interaction for all managers and team members. When the corporate communication and attitude survey was administered, the plant obtained some of the highest scores on communication by employees in Westinghouse history.

Effective team communication leads directly to action. The two most important aspects of team communication are interpersonal communication and the means of communication, especially for important information. Of all types of communication, two-way interaction is the most preferred and the most powerful. Engineers and scientists use interpersonal communication with their colleagues more frequently than formal communication methods.[1] Every interpersonal contact has the potential to build a positive relationship or to tear one down. Figure 7–1 shows that, initially, there is very little distance between ignoring a fellow team member and engaging in a friendly greeting. The distance, however, grows once one is on the negative path of using destructive behaviors versus constructive behaviors.

Effective interpersonal communication includes listening to a team member without immediately rejecting what is said. One team

FIGURE 7–1

Interpersonal Contacts Are for Better or Worse

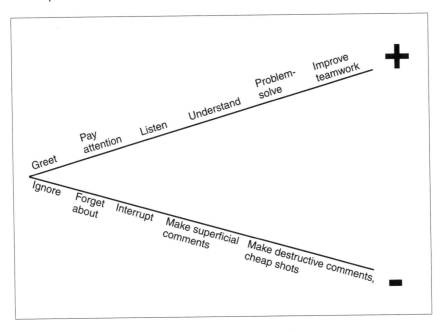

member told me, "When my ideas are not listened to, I feel like I don't count. If I don't count, maybe I should leave." If the leader communicates that his or her own ideas are the only important ones, people become passive and let the leader do all the work. People quit thinking and do only the minimum amount of work. Mistakes are made. The leader criticizes people and then the relationship gets into a vicious negative circle.

A different team member, Yolanda, said that when her manager communicated that he was not listening, she stopped sharing ideas. Because he also got mad when he was told bad news, Yolanda quit warning him of potential problems. This was a closed communication relationship instead of an open one, and it is all too common in many organizations.

Achieving an open communication relationship requires interpersonal skills training, the team context, and continual feedback to leaders and team members on how well they use the major skills. The most important skills are approachability, listening, being specific, and checking understanding.

Approachability

Team communication must occur during team meetings and outside of team meetings. In production work, when a team member needs help, he or she usually needs it now! The question or problem the team member has may be one that can severely hurt the achievement of one of the team's goals if it is not immediately addressed. Individuals need to be able to go to any team member or manager for help at any time. When a production team member needs to approach another team member who is working on a piece of equipment, an effective technique is to approach the person and quietly wait to be acknowledged. Machine operators who must keep their eyes looking straight ahead can be taught to shake their head to the side when they are ready to listen to a fellow team member who wants to present a pressing question or problem.

Managers of teams communicate their approachability through techniques such as the open door policy, managing by wandering around, and lunch with the boss. One very busy manager I knew established "office hours," a publicized office hour each day when anyone could walk in with a concern or idea. I observed how employees from all levels used that opportunity to go in with suggestions that could improve productivity that very day!

Managers and team members with offices communicate their approachability by looking up when someone comes in, coming from behind the desk, or having their desk arranged so that it is not between them and individuals who come to talk. One reason behind the move in business and industry to relax managers' dress codes was to increase the approachability of managers. Taking off one's coat and tie is a signal that often allows employees to perceive their managers as more approachable. Salespeople, executives, and other professionals who do not have the option to dress informally must learn to communicate approachability through their body language. Key behaviors are facing the other person, smiling, using open arm and hand gestures, and maintaining eye contact.

Regardless of the methods used, team members and their team facilitator or manager must sit down and decide together how and when to be approachable to each other. If team members and managers are not approachable, there will be little or no communication.

Listening

Listening is the foundation of all interpersonal communication skills. It requires paying attention to what the speaker is saying. Since people can listen at 600 words per minute but talk only at 100 to 150 words per minute, they are easily distracted.[2] The challenge is to use the extra time to listen more productively. Unfortunately, most people start planning what they are going to say next instead of listening to the speaker's concluding words. Ironically, the last sentence, which usually contains the meat or most important point, is totally missed by most listeners. In effective team communication, people learn to use the extra time to mentally repeat the speaker's key words and to understand his or her main points.

Recently I was helping a cross-functional project team from four different divisions develop a teamwork road map for the whole organization. One of the team members, named Rocky, had difficulty formulating his ideas when he spoke. The team used excellent listening and paraphrasing skills with this individual. The conference room was quiet whenever Rocky spoke. Team members' faces became still with concentration as they listened without interrupting. When Rocky was finished, one of the other team members paraphrased, using the skill of checking understanding to be sure everyone understood what Rocky intended to communicate. Sometimes it took two or three tries back and forth for us to grasp Rocky's idea or concern. As a result of these listening efforts, at least once at every meeting, one of Rocky's blockbuster ideas was used in the teamwork road map and plan.

During team training, I frequently ask the question "What are the most important ground rule behaviors team members need to demonstrate toward each other to have a great team?" The number one answer is "To respect each other." Because the word *respect* can have a variety of meanings, I always ask, "What does respect mean?" The answers are "To listen to the other person's ideas with an open mind," "To listen without interrupting," "To value each person's ideas and uniqueness"—all behaviors dealing with listening. To people in the workplace, *how* they are listened to goes far in building a team and creating the circumstances where potentially breakthrough ideas can be expressed and heard.

Being Specific

Communication at work must be fast and effective. Speed is enhanced when anyone speaking presents problems or ideas as specifically as possible. One organization's morale was suffering because people described problems this way: "Management never listens to our ideas," "No one cares about doing a quality job," and "Our management information system sucks." None of the above statements is specific. Being overly general not only is depressing, but it provides no platform from which to start solving the problem. Team members need to be specific—to state, for example, *which* manager is not listening to *what* ideas, or *which* person is making *what* quality errors on *what* work. When team members are specific, they are able to communicate and solve problems in a few minutes—even problems that previously took an hour just to identify and understand. Most managers whose teams have been taught effective team communication skills feel that the training helped bring about real teamwork and was responsible for many business and work breakthroughs.

The skill of being specific can improve delegating and help establish accountability. Most of each team member's daily work is organized around roles and responsibilities that have been developed as a team. If the team used good communication skills, these roles and responsibilities are worded in specific terms. But what about instances where team members or the team facilitator must ask another team member to do a task that lies outside his or her regular roles and responsibilities? Are the team members specific about *what* needs to be done and *why* the task will help the team achieve its goals?

Consider the phrasing of the following two questions:

1. "Would you finish that report by Friday?"

2. "Can you have a first draft of our current progress on our financial goals to Susan by 11:00 A.M. Friday?"

The second version reduces uncertainty and more clearly communicates the requirement. Companies can totally miss target dates on work goals simply because there was no completion time specified.

Presenting the *why* behind a delegated assignment increases the likelihood of a quality effort. Most people do not like to be told what to do by another person. When the reason for the assignment is explained, the importance of doing the task becomes obvious and resentment often disappears.

Speaking in specific terms also improves recognition. It may be easier to say to someone, "You did good work this week," than to say, "I liked it when you completed the Motorola job on time even though you received it late. Motorola prefers suppliers that meet their delivery commitments"—but the latter comment is preferable. Research on praise and verbal recognition is clear: when you want someone to know exactly what pleased you, and you want to encourage future repetition of the behavior, *be specific*. The increased specificity takes only an extra minute, but the power of the statement that is transmitted increases the likelihood of breakthrough performance many times over.

Checking Understanding

The skill of checking understanding is valuable in all team communication. Checking understanding is the two-way quality control step that occurs when a speaker has completed a statement and a listener summarizes back the key details or the main point. Some team developers call this skill active listening, empathetic responding, or testing understanding. On the surface, the value of summarizing and repeating what an individual has said is to ensure that the listener has accurately heard what the speaker intended to communicate. Figure 7–2 depicts the objective of the listener to match what is in his or her mind with what is in the speaker's brain to ensure that the message is being fully communicated. The listener may need two or three exchanges to completely understand the message.

A second, less obvious benefit of checking understanding is that it increases each team member's basic understanding of fellow team members' feelings, attitudes, knowledge, and hopes about the team and the work itself. The shared understanding creates emotional support that increases each team member's self-confidence, creativity, and openness to sharing problems and potentially valuable solutions. The esprit de corps frees people to act decisively.

FIGURE 7–2

Checking Understanding

The how-to steps for the checking understanding skill are as follows:

- Listen.
- Recall key words.
- Mentally summarize what the speaker is wanting and why.
- Indicate you are checking understanding.
- Concisely state your summary of the what and the why of the speaker's statement.

It is important that a team member preface his or her responsive remarks with the comment that he or she is checking understanding. The listener thus communicates that he or she is not necessarily agreeing with the speaker. He or she is only clarifying the speaker's statement.

Checking understanding is a valuable tool to use in resolving disagreements. Often two team members will be arguing with each other, and bystanders can hear that both parties are saying the same thing. The individuals in the disagreement are not listening or trying to understand their fellow team member's point of view. Calling a time-out and having each person check understanding of the other's statements has resolved many team conflicts.

Multicultural teams, especially those composed of individuals with different native languages, may need extra practice in checking understanding and more encouragement to use checking understanding. Without checking understanding, members of multilanguage teams often smile and nod yes as though they understand, when in fact they do not.

One other group needs additional encouragement to use checking understanding. Surprisingly, managers sometimes need more practice. Managers are used to talking, and they do it well, so they may think their job is to manage, not to listen. When managers check understanding, they demonstrate that they not only are listening but also accurately understand what is being said.

The team communication skills described in this section are crucial for breakthrough. Their use encourages team members to freely share potential problems as well as solutions. When team communication skills are used with customers, increased sales can occur.[3] Research indicates that interorganizational relationships, including joint ventures, are predominantly based on interpersonal relationships and teamwork among individuals from each of the firms, not on the companies themselves.[4] The teamwork and communication skills of the companies' representatives are pivotal to the success of the joint venture.

Research has repeatedly demonstrated that training supervisors in effective interpersonal communication skills improves the performance of their work groups. To be successful, self-managed teams need interpersonal communication skills training for all team members. These skills allow the team members to effectively manage their work and to utilize all 10 components of Structured Teamwork.

METHODS FOR SHARING IMPORTANT INFORMATION

After learning and using interpersonal communication skills, the next key ingredient of team communication is for the team to develop and implement efficient methods of disseminating important information. In a two-stage process, the team first identifies what information needs to be shared to achieve its goals, and then determines the most efficient way to do so. Sharing should include the use of less typical means of communication such as "huddles," e-mail, schedule boards, and of course team meetings. In one large high-technology company, the highest-rated and most powerful communication medium was the team meeting. Meetings allow simultaneous understanding and the interaction of all team members.

Information should be evaluated on its just-in-time utility to promote coordinated action to achieve or exceed team goals while avoiding information overload. The single most important piece of information is how well the team is achieving its goals. Some teams publicly display charts and graphs of the most current results in their work area. Other teams begin each team meeting with a brief report on goal progress. Awareness of progress on team goals increases motivation and performance of the goals, especially if the goals were set by the team members themselves. It may be wise to avoid or minimize other, more peripheral information.

Effective two-way communication is essential for good teamwork. In addition, it is a building block toward breakthrough teamwork because it helps teams achieve the other components of Structured Teamwork. Problem solving, decision making, goal setting, effective team meetings—all are vital ingredients for breakthrough teamwork, and all are impossible without good communication.

BREAKTHROUGH POINTS

- Effective team communication leads directly to action.
- The most important interpersonal skills for achieving effective team communication are being approachable, listening, being specific, and checking understanding.
- Important information must be identified and then communicated in the most efficient manner.

8

CHAPTER

Team Meetings

HOW TEAM MEETINGS CREATE ENERGY

Many of the improved business results due to Structured Teamwork occur because of the rapid and synchronized implementation of action steps. Team meetings are the starting point for rapid, synchronized action. Team meetings have the potential to be energizing and to meet a variety of employee needs. Individuals can leave a well-run team meeting motivated and recommitted to the team's mission and goals.

It is a pity that so few meetings achieve this. Many organizations cite meetings as the most frequent and consistent example of wasted time. And this is from companies that have spent literally millions of dollars on training in effective meetings. Why does this happen? My colleague Mark Henry believes it is because the teams were told "here is how to run a successful meeting." None of them were given the task of creating their own meeting procedures and structures, as is done in Structured Teamwork.

Team meetings succeed or fail based on how well the team's group dynamics are managed. In physics, *dynamics* is concerned with the management of powerful forces and energy. Whenever human beings congregate in a group, strong emotions and energy are present. If the group dynamics are effectively planned and facilitated, the resulting energy continuously flows during and between meetings. On the other hand, an unstructured team meeting can explode and unleash destructive forces equivalent to those of a bomb.

Too many meetings are boring, full of unmanaged conflict and negative emotion, and time-consuming. The major reason: the group energy is not managed. There is poor structure, no planned participation, and poor facilitation. The Structured Teamwork method, on the other hand, can bring meetings to life.

In one of the district offices of Amoco Canada Petroleum Company Ltd. prior to Structured Teamwork training, the meetings were eight or nine hours long once a week, and the office team still didn't get all the work done! The people hated Tuesdays because that was meeting day. After team meeting training, the district office team got all the work done in three-hour meetings. The mutual support of team members and the business results shot up like a rocket ship.

Structured team meetings are energizing because they do more than create an opportunity for communication. They meet basic needs of team members, create C^5 teamwork and get valuable work done. Figure 8–1 lists the benefits of a well-run team meeting.

Most managers do not want their employees to spend time away from work at team meetings. They do not realize that the basic needs listed in Figure 8–1 demand to be met. Some managers think they are getting more productivity by *not* allowing a one-hour team meeting once a week. But the invisible 30 to 90 minutes *each day* that workers socialize and communicate with each other to meet these basic needs in the absence of a regularly scheduled team meeting go unnoticed. Most of that time is totally unstructured and unconnected to any agenda that would help the employees' work group or the company. The genius of the well-run team meeting is that it can overlap meeting basic human needs with improving team performance.

Managers think team meetings are a waste of time because most of the meetings *they* attend do not accomplish very much. At best, one or two agenda items are completed in two hours. Structured team meetings, however, usually complete 10 agenda items, including solving problems and developing coordinated action plans, in less than an hour. When managers first sit in on such a meeting, they literally cannot believe it.

In Structured Teamwork training, we stress that team meetings are the heart of teamwork; they sustain the team members and

FIGURE 8–1

Benefits of Team Meetings

Fulfill basic needs of team members	Social and communications needs
	Need to be a part of a successful group
	Need to be involved in decisions that affect them
	Need for self-esteem
	Need for mutual support
	Need to be creative
Promote C^5 teamwork	Increase communication
	Improve cooperation
	Coordinate work and improvements
	Achieve creative breakthrough
	Promote continuous breakthrough
Get work done	Set goals
	Plan work
	Delegate work
	Measure progress
	Communicate results
	Solve problems
	Make decisions

provide the energy and coordination for great business results. Some managers, however, have prohibited their teams from meeting after the training was completed. They wanted the teams on-line and producing all the time. Those teams stopped making performance improvements. In contrast, the teams whose managers kept the team meetings going continued to achieve significant improvements in productivity, quality, and cycle time. One organization's teams achieved an average of $100,000 worth of improvements per team before they had even completed their Structured Teamwork training!

WHEN TO HAVE TEAM MEETINGS

People are social beings. If you follow people through their entire workday, you will observe that most have anywhere from 15 to 60 communication encounters. Most of the time these encounters are not work related. Productive time is lost in the natural course of meeting the social needs of humans. As mentioned in the preceding section, while some managers say, "We do not have time for team meetings," they are losing productivity throughout the workday due to unstructured social encounters. Short, regularly held meetings address some of these social needs at the same time that work is being done.

Some people take their aversion to meetings to extremes. I knew one manager who had one all-day meeting once a year. Throughout the year, individuals under his care were in constant conflict with each other and employee turnover was high. In contrast, managers and teams in the fast-changing world of computer chip manufacturing have short meetings every day. Some of the minimum and maximum frequencies for different types of meetings are presented in Figure 8–2.

The most important guideline in Figure 8–2 targets teams that must coordinate their daily work. They must have a meeting at least once every two weeks to maintain the continuity of work on projects and improvements and necessary updates.

FIGURE 8–2

How Often Should Meetings Be Held?

Type of Meeting	Minimum Requirement	Overload Point
Coordinating work with team members who work together: Goal setting Work planning Progress review Problem solving Etc.	Once every two weeks	More than once a day, especially if the meetings are long
Problem solving or quality circle–type meetings	Once every two weeks	Two or more times in one week
Communicating information from higher up in the organization or from other departments	Once every four weeks	Two or more times in one week
Technical training or technical information exchange (can be over lunch, coffee, etc.)	Once every two months	Two to six times in one week, based upon individual differences

Note: The above meetings can be combined with each other if total time is not over three hours.

HOW TEAM MEETINGS PROMOTE BREAKTHROUGH

Team meetings do not in and of themselves improve team performance. They have their greatest positive influence when they are structured to promote creative participation by all team members performing such self-management tasks as the following:

- Team mission development.
- Team goal setting.
- Team action planning.
- Team decision making.
- Team problem solving.
- Team work process improvement.

Communication and conflict management skills also can be practiced and improved in team meetings, and this positively impacts a team's productivity. A large number of organizations have provided interpersonal communication and conflict management skills training to their employees but have obtained little or no work performance impact. In those organizations, there has been no consistent place or opportunity to follow up on and reinforce the use of those skills. In Structured Teamwork, on the other hand, teams are taught skills that are immediately and continuously applied in team meetings.

Using the team meeting to decide which work improvement methods to implement and how to implement them is one ingredient that has produced significant performance improvement.[1] Likewise, setting team goals and reviewing goal progress in the team meeting helps teams improve their business results.[2] When teams set goals and develop action plans but fail to review progress toward their goals, the goals are often never met. Without regular reviews over time, team members forget about the goals, or the goals lose their priority status over "squeaky wheel" concerns.

Team meetings provide the glue that holds teams together. They must be held. Without team meetings, the team members will not feel ownership for the work and there will be no improvements in performance.[3] With team meetings, there is an increase in perceived influence on the job and a corresponding increase in job satisfaction.[4]

One study found a high degree of job stress for groups of nurses. Simply holding frequent meetings where there was group discussion resulted in improved attitudes toward work. In another study, team meetings with group discussions reduced employee turnover in a group of bank tellers.[5] Paying attention to employee needs is one of the key ingredients in successful team meetings.

Team creativity is required for the team to achieve breakthrough in any of its communication and self-management activities. The most important meeting climate condition for breakthrough is the participation of *every* team member in the meeting. Structured participation will get and keep each person mentally engaged and thinking.

HOW TO HAVE BREAKTHROUGH TEAM MEETINGS

Managing group dynamics, especially in the potentially volatile atmosphere of a team meeting, requires that every team member be trained in meeting skills. Some organizations take a shortcut and train the team leader or a full-time meeting facilitator, but team members remain untrained. The most frequent result of such training practices is the creation of leader-managed meetings, where the meeting leader is responsible for the success or failure of the meeting. If the entire team is trained, the team takes ownership for the success of the meeting. There is a corresponding major spillover effect of the team taking ownership for the team's work performance and results.

Figure 8–3 lists some advantages of team-managed meetings versus leader-managed meetings. Team-managed meetings are required for any team wishing to achieve breakthrough results. Leader-managed meetings may be good for sharing information with large groups of people, but teams function best with team-managed meetings.

In addition to being centered on the team, effective team meetings have three other important aspects: *structure, planned participation,* and *facilitation.*

Structure

Successful team meetings use structure. In 1992, Scott Poole, a professor at the University of Minnesota, summarized the findings of over 80 research studies of meetings for 3M.[6] A major conclusion emerged: Procedures and structure help groups perform significantly better. The only problem is that most groups will not follow the meeting procedures or structure they have been asked to use. The solution for team meetings is, of course, to have the team members themselves create the procedures and structure they will follow.

The most important structure is the meeting format. The format is the sequence of major procedures that will be followed in every

FIGURE 8–3

Leader-Managed Meetings versus Team-Managed Meetings

Leader-Managed Meetings	Team-Managed Meetings
The leader develops acceptable behavioral norms or helps the group or team decide what meeting behaviors are appropriate. The leader provides feedback when unacceptable behavior occurs.	The team owns the meeting; creates the meeting ground rules and norms and enforces them with constructive reminders.
The leader determines if and when to ask for participation from members. The 15-Minute Rule is followed whenever it is appropriate.	The agenda item requiring the most team participation is covered near the start of the meeting. 15-Minute Rule.
The leader presents information and makes sure appropriate information is presented during the meeting. The leader may influence final decisions and direction of the team or group. The leader may ask for help in problem solving, goal setting, planning, and decision making.	The team members do most of the talking and have equal say and status; team members select and participate in problem solving, goal setting, planning, and decision making.
The leader establishes and controls the meeting agenda. At the leader's discretion, the team or group may provide input into the agenda.	The team helps develop the meeting agenda; the meeting leader is a facilitator and helper to the team.
The leader is aware of most of the critical information that is needed and arranges for the information to be shared in order to reach the meeting's desired outcomes.	The team and individuals on the team have critical information to share: ■ Productivity results ■ Quality results ■ Scheduling or cycle time results ■ Data to solve problems
The needs of individual members are considered less important than arriving at a decision or sharing information. The leader uses good communication and facilitation skills throughout the meeting.	The needs, purposes, and perspectives of all team members are considered in arriving at decisions, goals, or giving information; team members use good communication and facilitation skills throughout the meeting.

team meeting. When a meeting format is used, every member of the team knows what will occur at the beginning, middle, and end of the team's meetings. The following are examples of procedures teams have found useful in each stage of their regularly scheduled team meeting.

Meeting Start-Up

- Introduce any new team members or guests.
- Tell a joke or recent humorous anecdote.
- Review the team's goals and progress on the goals.
- Agree on the meeting's desired outcomes.
- Finalize the meeting agenda, including asking for any new agenda items.
- Prioritize the agenda items with items requiring the most participation coming first, and estimate times for each item.
- Review or display team ground rules and norms.

Meeting Body

- Proceed through the prioritized list of agenda items.
- Summarize agreed-upon action items and decisions as they are made.
- Give reports.
- Make announcements.

Meeting Wrap-Up

- Summarize all action items and decisions.
- Plan next meeting:
  —Desired outcomes.
  —Agenda items.
- Identify roles and responsibilities for the next meeting:
  —Meeting leader.
  —Meeting recorder and minute-taker.
  —Timekeeper.
- Critique the meeting and the overall teamwork.

The above list contains possible elements in the team's meeting format. It has been useful for new teams, however, to develop their own meeting format before their first team meeting. Four of the most important elements of team meeting structure are the desired outcomes/goals, the meeting agenda, the meeting critique, and the meeting minutes.

Desired Outcomes of Meetings

Meetings often achieve so little because so little is expected. Normally those attending a meeting have very low expectations of what tasks and actions will be accomplished in the meeting. In most meetings, people just talk about things. They *talk* about an action plan rather than developing an action plan. They *talk* about problems rather than solving problems.

A one-hour meeting of a group of managers probably costs a company at least a few thousand dollars. How many of us would walk into a department store and plop a thousand dollars on the counter and ask the salesperson to give us something? The salesperson would ask what we want. We would answer, "Oh, whatever. Let's just talk." Yet isn't that exactly what many meetings do?

Ambitious desired outcomes or goals should be set for every meeting. Important work should get done in the meeting. One way to ensure that important accomplishments occur during the meeting is for the team to word the meeting goals in terms that describe the desired outcome or product of the meeting.

Good team meetings can be characterized by their products and desired outcomes. There are five major product areas of team meetings. Each item beneath the product area can be a desired outcome of an effective team meeting.

Reach Goals

Set goals.

Identify measurement indicators.

Identify and show baseline information.

Develop action plans.

Solve Problems

Specify the problem.

Identify and select causes.

Brainstorm solutions.

Select solutions.

Make Decisions

Brainstorm options.

Narrow options.

Do pro/con analysis for the two or three best alternatives.

Improve Processes

Identify the quality requirements of major customer(s).

Develop the process improvement goal(s).

Flowchart the current work process.

Evaluate the current work process.

"Imagineer" an ideal work process.

Develop an action plan for improvement.

Improve Teamwork

Communicate and coordinate.

Manage conflicts.

Recognize progress.

By setting more ambitious desired outcomes for the meeting, the team will get more work done and have a greater sense of accomplishment.

Meeting Agenda

A meeting is valuable when everyone agrees on *what* is to be accomplished (the desired outcomes) and *how* it is to be accomplished (the agenda). The agenda is the action plan for the meeting. It states the major activities, including the start-up and wrap-up activities. A valuable component of the agenda is the time each agenda item is scheduled to start. Even though teams do not always stick to the schedule, the presence of a schedule increases the meeting's productivity.

Most teams develop the agenda items for the next week's meeting at the end of the current meeting. This allows people to know ahead of time what is going to happen and how to prepare information that may be needed. New priorities can emerge between team meetings, so it is useful at the beginning of a meeting to ask team members if they want to add anything to the agenda. Another option is to tell team members that time will be available for new business, and show this on the agenda. At the end of the meeting, a required agenda item is to summarize the major points discussed, decisions made, and the items that were delegated, including who will do what by when. This activity supports the team being a high-performance action team.

Johnson & Johnson, the health care products company, had a ground rule that there could be no meeting unless there was an agenda. When the ground rule was implemented, some people did not believe the rule was for real. They called a meeting with no agenda. When the participants showed up in the conference room for the meeting, they asked to see the agenda. When the meeting leader said he did not have one, the participants got up and left the meeting. After this occurred once or twice, people got the idea that they had better prepare an agenda.

Sometimes emergency meetings must be called before an agenda is set. If this occurs, the first item of business should always be to develop the meeting's desired outcomes and the agenda.

Meeting Critique

The meeting critique is the last agenda item of the meeting. The purpose of the critique is to evaluate the meeting. If a team consistently evaluates its team meetings, the meetings will gradually increase in both effectiveness and efficiency. The foremost way to conduct a critique is to ask each participant in the meeting to reflect on what went well in the meeting (the pluses) and what should be done differently to make the meeting better the next time (the "deltas" or areas of improvement). Some teams misinterpret the critique to be an evaluation of pluses and "negatives." Deltas are different from negatives. Deltas or areas of improvement are worded to describe what should be done differently the next time to make the meeting better. Delta comments require individuals to think not only about what went wrong (the minus) but also what should occur next time (how to get a plus). For example, if the negative aspect of the meeting was that one or two people did most of the talking, the delta might be "Our next meeting should have more participation by everyone on the team."

The difference between a negative and a delta is subtle, but the results are profound. The delta does not offend anyone, whereas negative wording in the above example could result in angry or defensive individuals (those who talked too much). The delta wording is positive, forward-looking, and immediately acceptable as an action item for the next meeting.

Pluses and deltas should occur in the last three to five minutes of the meeting. The activity should allow each person to reflect quietly on the meeting for at least a minute or two, jotting down any thoughts. This simple activity models the principles of both continuous learning and continuous improvement. For team meetings, the critique is especially important because the activity is broad, encompassing not only how the meeting can be improved but also how the team members can work together better. The critique is an opportunity to comment on any observed strengths or areas of improvement related to the team's communication, cooperation, coordination, creative breakthrough, and continuous breakthrough.

Minutes

The fourth required meeting structure is meeting minutes. No one likes minutes. No one likes to take them; no one likes to read them. Usually meeting minutes are too detailed and too long. There are, however, ways to make minutes meaningful. The following items represent the most important information to preserve in the meeting history:

- The decisions that were made.
- The action items that were assigned to whom, to complete by when.
- The desired outcomes, agenda, time, and place for the next meeting.
- The results of work done by the team (action plans, brainstormed solutions, etc.).
- The meeting's pluses and deltas.

Most team meeting minutes can be written on one page, accompanied by the products created in the meeting such as the list of solutions or pro/con analysis information, especially if they will be needed in the future. Teams should develop a minutes form that includes the above information and anything else the team thinks is important to record. The form should be used to record the team meeting minutes. The meeting minutes should be published and disseminated within 48 hours. If actions were identified and delegated or decisions made during the meeting, the team members need to see the future action items as soon as possible in order to get to work on the tasks.

One of the most successful teams in IBM's history was the IBM 360 mainframe computer team. The team designed one of the best computers in the fastest time up to that point in IBM history. Part of the team's emphasis on reduced design cycle time was the ground rule to have meeting minutes published within 12 hours of the meeting!

The team meeting structures described above create a framework for creativity, honest communication, and productive work to occur. The next most important ingredient of effective team meetings is planned participation.

Planned Participation

The foundation principle of employee involvement and empowerment stresses that when employees participate in goal setting, work planning, and other work decisions, they are more committed to helping the goals, plans, and decisions succeed. Early group dynamics research conducted by Kurt Lewin found that participant involvement in meetings increased the motivation to act on the information by 10 times![7] That is a 1,000 percent increase in implementation effectiveness. Participative meetings are clearly better than one-way communication meetings when participant commitment is a desired outcome.

Recent research has found that structured or planned participation obtained superior results on solution implementation than open discussion. Planned participation ensured that all team members participated, not just the more verbal members.[8] A key to group dynamics and the effective participation of every team member is planning. Obtaining participation in team meetings without planning is like pulling the containment rods out of a nuclear energy plant—the energy is unpredictable and a meltdown results!

To ensure planned participation, the team first identifies the meeting's desired outcomes. The team then develops the corresponding agenda item, which encourages every team member to share ideas. For example, many teams use a portion of the meeting to solve work problems. Planned participation can occur around any of the six steps of structured team problem solving, which will be presented in Chapter 13 (p. 177). The specific agenda item for step two, analyzing causes, could be: "List as many causes as possible for why our division's new products are delayed in getting to the marketplace." The planned participation activity itself uses the steps of structured brainstorming. Team members initially write down their ideas and then take turns presenting one idea per person. The main goal is for every team member to effectively contribute his or her ideas on the agenda item.

The 15-Minute Rule:
Plan Participation within the First 15 Minutes
People like to talk and participate in meetings. On the average, individuals can usually listen without talking for 15 minutes. After that, people want to talk or do something in response to what they have heard so far. If an opportunity for participation is not provided within the first 15 minutes, some individuals will begin talking anyway. No matter what is being discussed, at some time around the 15-minute point of the meeting individuals will start talking, usually somewhat off the topic. Mark Henry, a teamwork consultant with high-technology companies, has noticed that if people do not get an opportunity to participate in the meeting, they will mentally participate somewhere

else. Their minds wander. It is noticeable when someone brings something else to work on during the meeting—a surefire indicator that participation is not necessary.

Most managers think it is important to do announcements and one-way communication items at the beginning of meetings. A problem occurs. Because of the innate drive to get involved, individual participants will get meetings off track just so they can participate. People may ask questions. They may agree with the speaker and then bridge over to present something completely different from what was being presented. Many times meeting participants will disagree with what is being said because of being frustrated at not being allowed to contribute their ideas. At this point many agendas are derailed and the meeting becomes unproductive.

This is why we devised the 15-minute rule: Plan participation within the first 15 minutes. All meetings, but especially team meetings, cry out for planned participation that occurs in the early part of the meeting. In addition to capitalizing on people's intrinsic desire to participate early in meetings, early participation prevents team members from slipping into the passive observer mode. At one midwestern organization, the manager talked and presented one-way information for almost an hour of the team's scheduled two-hour meeting. At the start of the second hour, when he asked for people's ideas for a new project that was being implemented, no one wanted to talk. They had sat in the passive role for an hour and it was difficult to shift to the role of active participant.

When the 15-minute rule was presented to Jim Doran, a vice president at Advanced Micro Devices in Sunnyvale, California, and his team during the team meeting training, he exclaimed, "Our quarterly all-employee meeting!" He went on to describe how, at this meeting, one-way information was presented in a large room to almost 150 employees. Near the end of the meeting, Jim and his boss, Bill Siegle, would ask, "Are there any questions?" Usually only one or two people from the audience asked questions, often not very good ones.

The next quarterly all-employee meeting (after the team meeting training) was held in a large room with round tables, with 8 to 10 people seated at each table. After presenting introductory information, at the 15-minute point of the meeting, Jim asked everyone to write the answers to two questions that were relevant to the organization's performance. Jim and Bill then solicited the answers and wrote them on flipcharts in front of the room. The audience's answers were incorporated into the normal reporting presented during the last half of the meeting. Energy and excitement filled the meeting! Bill Siegle remarked that it was a lot more fun, and Jim and Bill agreed they would never go back to the old way.

Participation doesn't just happen; it happens because it is planned. In the case of the quarterly AMD meeting, considerable time was spent planning the participation of 150 people in a large room. The planning involved much more than just logistics: the right questions needed to be asked. It worked because the participation was planned and was pursued early in the meeting.

Likewise, every team meeting should activate participation of all team members at or before the first 15 minutes. The participation should be planned around the most important agenda items. One-way communication items should be delivered at the end of the meeting.

All team members should be intellectually engaged throughout the meeting. Placing writing materials in front of participants in team meetings encourages engagement and participation. Team members can be encouraged to write down reflections or ideas throughout a meeting. People can share their insights during breaks or at the end of the meeting. Team participation and learning are cornerstones of breakthrough teamwork.

Facilitation

Individuals engaged in the content of the meeting sometimes lose perspective and discipline. When heavily engaged, they find it difficult to stay within the meeting plan and within team guidelines about how to treat fellow team members. Scott Poole asserted that meetings have two goals: contributing to the discussion at hand and working together as a team.[9] Structured Teamwork skills help team members work as a team. Specifically, ground rules, norms, meeting skills, and the other Structured Teamwork skills help the individual team members function together. It is necessary for each team member to actively support the task of enforcing ground rules, norms, the meeting structure, and the agenda. All team members need to use the facilitation skills.

Poole and DeSanctis found that 50 percent of the groups they observed did *not* follow established meeting procedures or stick to an agenda.[10] This is the role of facilitation—to encourage the team to use its skills and procedures/structures to ensure a productive meeting. One person should be designated as the meeting leader, who will help the team follow the team's meeting format and the team-developed agenda. Facilitated meetings are more productive in terms of absolute quantity of work achieved.[11] Every team member, however, must share the role of meeting facilitator—and will, if taught how. Groups that use shared meeting facilitation are high-performing groups.[12]

Facilitation skills are behaviors used by all team members to help meetings be successful. There are many facilitation skills. One facilitation skill is summarizing, where someone on the team outlines what has been discussed for the last few minutes. This behavior decreases the likelihood of misunderstandings, and it often helps team members get closure on the topic and move on to something else. We use facilitation skills to keep meetings running smoothly, and to keep meetings on track and productive.

Facilitation skills help:

- Encourage participation.
- Get the meeting work done.
- Get participants back on the topic.
- Manage conflict.
- Create a good team-managed meeting.

Every person in a team meeting has two roles: (1) to participate in the agenda items and (2) to help facilitate other team members' participation and the achievement of the meeting agenda on time. You will often be in meetings where the topic under discussion is not one to which you can contribute. You can still participate by helping facilitate the meeting process using the facilitation skills found in Figure 8-4.

Research conducted for Xerox by Neil Rackham of the Huthwaite research group in England[13] found that the frequent use of summarizing and checking understanding significantly reduced misunderstandings in meetings. The average number of misunderstandings per person dropped from five in a typical one-hour meeting to one. Most workplace meetings have little checking for understanding and summarizing because someone besides the presenter or main contributors has to do those tasks. When they are not done, people walk out of meetings and ask each other in the hall, "What did he say?" or "What was that all about?" It also explains why action items delegated in meetings do not get done unless they are summarized at the end of the meeting.

At the beginning of team meetings, it is useful to review the previous meeting's minutes and check on the progress that has taken place on previous action items. This technique of reviewing progress at the beginning of the meeting builds a platform of momentum upon

FIGURE 8–4

Meeting Facilitation Behaviors

Behavior	Description	Example
Changing the meeting process	Making recommendations regarding the meeting process	"Let's go on to the next area."
Building on someone's idea	Adding to someone else's idea or proposal	"I want to add to Bill's suggestion."
Supporting others	Praising someone's contribution	"Good idea, John!"
Checking understanding	Asking a question or summarizing to check or review your understanding of what someone has just said	"Jane, are you saying we should discontinue the reliability tests?"
Summarizing	Presenting an overview of key points just discussed, agreed to, or delegated	"This test appears to be a major problem."
Requesting action	Asking someone on the team to be responsible for an action item	"Jack, would you have an answer for that at our next meeting?"

which the team will work to continue solving the problem or developing the action plan. The process of reviewing past achievements first also creates a positive momentum for addressing subsequent activities with enthusiasm.

In Washington State, I successfully used this method in meetings for a joint venture project composed of diverse personalities from different organizations among whom there was considerable conflict and for whom certain issues were potentially explosive. The facilitation process included the initial review of the team's goals, what had been achieved in the last meeting, and progress toward the goals to date. A positive momentum was created in the meeting for dealing with the tough issues that held considerable conflict. This process is especially important when teams meet only once a month or even less frequently. Team members were also trained to check understanding and to ask clarifying questions to peacefully try to understand the grains of truth in the different viewpoints.

CONCLUSION

There are many positive spillover effects of well-facilitated, participative team meetings. The team meeting is a miniature representation of the team's entire culture. Every element of successful teamwork can be seen in the team's meeting. For this reason, if we want to evaluate a work group's effectiveness and overall culture, we should observe its team meetings.

The culture of the entire organization can be influenced by the effectiveness of team meetings. Figure 8–5 shows this spillover effect. Team meetings reflect, and can positively or negatively influence, an organization's culture. For instance, in organizations where team members are always late to meetings, the organization itself is late in getting work completed and meeting customer delivery deadlines. When getting to meetings on time is an expectation, it often spills over to the organization and work deadlines are met. It's a value that transfers from meetings to the workplace.

Team meetings are where it can all come together for the team or where it can all break down. If you implement the methods described in this chapter, your meetings will become catalysts for breakthrough results.

BREAKTHROUGH POINTS

- Without proper structure, meetings can be boring, divisive, and time-consuming.
- Many managers have a poor opinion of team meetings because the meetings they attend accomplish very little.
- Depending on the type of meeting, frequent, short meetings are more effective than long, infrequent meetings.
- Team meetings are the heart of effective teamwork.
- Every team member should actively participate in team meetings.
- Effective team meetings require structure, planned participation, and facilitation.

FIGURE 8–5

Team Meetings That Influence Organizational Culture

Team Meeting Behaviors	Organizational Culture Behaviors
A. Structure	
Team members adhere to ground rules and norms.	The ground rules and norms are followed outside the meetings.
Team members are on time to meetings.	Work is done on time; all deadlines are met.
The team reviews minutes and delegated/follow-up items from last meeting.	All employees are held accountable for their job duties, responsibilities, and work tasks.
The team uses an agenda/plan to achieve meeting goals and adds new agenda items.	Project plans are used and daily work is prioritized according to the requirements of the project plan.
The team reports results.	The organization communicates the results of meetings, decisions, goals, strategies, etc. to employees.
Team members critique the meeting for continuous improvement of meetings and the team.	Continuous improvement occurs for all high-leverage activities.
B. Planned Participation	
Meetings are team centered instead of leader centered.	Leadership in the work and for continuous improvements is shared by all employees.
C. Facilitation Skills	
Guests or new team members are introduced.	The atmosphere of the organization is friendly and supportive.
Checking understanding is used to manage conflict in meetings.	Checking understanding is used to manage all conflicts at work.

- The structure of an effective meeting includes establishing an appropriate format, reaching a desired outcome, using an agreed-upon agenda, critiquing the meeting, and taking minutes.
- According to the 15-minute rule, all members of the team should be encouraged to participate within 15 minutes of the start of the meeting.
- Certain facilitation behaviors by all team members are necessary for successful meetings.

9
CHAPTER

Conflict Management

UNMANAGED CONFLICT: THE ENEMY OF C^5 TEAMWORK

An executive had just taken over as the leader of a large organization. One of the middle managers in his organization had developed an innovative solution for a major problem facing the parent organization and similar organizations all over the world. The middle manager received high amounts of recognition from headquarters staff and other outside organizations. Concerned about some potential dangers of the manager's new approach, the executive voiced his concerns to the manager. The manager disagreed and thought the new executive was meddling.

Both parties quit talking to each other and went to headquarters staff to generate support for their respective positions. The conflict went on for months. In the end, the executive got authority from headquarters to force his position on the innovative manager. The manager withdrew from developing any further innovations, and the approach that was once revolutionary became mediocre. Unable to get support from his other middle managers for new breakthroughs, the executive did not benefit, either. The organization, once one of the best, became the worst. The executive was removed from leadership of the organization. Neither the executive nor the manager advanced any further in his career. The opportunity for greatness was lost because the two individuals could not manage their conflict, which, when compared to the ultimate consequences, was absolutely minor.

Does this story sound familiar? Conflicts between leaders and their teams are occurring in one company after another. And as executives and managers fight among themselves, their companies are crumbling around them.

Several years ago, one of my consulting clients asked me to summarize the research and develop a course on how to effectively manage conflicts at work. Like many people, I do not like conflict, so I was not enjoying the project. But as I plowed through the research and read case studies from business, several insights sparked my enthusiasm.

First, unmanaged conflict is the enemy of teamwork. In certain cases, when team members either totally avoided their conflicts or allowed themselves to become angry and out of control, the resulting negative emotion destroyed the supportive work climate. Team communication decreased in frequency and openness. Offering to help each other was totally out of the question. There was little coordination of work to achieve mutual goals and solve shared work problems. Without feelings of confidence and supportiveness, creative thinking and breakthroughs were nonexistent. Overall goal achievement and team performance became negative or at best average.

If conflicts are properly managed using team creativity, business breakthroughs can occur.

I then gleaned a second major insight from the research on conflict management. If conflicts are properly managed using team creativity, business breakthroughs can occur. Work conflicts can serve as a stimulant for innovation. As Alfred P. Sloan led General Motors from near bankruptcy to become the world's most successful corporation, he continually used the creative management of conflicts to generate new business innovations. One example was the autonomy of the local GM dealer. The dealers wanted to be free of control from Detroit, yet they wanted to provide input into major GM decisions. Neither side looked like it was going to win. The creative solution allowed dealers to be autonomous as long as they followed certain GM requirements. It also provided for an advisory council to be selected by the dealers to provide input into major GM decisions. GM maintained the control it wanted and the dealers had a say in anything that might affect their freedom as independent dealers. The solution improved communication of sales strategies, which improved business both for the dealers and for GM.

Effectively managing conflicts can result in business and work breakthroughs. Most people see conflict as win–lose: If I'm right, then you must be wrong, or vice versa. They miss a third and much more useful alternative: We are both right, and if we can put our two rights together, we'll come up with a real breakthrough.

WHAT IS CONFLICT AND WHY SHOULD IT BE MANAGED?

Performance Resources, Inc., has asked hundreds of teams to define conflict at work; the most frequent answer has been: "Conflict is a disagreement between two or more people accompanied by strong emotion." Conflicts evoke anger, hurt, outrage, disgust, hopelessness, and feelings of being trapped, threatened, or betrayed. After two days of Structured Teamwork training, a supervisor at one company asked in a voice filled with some emotion, "When are we going to have the t-group or encounter group?" He wanted a time when everyone could really go at it with each other and let out all of the bottled-up negative emotions. I replied that we did not do emotional encounter groups because they neither manage the conflicts nor improve teamwork performance. He then stated that the team had some problems with each other that must be dealt with if there was to really be a team. I asked if the group wanted to learn skills that would help them manage the conflicts. There was unanimous consent.

> Conflict is a disagreement between two or more people accompanied by strong emotion.

Team members expect conflict to be reduced automatically as their team is developed, empowered, and shown how to achieve more ownership. This is a false expectation. Instead, conflict increases—as everyone cares more and verbalizes more about problems and solutions. We usually have conflicts over things we care about. Management may have the *perception* that there is less conflict after team development because the focus of the conflict has changed. Conflicts shift from *whether* to pursue the needed vision and goals to *how* to reach the vision and goals. Instead of personal conflicts or conflicts between competing departments, the conflicts center on which breakthrough ideas are the best to implement for a particular problem. Perhaps because managers and executives are so relieved by the more action-focused conflicts versus resistance conflicts, they sense that there is decreased conflict.

Unmanaged conflicts cost money and time.

Unmanaged conflicts cost money and time. One organization experienced unmanaged conflict between the engineering organization and the product marketing organization. Key managers and contributors spent 50 percent of their time on an unmanaged conflict that delayed their new product for 18 months. They totally missed the market window on that product and lost the time that could have been spent on the launch of another high-profit product. The estimated loss of revenue was in the hundreds of millions of dollars for the organization. Unmanaged conflict can kill a business.

MANAGE CONFLICT TO MAINTAIN HARMONY AND ACHIEVE BREAKTHROUGH

Conflicts between members of the team must be managed to maintain long-term relationships and teamwork. Teams that effectively manage major conflicts improve their confidence in overcoming future challenges. Groups that effectively manage conflicts experience two sources of satisfaction: having influenced the outcome and finding resolution to conflicting points of view.[1] Teams get great satisfaction from successfully handling team conflicts.

In a survey of 22,600 employees of Fortune 500 companies, respondents rated conflict resolution as an area of work with which they were *most* dissatisfied.[2] My colleague Terry Ross has remarked, "Conflict is a reality of work, but few organizations install a vehicle to deal with this reality." Conflict is especially a reality of employee empowerment and self-managed teamwork. If organizations desire all of the business benefits of employee involvement, then both conflict management skills training and teamwork training are required.

HOW CONFLICT MANAGEMENT FITS WITH THE OTHER COMPONENTS OF STRUCTURED TEAMWORK

Conflict management skills are required to enable teams to do their work, set goals, develop the team mission, solve problems, make team decisions, improve work processes, and define roles and responsibilities. For instance, because setting goals and team priorities is important, team members have strong feelings about what they think the priorities should be. Conflict management skills should be used to manage the disagreements on goals and priorities. They can be helpful when teams do any of the team tasks where there is more than one option.

Many times, however, teaching conflict management can be useful later in the Structured Teamwork training sequence. If a team is able to work toward accomplishing its team goals as it is being trained and facilitated without much conflict, the conflict management skills training can be the transition for the team to become independent of the team trainer/facilitator. As a team spends time together working toward and achieving the team's business and work goals, the C^5 teamwork framework is created within which team conflicts may be managed. The C^5 framework clearly establishes that the purpose of the team is to communicate, cooperate, and coordinate to achieve continuous creative work performance breakthroughs. In the absence of the C^5 framework, team conflict management may degenerate to focus only on low-priority individual team member personality conflicts.

> **Never open a conflict unless there is enough time to manage it without anyone feeling rushed.**

The conflict management skills themselves build on and use team communication skills, especially listening, checking understanding, and being specific. Goal setting is used by all sides in a conflict to specify what each side really wants. Team creativity skills are used to identify how the differing parties can all achieve what they want.

WHEN TO MANAGE TEAM CONFLICTS AND WHEN NOT TO TRY

Conflicts need to be resolved as soon as possible to keep the good teamwork flowing. Conflict management establishes agreement in the midst of disagreement. It helps identify the facts in the midst of emotion. The only problem is that quite often team conflict management takes a lot of time. A rule of effective conflict management is this: Never open a conflict unless there is enough time to manage it without anyone feeling rushed. There is more than enough emotion involved in the conflict without putting it in the pressure cooker of limited time.

Because the work must get done to achieve the team's goals, and since conflict management takes time, the team must be selective about which conflicts it handles, and when they are handled. Many conflicts may have to be ignored until there is a break in the work demands. Sometimes addressing a major conflict after the team has achieved a breakthrough in performance creates a positive platform for addressing the conflict. The main showstopper conflicts that must be addressed immediately are the ones that most team members feel will severely impact the achievement of the team's goals.

But many conflicts do not involve the whole team. Conflicts often involve only two team members, who can manage the conflict off-line, by themselves. If that proves unfruitful, the two individuals can request a third team member to help facilitate them through the conflict management skills presented in this chapter.

If two individuals have a conflict that is not resolved, the tension between them can affect the entire team. Everyone on the team will know it's there, and although the team may not need to be involved in solving it, the team can and should hold the two individuals responsible for working it out. For example, on one team two operators had refused to talk to each other for months. Everyone else was walking on eggshells to avoid provoking another blowup. A lot of team issues were being ignored out of fear of these two getting into another fight. Using the conflict management skills, the team leader got them together off-line and resolved the issue. Bingo—the team really surged forward after that.

Effective conflict management hinges on another important rule: Never try to manage a conflict when team members are tired, hungry, or feeling weak. The best times to manage conflicts are at the beginning of the workday or after lunch. Teams do a tremendous job with volatile issues right after a big lunch. Remember, too, that dealing with emotional issues is mentally and physically exhausting; conflict management is difficult, if not impossible, to do creatively and well when team members are tired.

One organization asked several executives and me to observe a new team that another company had trained. The team trainers were proud of the work the team had done and scheduled a meeting at the end of the workday for the team to show off the skills of its members. Along about 5:00 P.M., after meeting for an hour, the team members had a major conflict. They had been taught that no matter when a conflict occurs, they need to stop immediately and address the conflict until it is resolved, even if it means going overtime. The team members became very emotional and argumentative with each other, and things went downhill from there. For another hour, we observed the escalation of the team's verbal attacks and frustration. Even though I was a guest, I felt so frustrated for the team I intervened. I suggested that the team be allowed to go, eat, rest, and take on the conflict the next day when they were fresh. Fortunately, the executives quickly added their support. The team and the trainers requested that we return the next morning to observe the resolution of the conflict. We did. The team took 15 minutes to find a creative solution that made everyone happy. Teams should address conflicts only when they are rested and feeling strong.

Structured Teamwork uses the potentially explosive energy of conflicts to discover and implement creative breakthroughs. If the team members can facilitate themselves through a conflict using the steps of team conflict management outlined in the following section, anger and frustration can be transformed into achievement and pride.

HOW TO MANAGE TEAM CONFLICTS

Skill training in conflict management increases teams' effectiveness. Listening and other interpersonal skill training has been found to improve conflict management ability and work group productivity.[3] The skill training includes observation of correct performance of the skill, individual practice, and feedback on the practice performance. Conflict management skill training also requires frequent practice. The most important skills will be presented below.

Research has revealed that the more intense the conflict, the greater the degree of formality that should be used to try and manage it. The extreme example is international peace negotiations; it can take months of planning to decide how the parties will be seated and what topic each day's session will cover. Interestingly enough, international negotiations usually last two hours in the morning and two hours after lunch. The planners prevent fatigue by structuring the time allowed for direct communication.

Unlike international peace negotiations, teams cannot spend months planning to address a conflict. They can, however, use a structured process to manage team conflicts successfully. The synthesis of the best research and experience has uncovered five steps:

1. Manage feelings.
2. Create a supportive climate.

3. Describe the conflict.

4. Understand the goals.

5. Create solutions.

Step 1: Manage Feelings

Feelings and emotion can convert a simple difference of opinion into a conflict. The predominant feeling of team conflicts is anger. Team members become angry with each other both in and out of team meetings. Unfortunately, there are destructive physiological and psychological effects of anger that interfere with resolving conflicts between individuals.

When humans get angry, blood pressure goes up, adrenaline is released to the large muscles, and other internal chemical reactions occur—all of which prepare the body to fight or run. Dr. Redford Williams of Duke University Medical Center found that individuals who display their anger are more likely to develop serious heart trouble.[4] In a 25-year follow-up study of law school graduates, those who frequently expressed their anger were four times as likely to die as their colleagues who did not display anger. The study did not find that being a workaholic, being aggressive, or being impatient caused heart problems. It was pure and simple unmanaged anger that caused heart disease. Research has discovered no benefit to expressing anger, despite the myth of "letting it all out."

On the other hand, there's an equally dangerous outcome to the individual if we just "bottle it up" inside and don't deal with the conflict. Blowing up or bottling up—neither one is healthy, and it discredits the other parties with whom we have the conflict. Bottling it up basically says, "I don't trust you or me enough to confront this." That's pretty destructive for a supportive work climate, hence the need to know how to manage our feelings.

Anger brings on other dangerous physical and psychological effects. It causes the pupil of the eye to constrict, reducing peripheral vision. The reduction of vision is potentially dangerous for persons who work around heavy machinery or drive any type of vehicle. There are parallel psychological reactions. One of the most damaging is that anger increases an individual's feeling of total certainty about his or her own position. There is, in effect, a loss of *psychological peripheral vision* and the ability to see other people's points of view. In the final and most serious reaction, anger appears to freeze the brain's reasoning and creative abilities. Consequently, soldiers readying for combat and athletes in a pseudo conflict are repetitively drilled on how to respond to certain situations. Under conditions of anger, individuals lose the ability to think and can only react.

The feelings that conflicts provoke, especially anger, must be managed. There are several actions team members can take when they become angry and feel the need to discharge negative feelings. The following are some ways to manage feelings before discussing a conflict:

1. Do something relaxing.

   a. Go for a walk or other exercise.

   b. Use positive visualization.

   c. Use positive self-talk.

   d. Listen to relaxing music.

   e. Meditate.

2. Sort out feelings with a friend.

3. Identify your goal: "What Do I Want?"

Different techniques are helpful to different individuals. Therefore, team members should find and use the most effective method for themselves.

The above tips can help individuals calm down before discussing a conflict, but what can someone do if verbally attacked or provoked during a meeting, when it would be inappropriate to get up and go for a walk? The most potent behavior is to take a slow, deep, relaxing breath. Anger causes the heart rate to go up and breathing to become fast but shallow. Taking a slow, deep, relaxing breath calms the body and allows the mind to refocus on the work at hand. The relaxing breath calms the brain so it can again think rationally and creatively.

One manager related the following story: Because of a computer problem, members of his team were unable to access necessary work information from the computer. He spoke with the information systems support person and was assured the problem would be fixed that day. The next morning, a similar computer lockup occurred that was even worse than the one from the day before. The manager described his anger as so great that he "hit the ceiling." As he went down the hall to the information systems offices, he remembered the training and took several relaxing breaths. As a result, when he got to the information systems office, he was able to describe what had happened in a calm tone of voice. The support person in turn apologized, dropped his other work, and fixed the problem with the manager's help in five minutes! Good solutions start with managing feelings.

Some people are unable to manage their anger and relax enough to handle their feelings at work. Often their lifestyles at home are not relaxing and do not adequately recharge their emotional and physical batteries. A lifestyle that creates the capability of managing feelings includes physical fitness, good nutrition, relaxation, priority management, and a positive attitude. Early in his work, Dr. Kenneth Cooper described how aerobic exercises like running, walking, and swimming reduce the amount of time it takes for individuals to recover from emotionally charged situations. Unfit individuals who become upset at work may stay upset for as long as 12 hours. The words or pictures that stimulated the conflict continually go around in their heads, their blood pressure and heart rates stay high, and their muscles stay tight and tense. Aerobically fit individuals can bring their anger responses down in minutes. All of the relaxing lifestyle attributes help team members do Step 1, manage their feelings.

Step 2: Prepare a Supportive Climate

After all of the team members involved in resolving the conflict have sufficiently managed their feelings, the meeting can be planned in which the discussion will occur. Several techniques are available to plan a meeting that creates an emotionally supportive atmosphere, which in turn can help manage negative emotions. The first step is to identify a mutually agreeable time and place to discuss the conflict. When all individuals involved in the conflict agree to the time and place, a feeling of equality is established.

The meeting agenda should be planned with enough time available to avoid time pressure. Be sure to schedule the meeting at a time of the day when the participants are not tired or hungry.

Identifying a mutually agreeable place is just as important as agreeing on the time, especially if a manager or supervisor is one of the participants in the conflict. An equal meeting environment is not established when the manager has the meeting in his or her office, and he or she sits behind the desk. Plan to use a place with some degree of privacy. Individuals arguing their viewpoint in front of others sometimes "play to the crowd" instead of trying to understand the other person's position.

Football players talk about putting on their "game face." Team members should put on an open and optimistic face as they prepare to manage a conflict. All participants should have an attitude of open-ness versus "I know what I am going to demand." Each person should anticipate that together the team can create breakthrough solutions.

Step 3: Describe the Conflict

Research suggests that certain ways of talking about the conflict can maximize the possibility of a creative, breakthrough resolution. For example, most people begin the discussion with, "Here is my problem with you . . ." They present their emotion-filled conclusion first—the opposite of the best way to begin. A far more effective approach is to present the facts of the situation in chronological order. Begin by describing what happened first. Usually, at first there was a feeling of agreement. Then at some point an event occurred that started the conflict. Present as accurately as possible what happened in the order that each event occurred. The best descriptions are like a playback of a video camera recording. The team or person is led to the conclusion step by step.

This approach also includes the "Joe Friday of *Dragnet*" method: "Just present the facts, ma'am, just the facts." After the other parties in the conflict describe the situation in chronological order from their viewpoint, the team or individuals can pinpoint the specific reason the conflict occurred.

Describing conflicts in factual chronological order works! In especially intense conflicts, team members can outline the "story" on paper before the discussion. In this way, all parties in the conflict can focus on how they present their viewpoints rather than worrying about recalling all of the facts.

Research defines the most effective methods to use to describe conflict situations. For instance, almost 40 percent of the emotional expression is communicated by the tone of voice we use as we speak. With this in mind, team members who want to manage the conflict by reflecting emotional calm and confidence should speak quietly, slowly, and in a low tone of voice as they describe the conflict. The opposite happens in most arguments. We have all seen two people arguing. As one person starts to talk louder, the other speaks even louder and faster, until they are both yelling in shrill, high-pitched voices at the tops of their lungs. A quiet, slow, low tone of voice brings down the emotional intensity of the conflict.

Research also indicates that the speed of talk affects the listener. Talking fast creates excitement and is useful in motivating team members in a meeting. With conflicts, however, speaking slowly is best because it lowers the emotional intensity. Remember that in conflict situations, the people involved have trouble really listening to each other because of the emotion of the conflict and their natural inclination to try to think of what to say next. Speaking slowly solves both of these problems.

There is a final rule for effectively describing conflict situations. Do not use emotion-laden words. This advice is the opposite of what some schools of assertiveness training and pop psychology fads have advocated. In these schools of thought, people are encouraged to be honest and tell other people exactly how they feel. For example, someone might say, "I feel totally furious because you did not relieve me at my machine so I could go to lunch." Using emotion-filled words or phrases like "totally furious" or "mad" is like waving a red flag in front of a raging bull. Such language inflames and agitates the other participants in the conflict. Instead, team members should keep the emotional words and expressions out of their discussion. For example, a team member could begin a discussion by saying, "I would like to discuss a situation that happened this morning. When would be a good time for you?"

During this step of describing the conflict, all parties involved should listen and interact. The purpose of the step is to clarify and understand each person's facts and point of view regarding the conflict. The main skills are summarizing and checking understanding to ensure that both parties understand the other's viewpoint. Many times conflicts are resolved after Step 3. However, if the conflict is still present, the team proceeds to the next step.

Step 4: Understand the Goals

When all participants in a conflict understand one another's goals and remember and support the team's goals, the likelihood of resolving the conflict improves. Team goals must be in the forefront at all times. Research and development teams that create new products experience high amounts of conflict as they select from an array of possible products and features. When project teams refer to their team goals, conflicts are resolved faster and teamwork performance increases.[5] Teams that have an especially challenging goal can appeal to the need to work together to achieve the challenge as a means of managing the conflict.

Sometimes simply hearing each other's goals results in a break-through in the conflict between two people. There is a folktale of two sisters who fought over the last orange in their home. The obvious compromise solution was to cut the orange in half, giving each sister one half of the orange, but the wise grandparent asked each why she wanted the orange. One sister needed the slices of the orange for a fruit salad she was making. The other sister needed the orange peel to make jam preserves. When they heard and understood each other's goals, a win–win solution emerged. One sister got the orange peel, the other the fruit.

There is a structured pattern to follow when trying to under-stand goals in a conflict situation. First, members of one group present their goal(s). Then the other group checks understanding of the goal(s). Only after the group that presented the first goal(s) feels that the other group's understanding is accurate can the second group present its goal(s). After the second group has presented its goal(s), members of the first group must demonstrate that they understand the goals by verbally repeating them back in a checking-for-under-standing format. An easy way to remember this pattern is to see it. Figure 9–1 helps team members follow the pattern.

FIGURE 9–1

The Path to Conflict Management

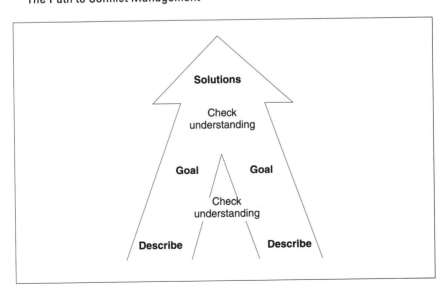

Sometimes the win–win solution for all parties is not created from hearing each other's goals. When this happens, the joint identification of the overarching, overlapping, or team goal is needed. If an overarching goal *cannot* be identified, the next step is still valid: both sides in the conflict place their separate goals on the table as the team participates together to create winning solutions.

Step 5: Create Solutions

In Step 5, when there is a conflict within the team, other team members make valuable contributions as they identify breakthrough solutions. Team creativity and structured brainstorming help the team develop a variety of solutions that will help the parties in the conflict achieve their separate goals or the overarching goal(s). Conflict management using structured brainstorming tends to be less personalized because ideas are listed on a flipchart, and they become disassociated from individuals.[6] They become team-suggested solutions. Teams need to be instructed to brainstorm wild or paradigm-busting ideas. The wild ideas are particularly valuable in creating breakthrough solutions for conflicts. Sometimes funny ideas promote a healthy perspective by all of the participants, and sometimes the feasible spin-offs of the wild ideas may be the best solution.

T. Don Stacy, the former chairman and president of Amoco Canada, described a situation that occurred when he was responsible for production in South America for Amoco. The government of one of the countries in which Amoco had interests asked the company to drill a new well on some property where oil was suspected. Amoco headquarters was reluctant to approve the project because the proposed well was not in a prime area and because the government had refused to reduce the very high royalty rates it received from Amoco. As a matter of fact, Amoco was reluctant to invest further because of the low rate of return the company received. A situation existed where everyone was losing.

A group of Amoco staff met to brainstorm solutions to the problem. A creative solution emerged. Amoco projected the costs of all conceivable future production investments for the next three to five years in the country. It also documented the investments it had made in the past three years or so. The group developed a presentation and took it to the government. Amoco offered a package deal where the company would drill not only the well that the government wanted but also other wells that would significantly increase the total revenue because of increased production. In turn, the government was asked to reduce its royalty rate in order for Amoco to make back the return on the new drilling investments. The solution made Amoco more willing to invest additional money for the desired well and for future exploration and production. All parties agreed to this innovative approach and the rest is history—everyone made a lot of money.

This story is an example of how creative solution development by a team of managers resulted in a business breakthrough for both of the parties involved. Each of the key managers who were part of the team that developed and implemented the solution thought that he or she played a significant role in developing the innovative solution. There was therefore tremendous ownership by each person on the team to implement his or her assigned role in a timely and effective manner in order for the project to succeed. The created solution is valuable only to the extent that it is effectively implemented.

Sometimes teams and individuals need to take a break for a week or more before doing Step 5, Create Solutions. In extremely emotional conflicts, completing Steps 1 through 4 can eliminate the perception of an adversarial relationship. Team members may then need time to become comfortable with the new situation and to incubate the possibilities before taking the positive step of creating solutions.

Teams and team members cannot force solutions. If they do, the fabric holding the team together is torn apart. The Structured Teamwork approach, which uses problem solving, is more successful than the smoothing approach or the forcing mode.[7] Supportive relationships of team members are maintained, and breakthrough solutions are created.

CONCLUSION

The basic approach to preventing conflicts is to keep the other nine components of Structured Teamwork healthy and working. Teams can prevent a high number of volatile conflicts by referring back to the team's mission and goals. Having and communicating good measures of goals can keep the stress level down. Regularly scheduled team meetings that promote good team communication and team creativity can keep cooperative behavior alive and recognized. Using structured methods to solve problems, make decisions, and improve work processes can reduce negative emotion and resistance to changes the team must make.

Fortunately, a high percentage of teams trained in both conflict management skills and the other components of Structured Teamwork do an excellent job of both preventing emotionally charged conflict and, when conflict does occur, creating breakthrough.

BREAKTHROUGH POINTS

- *Unmanaged* conflict is the enemy of teamwork.
- Properly managed conflict can lead to business breakthroughs.
- Conflict is a disagreement between two or more people accompanied by strong emotion.
- Never open a conflict unless there is enough time to manage it without anyone feeling rushed.
- As a conflict becomes more intense, the degree of formality necessary to manage it should be increased.
- A structured five-step process for resolving conflicts includes managing feelings, creating a supportive climate, describing the conflict, understanding the goals, and creating solutions.

10

CHAPTER

Team Values,
Vision, and Mission

COORDINATION

Chapters 10, 11, and 12 address critical issues that relate to team coordination. Researchers consistently discover that effective teams need direction. This chapter deals with the importance of team values, vision, and mission. Chapter 11 speaks to the significant issue of team goal setting. The importance of roles and responsibilities and team organization is captured in Chapter 12.

Team values, vision, and mission statements can be used to motivate team members and set the team's direction. The ideals articulated by the team inspire team members to reach inside themselves to find the best. In his landmark book *Working*, Studs Terkel presented the results of interviews of people working in a variety of jobs.[1] He described how individuals in certain professions such as nursing and education could work long, hard hours and yet remain positive and energized because they believed their jobs had a valuable purpose. On the other hand, Terkel described individuals with jobs such as government administrator or bank teller who were unhappy and burned out because they felt they were little more than a "machine."

The most famous example of the way meaningful work can literally achieve miracles is Viktor Frankl's description of life in a World War II concentration camp. He describes his ability to survive on a semistarvation diet in a disease-ridden, drafty, freezing barracks because of his conviction that the book he was writing on psychiatry would help mankind. The major conclusion of Frankl's book, *Man's Search for Meaning*, was that individuals who had a personal mission or purpose for which they were living were able to survive the harshest deprivations encountered by anyone.[2]

Charles Garfield conducted an analysis of a variety of peak performers, primarily from athletics. He studied Olympic champions and world champions of all sorts. He offered this major conclusion: "the one characteristic that appears in every peak performer I have studied: a sense of mission."[3] Teams can achieve this powerful sense of purpose when they develop the vision or mission for their work group.

The team vision or mission is the idealistic North Star the team strives to reach. Teams at ABB Coral Springs adopted mission statements such as "To manufacture the best quality product for our customer through teamwork" and "Work as one to be #1."

WHAT ARE TEAM VALUES, VISION, AND MISSION?

In Chapter 16 of *A Passion for Excellence*, Tom Peters's sequel to *In Search of Excellence*, Peters describes how companies obtained superior business results when they used a variety of methods to get all of their people excited about the organization's direction. Values, vision, and mission are direction-setting tools that have the potential to energize teams and organizations.

Values

The *values* of an organization or team are the shared beliefs or expected behaviors of all members of the organization or the team. The team's values may be explicitly listed and agreed to, or they may be implied in the team's mission statement, ground rules, and norms. In most teams, the members develop the list of written values off the tops of their heads.

Research produced by John Kotter and James Heskett suggests that the values an organization and perhaps even a team select may have a profound influence on business results. In *Corporate Culture and*

Performance, Kotter and Heskett described four extensive studies they conducted between August 1987 and January 1991 to determine whether a relationship existed between corporate culture and long-term economic performance.[4] The first two studies examined 207 firms, including the largest 9 or 10 firms in 22 different U.S. industries. The third study considered 20 firms that appeared to have cultures that seemed to hurt their corporate productivity, and the final study looked at 10 firms that had experienced a cultural change that had a positive impact on their companies economically.

Kotter and Heskett concluded that firms whose cultures simultaneously emphasize customers, employees, and stockholders throughout all levels outperformed companies that did not stress these three constituents equally. The companies that valued customers, employees, and stockholders had income gains of over 750 percent during an 11-year period. The income improvement of firms without this simultaneous emphasis was near zero over the same period of time. Organizational values do make a difference.

AT&T, the giant telephone and communications company, was so impressed with the above research that in 1993, the board of directors linked Chairman Robert Allen's salary and bonus to how well AT&T performed on the values of the three major stakeholders: customers, shareholders, and employees.

Teams as well as organizations must simultaneously emphasize customers, shareholders, and the employees themselves in their values. Successful teams agree on values that relate to how they want to be treated when they develop their team ground rules and norms. The ground rules and norms are, by definition, the behavior expectations all team members agree to uphold in order to achieve a successful team. Teams usually express their values relating to customers and shareholders in their team mission and goals. If a team is performing poorly, a good starting point for improvement is to assess what its values are (ground rules, norms, team mission, and goals) and how consistently it is adhering to them.

Vision

Vision is a positive and idealistic description of the future that achieves a team's or organization's priority values. Naturally, because of the Kotter and Heskett research described above, the vision should include achieving the major values of customers, stockholders, and employees. An organizational vision is usually developed by the executive staff of the organization and provides the direction in which the organization will grow in the future. Team vision statements are descriptions of what the team members would like their work, their performance and results, their relationship to each other, and their work area to look like.

Research on the topic of the utility of vision statements comes from studies of high-performance athletes and musicians and their performance as related to their individual visualizations. To perform the art of visualization, one must create a complete mental description, picture, or movie of the desired performance. Olympic high-platform divers especially have benefited from visualizing each movement their bodies should make to achieve the perfect smooth dive into the water.

The use of vision can benefit a team in a similar way. When the team obtains agreement of all team members to the vision, the members function as one body to achieve it. The vision statement becomes another tool for establishing and guiding the team's direction. Without a team vision, teams may lack the idealism of a positive future to fuel their actions of today.

Mission

The most useful of all team direction-setting tools is the *mission*. The team's mission states what the team does to help reach the larger organization's mission and vision. The team mission also summarizes the idealistic benefit of the team's activities and establishes the motivating purpose the team desires to pursue.

The team mission is important because it:

1. Describes how the team helps the organization reach its mission and summarizes what the team does.

2. Describes the idealistic purpose of the team's activities. It describes the reasons the team does what it does, the team's values, and the idealistic benefits the team wishes to achieve.

3. States in concrete terms the direction so that team members and others can relate to it and move toward it.

4. Is concise enough for team members to remember. It may be helpful to state the team's mission in a short slogan. Some teams also like to have a paragraph or long sentence that describes what the slogan stands for.

The mission of Sony, the consumer electronics giant, is "To utilize the most advanced technology for the general public." This mission statement, created almost 40 years ago, guided the company as it developed its highly successful Walkman portable radios and other high-tech consumer electronic products, and it still guides the company today. It is an example of a mission statement that articulates the values that are important to customers, shareholders, and other stakeholders.

John Pearce and Fred David's 1987 research on mission statements found that companies whose mission statements articulated philosophical idealism and their desired public image had greater performance than companies whose mission statements described only the product or service or focused on financial survival.[5] Idealism appears to be an essential ingredient.

HOW TEAM VISION AND MISSION SUPPORT BREAKTHROUGH

Team vision and mission capture the idealism of the team members. The idealism motivates all members to strive to do their best. Such motivation encourages creative ideas on how to do the work faster or with higher quality. Modern sailboats have the amazing ability, most of the time, to stay upright no matter how high the winds or how furious the seas. This stability is partially due to the specially designed and weighted keel on the bottom of the boat. The mission statement is a team's keel; it keeps the team upright and headed in the right direction regardless of changes that might upset the team.

Renu Rastogi describes work in most organizations as being characterized as uninteresting or meaningless, performed in a contractually determined climate with frequent disruptions.[6] He suggests that organizational goals must be linked with idealistic social goals, that the moral basis of work be elevated, that intrinsic motivations be recognized, and that shared values and concerns be acknowledged.

The team mission, combined with a sense of purpose, helps the team members manage the stress of always pushing themselves and their performance to higher reaches of excellence. Thomas Holmes and Richard Rahe, two stress-management researchers, developed a widely used scale to measure the amount of life stress individuals experience.[7] Major traumatic events like the death of a spouse secured the maximum score of 100 points. Even positive changes (such as getting married, moving into a new home, receiving a promotion, or taking a vacation) earned stress points, though at much lower levels. The two researchers discovered that if an individual scored more than 300 points within a year, there was an 80 percent likelihood that he or she would experience a major physical or emotional illness. For individuals with points between 150 and 300, the probability decreased to approximately 50 percent.

Two other researchers, Salvatore Maddi and Suzanne Kobasa, were puzzled by a major contradiction in research using the stress management scale. Consistently, certain executives scored above 300 points every year and yet never had a physical or emotional breakdown. They were transferred by their companies, were promoted, had to sell and buy new homes, and weathered all manner of major life changes. The researchers wanted to know what was protecting these executives from the normal consequences of so much change and stress. Using interviews and personality tests with the executives, they identified several differences between the "hardy executives" and those who had emotional or physical problems:[8]

1. The hardy executives had a commitment to a personal mission or purpose in their lives.
2. The hardy executives viewed change and challenges as exciting rather than threatening.
3. The hardy executives felt a sense of control over the changes that occurred versus feeling like helpless victims.

Their mission insulated the hardy executives from the negative effects of stress due to change.

In a similar fashion, a team's idealistic mission can buffer the team from the stress of too much change, even if it is good change. Maddi and Kobasa's third research finding may partially explain why self-managed teams get good results for long periods of time as opposed to teams that get a one-shot breakthrough. Self-managed teams have a sense of control over their own work life because management has given the team members decision-making authority for most of the decisions in their work area. Employee involvement and empowerment are good for employees because they provide the opportunity for individuals to have some control over what happens in their work life. This keeps the team members mentally engaged and contributing rather than causing them to become helpless and apathetic, as when too much uncontrolled change occurs.

A sense of purpose and mission is the foundation of an individual's personal mastery of life and work, writes Peter Senge in Chapter 11 of his book, *The Fifth Discipline: The Art and Practice of the Learning*

Organization. Team vision and mission are foundations for team learning and mastery.

DEVELOPING THE TEAM MISSION

The team mission should be produced in the early stages of a team's formation. A short-term project team needs a team mission just as much as an ongoing self-managed work team or an executive team.

All teams require a team sponsor to be effective. The sponsor is the individual who has the authority over the work and the resources the team is being asked to use. In addition, the team sponsor provides the team with its initial objectives and overall direction, and identifies why these individuals are being formed into a team. This information is communicated to the team personally or in writing at one of the team's first meetings. The sponsor is responsible for a smooth and rapid team start-up.

Unfortunately, teams have no initial ownership of the objectives or the team charter that was developed by the sponsor. Teams can waste as much as 15 hours of valuable team meeting time arguing about the sponsor's objectives. Contrast this with another strategy of introducing the objectives to the team, in which the team sponsor spends an hour or less explaining the desired objectives and the team then immediately develops its own mission statement that achieves the sponsor's objectives. In a short amount of time, the team is aligned with the sponsor and has developed a team mission that captures the team's idealism and ownership for what it is being asked to do. Team mission statements should be developed using a *structured process* that includes the following elements:

- Create a specific focus.
- Identify an idealistic purpose.
- Generate excitement.
- Be concise.
- Identify team boundaries.
- Be evolutionary.

Create a Specific Focus

A team mission statement can achieve focus in a number of ways. First, it should be linked to the organization's mission. The statement should also focus on satisfying the team's external or internal customers.

Third, the team mission statement should center on the team's current and future work activities and major work processes.

Recall from Chapters 4 and 5 the story of the highly successful Team Engineers team at ABB Coral Springs. Initially, the individual assemblers and testers worked in a secluded fashion, supporting three different product lines. They thought there was no way they could help each other. A tester would fail a part and then not tell the assembler the specific problem that caused the part to be failed. After the team developed its mission "to deliver high-quality parts on time to customers," the testers and assemblers found ways they could support each other's success. The team members in the three different product lines discovered they could cross-train and then help each other when the customer had a greater need for a particular line of relays and the other lines were not that busy. The assemblers from the three different lines discovered shared problems that, when solved, improved every line's quality and on-time delivery.

Team missions should have a narrow focus to ensure success, especially when a new team is forming. In Chapter 10 of their book *In Search of Excellence,* Tom Peters and Bob Waterman presented eight attributes of highly successful companies, one of which was a narrowly focused organizational mission. Peters and Waterman described the importance of businesses having a narrow, laserlike focus by using the down-home adage "Stick to the knitting." Businesses should focus on what the organization knows best. In our modern global society, a negative connotation seems to surround the idea of having a narrow focus for a team's activities. But it is better for a team to select a few areas of work or business on which to focus and become the very best at those, rather than being too broad and involved in too many activities, doing none of them very well.

Identify an Idealistic Purpose

After the team has developed and agreed to its central activities and focus, the team members should identify the idealistic purpose of their team, which includes the personal, idealistic meaning the team can have for each member. Individual team members can develop any purpose they want. Usually teams develop something that focuses on satisfying external or internal customers. Internal customers are those individuals who receive the products or services of the team and do the next stage of work on it. In a restaurant, the waitresses are the internal customers of the cooks. Team members must interact with their customers or other stakeholders to find out what would satisfy them the most. Direct customer feedback can help the team develop the idealistic purpose part of the team's mission. One team at ABB Coral Springs integrated customer satisfaction into its mission directly; the mission of the team was "To manufacture the best quality product for our customer through teamwork."

Generate Excitement

Team missions should create energy. Mission statements should not only capture idealism but also create some excitement and fun about work. The video segment on Walt Disney World and the Disney company from the video *In Search of Excellence* provides a good example. Disney has every employee, including the street sweepers, pursuing the Disney World mission of "creating the most wonderful place in the world," and the employees have fun doing it. After I showed the video to the executive team of a mid-size family-run company, the young son of the president, looking haggard and beaten down, said, "We are not having any fun here." The team members then had a candid discussion about why they were not enjoying their work.

A major problem that prevents many executives from having fun at work is the perceived burden of carrying every aspect of the company on their shoulders. This perception usually occurs because there is no participative management or ownership by the rest of organization. After the discussion, the leaders of the family-owned company created a team mission for themselves to develop a sense of ownership on the part of all of the employees.

Another way to create an exciting team mission is to develop one that challenges the team. Jon Katzenbach and Douglas Smith described in *The Wisdom of Teams* how a challenging business mission, namely, to create a new type of business unique to the railroad industry, played a role in turning around the intermodal container division of the Burlington Northern Railroad.[9] The mission helped the division transform itself from the lowest performing division to the one with the highest profit and revenue. The challenge of the mission created a bond of mutual support among all team members. They believed in doing whatever it took to achieve the mission, including bypassing some of their own company's bureaucratic policies and procedures that stood in the way.

Teams can also create excitement in their missions by identifying the competition who is winning their customers away from them.

When Motorola began its corporate march to quality excellence and breakthrough teamwork, the company's management communicated that Texas Instruments and certain Japanese electronics companies were doing a better job than Motorola. The information on competitors unified Motorola managers across many divisions who previously had been so competitive with each other that external competitors had no need to worry. Their new unified mission to beat the competition helped cut through resistance across different divisions to support the quality march.

Be Concise

In 1992, Mark Henry, one of my colleagues, was asked to help a marketing group that was feeling overwhelmed by problems. The group members had asked Mark to train them in team problem solving and then facilitate the group to solve their most important problems. After two hours, the executive vice president of the group said, "I have been thinking about our session. We are doing the right thing but at the wrong time. We should agree on what our business is first." Someone said, "You mean like a mission statement?" The room was quiet and then someone said, "Yes." The group members admitted they had a written mission statement but no one could remember it. In fact, the executive vice president was challenged by one person to explain what the mission statement meant. He could not because he himself could not remember it. As stated earlier in this chapter, team mission statements need to be short enough so that everyone can remember them.

Preston Snuggs, the wafer Fab director of the highly successful Fab 14 of Advanced Micro Devices, was participating with his management team in its team mission training. The team had reached the point where the mission statement read, "Fab 14 manufactures advanced EPROMs and other memory devices and will satisfy its customers by shipping them on time." The mission was OK, but it was not concise. Preston and the team spent about 10 minutes brainstorming how to shorten the statement and came up with "Fab 14: Advanced EPROMs on time all the time." This mission was flashed on computer screens, banners were made, and T-shirts were printed. Everyone could remember it, and everyone tried to achieve it!

Identify Team Boundaries

Another value of organizational mission statements is to let all members of the organization know what business they're really in. It answers the question "What is the real focus of the business?" Such a statement can be used to set boundaries on what is important to them—what they should be paying attention to as a team or organization. Originally, General Motors managers thought they were in the *car* business. Under Alfred P. Sloan, General Motors realized it was in the *transportation* business. This new breakthrough mission opened the company up to include trucks and buses. Because of the new mission, General Motors created one of the major lines of school buses and built vehicles for transporting military troops.

Likewise, the mission for any team sets the boundary or fence around that with which the team should be most concerned. The boundary-setting aspect of the team mission is critically important for deciding which problems to solve, which work processes to improve, and even which agenda items to address in team meetings.

Be Evolutionary

Mission statements should evolve with the team. For new teams, mission statements should have a very narrow focus. As the team consistently achieves successes within the boundaries of the initial mission, it can be expanded. Teams can refresh missions as customers change what they want and need. As individual team members and the team do an outstanding job of supporting the team's mission, the team should recognize its own accomplishments. Remember, the team mission will provide overall direction as the team does its other activities, especially the next component of Structured Teamwork, goal setting.

HOW TEAM MISSION FITS WITH THE OTHER COMPONENTS OF STRUCTURED TEAMWORK

The team mission is the overall umbrella for the team's direction. The team goals should be developed after the team mission and should directly help achieve the mission. Figure 10–1 shows that team action plans are needed to attain team goals; team goals in turn help achieve the team mission.

The team mission statement should be written on the cover of the team notebook or displayed in the work area. It is the focus for all major decisions, including which work processes have the highest need for improvement and which problems should be solved first. Team member roles and responsibilities are established to achieve the mission and goals, rather than simply to perform a work function. A team's mission statement can be developed in one to six hours when

FIGURE 10–1

Alignment

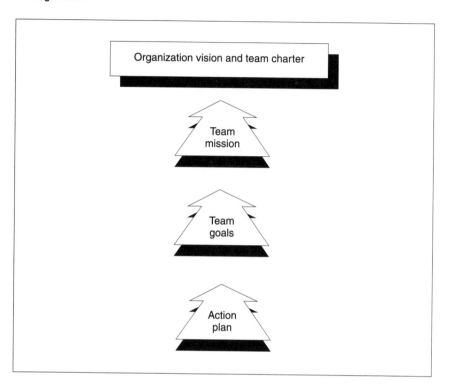

the Structured Teamwork methodology is used. Forming the mission statement is the foundation of team coordination: team creativity, communication, and cooperation skills are required to do it well.

BREAKTHROUGH POINTS

- Team values, vision, and mission statements motivate and set the team's direction.
- Mission statements should be developed using a structured process; they should create a specific focus, identify an idealistic purpose, generate excitement, be concise, identify team boundaries, and be evolutionary.
- The team mission statement should be prominently displayed.

11
CHAPTER

Team Goal Setting

TEAM GOALS CREATE WINNERS

A sports team wins when it has more points than its competitors. A business team wins when it sets appropriate and challenging goals and achieves them. Goals provide a yardstick a team (and management) can use to measure its accomplishments. What goals the team sets and how they are set can make a profound difference in the team members' work performance and in their coming together as a team. Team goal setting and the achievement of those goals build strong teams and esprit de corps. Sometimes people reverse this cause-and-effect relationship, but let me emphasize that the goals make the team; not the other way around. A team decides to win the Super Bowl, and then the team members work together to become champions.

Team goal setting includes talking about and agreeing to what each team member wants to achieve that will lead to the team mission. Goal setting and the frequent review of results help the team avoid wasting time on distractions and activities of minor significance. When there are *no* mutually supported goals, a group may degenerate into political factions where issues are no longer based on information. In the absence of team goal setting, each individual pursues his or her own independent direction, which may or may not help the organization reach its goals.

Team goal setting requires a structured process that includes the following:

- The team develops goals that directly align with the organization's desired business results.

- The entire team is involved in using team creativity to identify and select goals.

- The team develops a challenging "reach-out" goal that is worded as specifically as possible.

- All team members use team creativity to develop goal measures that are feasible and that will determine whether or not they are achieving their goals.

- Each team member participates in developing a creative action plan.

- The team identifies champions for the action steps.

- The team creates and tracks target dates for action step accomplishment.

The Structured Teamwork success stories presented in this book all had team goal setting as a key ingredient of their team development.

HOW TEAM GOAL SETTING SUPPORTS BREAKTHROUGH

Research and development teams responsible for new product launches benefit significantly from team goal setting and alignment. The number one predictor of success of R&D teams is the quality of the involvement and communication of the team in developing project goals.[1] Hundreds of millions of dollars are lost each year because of delays in the delivery of new products by teams of engineers, scientists, and technicians. The first major cause of the delays is the misunderstanding of and lack of agreement on the product development goals; the second major problem is the lack of clear metrics for measuring project progress; and the third major problem is the absence of jointly developed project plans with clear roles and responsibilities.

Unstructured work groups and project teams can waste up to half of their total project time getting oriented to their project.[2] Team goal setting accelerates project start-up. Product development teams that have used Structured Teamwork to jointly establish project goals and action plans have created and launched new products at lightning speed!

Teams that base their team development around structured team goal setting obtain 20 percent to 75 percent improved work performance.[3] Structured team goal setting works because it provides team members with more knowledge about the goals than when goals are simply delegated. Additionally, team goal setting is motivating and energizing to teams. Team members walk out of the team meeting committed to achieving the goals because they helped set the goals themselves.

Skill training for the ABB Team Engineers team progressed on track until a major conflict occurred during a team goal-setting session. Just as with every component of Structured Teamwork, the team members are taught the skills and, in a just-in-time fashion, then apply the skills in the training. During the goal-setting module, the team members narrowed their goals to improving either their scheduling or the quality of the electrical relays they produced. The team was in a deadlock. The majority favored working on the scheduling problem because they had a high number of late orders to customers. Four team members, however, wanted the group to work on improving the quality of their work.

The team was trying to practice their ground rule of making decisions by consensus, so that the decision would be agreed to and supported by every team member. Because of this expectation, a considerable amount of time was spent discussing both goals. That time would not have been expended in a "majority rules" decision-making mode. The team members, and even Mark Casner, their supervisor, were getting impatient with the conflict and disagreement. During team meetings, Mark was just another team member; even though he had his preference, he knew that for ownership to occur, the team as a whole had to support the decision. The team experienced firsthand the fact that when people are empowered, they have strong feelings and care about their ideas. As the clock approached 11:00 A.M. and time to adjourn, those who favored working on the quality goal backed down and agreed to support working on the goal to improve work scheduling.

During the lunch break, however, the team members who initially supported the scheduling goal felt concern for the four people who wanted to work on the quality problem. Between bites of their sandwiches, they discovered that a major quality problem was caused by their installing the wrong parts in the relays. As the team continued to talk about why it was happening, they realized the main cause was that many of the parts bins in their Kanban supermarket were mislabeled. It was a problem that the engineers had promised to fix. The team members said to each other, "We can fix that! We know better than anyone else what the correct labels are supposed to be!"

That afternoon, the team completed the relays required for shipping ahead of schedule. During the extra time, they correctly relabeled all of the parts bins. The team's on-time shipping results notably improved, but so did their product quality. Because the team members had an active role in setting team goals, they took an active role in making them happen. That is commitment and ownership.

WHEN TO USE TEAM GOAL SETTING

All work teams and project teams should develop team goals early in the team's development, usually immediately following team mission development. Goal setting improves team work performance because of increased team member motivation to attain the team goals. A review of 70 goal-setting studies confirmed Edwin Locke's theory that goal setting is one of the most powerful motivational methods in the workplace.[4]

There are two instances, however, when team goal setting should be delayed. The first is when the team is predominantly composed of new or inexperienced team members. When team or participative goal setting is used with individuals who have little or no knowledge of the area in which goals are set, the results are not successful. Educating employees in factors that influence productivity goals and letting them set and measure work goals leads to significant productivity improvement.[5]

A more effective method is for the leader to assign the goals to new employees and to carefully discuss with the team why the goal and its target level are important to the team. Even in this situation, however, the team leader should obtain a verbal or other type of commitment of support from each team member. Many times new teams are given the exact goals. In these cases, the team builds its commitment by developing subgoals, goal measurements, and/or an action plan for how to achieve the set direction. This type of involvement usually creates the necessary understanding and support for the team to be successful.

My colleague Bob Watt wanted to form a new team with the managers he directed. He had each team member stand and blow up a balloon. Bob then instructed everyone to let the balloons loose. There was a lot of laughter as the brightly colored balloons were propelled in various directions all over the conference room. Each person was given a new balloon and told to tie a knot in the balloon after blowing it up. As each person held up a knotted balloon, Bob described how the knot represented the team and the members' commitment to one another. Without the team, all of their efforts are like loose balloons, which shoot off in different directions. This is just an example of the creative ways leaders can have team members demonstrate support for the team and its goals when it is not possible to have them actively involved in setting the goals themselves.

The second time team goal setting should be delayed is when the team members do not have the basic team communication and conflict management skills to talk about and agree on goals. I have seen both frontline work teams and management teams that had so much conflict they could not agree on their team goals or where goals were needed. In such instances, success was possible only after the teams completed team communication and conflict management skills training. It was also useful to give team members the assignment to talk to some of their internal or external customers and discover what their customers wanted. Then the team was able to proceed with team goal setting.

HOW TO SET TEAM GOALS

A few research studies have reported that participative team goal setting did not result in improved work performance.[6] In most cases, however, a structured goal-setting process was lacking. A structured methodology is required to ensure that team goals:

- Are aligned and focused.
- Are creative.
- Are challenging and reach-out.
- Are specific.
- Are time based.
- Have goal measures.
- Use a plan composed of bite-sized action steps.

Each of these key elements is necessary to support breakthrough.

Goals Must Be Aligned and Focused

The beginning point for team goal setting is learning the priority business goals of the organization that the team must support in order to achieve organizational success. The team uses this information to identify the goals it can accomplish that will lead to the achievement of the organization's goals. Executives and managers must communicate the business and organizational priorities to the teams. Many of the organizations with which I have consulted in the 1980s and 1990s had one priority—to make a profit in order to survive. The self-managed work teams developed whatever goal could best promote profitability at that time. The teams at Monsanto and Westinghouse set goals to improve quality and reduce scrap. ABB teams decided to reduce manufacturing cycle time and to greatly increase productivity. Motorola groups set goals to help improve their position with strategic customers. In each case, the teams set goals that were aligned with and supported the organization's most important priorities.

Goal alignment is not only necessary for team goal setting but has become an essential ingredient in strategic planning and in almost any type of organizational development. Major organizational development activities that directly support business goals increase the likelihood that positive business results will occur.

Another aspect of alignment critical for goal-setting success is to limit the number of goals teams set. One department I knew of developed 60 goals to achieve in one year. No organization can simultaneously work on 60 different goals; setting so many goals is not only a waste of time but discouraging for the team. The department that attempted such a feat not only did not achieve any of the goals but also lost so much money that the entire organization was put at risk.

The negative business impact of poor goal alignment is confirmed by research done on executive teams. Research conducted by two IBM internal consultants found that profitable companies had greater agreement and alignment on a few priority goals versus many goals.[7] The top managers of each of the 40 most profitable companies in their study had agreement on only 6 to 12 goals. Everyone could recall the goals from memory and agreed they were the priorities. On the other hand, the top managers of the 40 least profitable organizations had 26 to 43 separate goals per organization. These managers had their own priorities and were not in agreement with each other on the vital few priorities. Without agreement and mutual support, there was no way their organizations could achieve business success.

After learning about this research, one of my clients decided that no department or division would have more than six goals at one time. The leader and management team of each department or division are together responsible for creating agreement for a small number of priorities for their unit. Having fewer priorities generates team focus.

Every team must obtain agreement on the few priority goals for a given time period. Overlapping goals is one way to reduce the breadth of focus. Achieving strategic objectives by overlapping them with tactical goals is another way to reduce the number of priorities at one time. AMD's Austin Wafer Fab Division overlapped its conversion of operators to technicians with giving them teamwork skills training first. This was one of the steps in the strategic plan. Doing it first overlapped with several immediate tactical objectives: improving worker discipline in following specifications, improving communication, and getting improved results on continuous improvement project objectives.

Goals Must Be Creative

Goal setting without team creativity is a boring, bureaucratic, paperwork task. The lack of creativity and team participation is why a similar management innovation—"management by objectives"—was not always successful. Using team creativity provides energy, enthusiasm, and breakthrough ideas for possible goals. For research and development engineers and technical support people, the team approach is one of the best methods for achieving goal alignment and creative goals.[8]

Participative goal setting in and of itself, however, does not lead to improved performance.[9] Participation using brainstorming does improve results. Brainstorming puts creativity into team goal setting. When structured brainstorming is used, teams set more specific, relevant, and challenging goals than groups using goal-setting discussions when setting goals. Team goals that are set by use of structured brainstorming improve team performance.

While brainstorming, teams should focus on possible goals that would help the organization achieve its mission. After the team members have generated and listed their goals, they should combine the duplicate and similar goals. Often the members will realize that some of their goals are actually action steps that fit under one or more of the goals.

The team then selects five to seven of the most important goals on which to work at this time. The team uses team decision-making skills to select the goals that have the highest leverage for helping the organization achieve its goals. One of the best ways to narrow the list is to have team members vote on their top choices. A brief discussion may accompany the voting to ensure that the best goals are selected. Another narrowing tool is to identify specific criteria to use when considering which brainstormed goals to keep. Goals are kept or eliminated based on how well they conform to the set criteria. The most important criterion should be whether the brainstormed goal will help achieve the organization's mission.

Goals Should Be Challenging and Reach-Out

Early on, research revealed that teams that set challenging, reach-out goals outperformed teams that set easy goals.[10] Specific and challenging goals had an average of 16 percent improvement in productivity across 10 studies versus "do your best" goals or no goals.[11]

An irony is that teams with reach-out goals did not necessarily achieve their goals, but their absolute performance was usually better. One set of teams at Motorola set reach-out goals for approximately 50 percent improvement in productivity. They achieved only an average 35 percent increase during the first three months. However, their performance was great compared to the teams that set 10 percent improvement goals and achieved between 12 percent and 15 percent improvement. Usually teams set goals that are more challenging than those set by their managers or supervisors. The challenge can be motivating and bring the team together. Challenging goals were a major ingredient in the success of the management teams studied by Jon Katzenbach and Douglas Smith.[12]

However, setting the reach-out goal without doing anything else is not enough. Teams that set extremely difficult goals are often forced into major paradigm shifts. These shifts are one of the most valuable aspects of extremely difficult goals. Teams must change the way they view the work processes and the action plans necessary to achieve the goals. Soon after completing goal setting, perhaps during action planning, teams must challenge themselves to find creative, breakthrough ways to do the work, which will result in the achievement of the reach-out goal.

The art of setting a reach-out goal is to discriminate between that which is attainable and will stretch the ability and creativity of the team, and that which is impossible and therefore self-defeating. If the team feels at the beginning or sometime later that the goal is impossible, the members will become apathetic and have an "I don't care" attitude. Consequently, teams must creatively examine how the work is done when reach-out goals are set.

Goals Should Be Specific

A team does not have a goal unless it is worded specifically enough so that every team member has exactly the same goal in mind. Goals that have specific targets and measurable outcomes significantly increase team performance. Edwin Locke and his colleagues conducted or reviewed over 50 goal-setting studies. They concluded that setting specific goals resulted in tremendous improvements. Specific goals, such as "increase productivity by 50 percent in three months," are much easier to measure and plan than general or "do your best" goals.

In fact, goals in business and industry traditionally were "do your best" goals until the Du Pont family adopted a management team approach to running the Du Pont Corporation early in this century. A key ingredient in their management methodology was to set a specific financial target of total sales and profit to be achieved each year. The Du Ponts found that specific financial goals made all of their business planning more efficient, as every decision was logically aligned to support those goals. Du Pont became one of the most successful corporations in the United States, and the Du Ponts' leadership on the board of General Motors took GM from near bankruptcy in the 1920s to a position as the world's most successful business enterprise in the 1950s. Goal specificity was a chief element in their success.

Goals Should Be Time Based

You may have noticed that all my examples of challenging or specific goals involved a time element. Goals require due dates. Team members work on goals with time deadlines more readily than on goals with no such dates. We are conditioned to believe that goals with specific deadlines must be urgent. As teams develop goals, they should initially set the target date as a preference in draft form. It should be finalized after developing the action plan to ensure that all critical steps can be achieved within the specified time frame.

Teams Should Have Goal Measures

Both goal challenge and goal specificity positively influence team performance. Goal measurement development is critically important because it is the concrete representation of both. Measuring goals and publicizing attainment results can increase performance. In one organization, for example, providing daily visual and public feedback on quality goals resulted in a 66 percent drop in rework.[13] Team measures create the feedback loop the team needs. Performance feedback combined with team goal setting increased productivity 75 percent in another organization.[14]

Monsanto Chemical in Addyston, Ohio, emerged as one of the first self-managed team implementations. The team members began by identifying performance measures for their goals. Setting team goals and specifying how they are to be measured form the foundation for empowered teams. Stated goal measures help ensure that the goal is specific and achievable.

However, just as teams should not have more than five to seven goals at one time, they should not have too many goal measures in total. Having 9 or 10 goal measures at one time is close to ideal, as these allow the team to regularly measure and react to the results.

Measuring a team's performance is a key to unifying the team. Therefore, time should be spent carefully developing measures of the most important team goals. Most goals should have both a quantity measure and a quality measure. Developing good goal measures around which feasible data can be collected requires hard work and team creativity. The team should use creativity methods to develop and agree on the best and most specific measures possible.

The ABB Line 5 team achieved significant business results even though the team was asked to begin producing a variety of new products. The Line 5 work team collected its own manufacturing results data. Every manager knows that one of his or her hardest tasks is to get employees to enter or track performance data on their work. The Line 5 team members not only tracked the data but also used the data to respond rapidly to problems or to continue what they were doing if the data was positive.

All too often, team performance data are collected for the benefit of managers who are three layers removed from the work itself. This all too frequently results in no tangible improvements. Data need to be collected and provided at the point of attack, where the service is delivered or the product is made. When a team tracks its own performance, it has the opportunity to correct problems immediately!

In fact, the adjustments a team makes after receiving feedback on the goal measures create improved performance. Studies have shown that feedback on work performance achieves significant results only when the team uses the results to modify its goals or how the work is being done.[15]

Every team, in fact every employee, wants to know the answer to the question "Are we winning or are we losing?" The goals and the goal measures provide the score. The team needs to know, accept, and act on the score. Key to accepting the judgment is the team's initial involvement in developing both the goals and the measures. The organization must allow the main form of evaluation to be the measures that each work team develops to assess its team goals and work processes.

Plans Should Be Composed of Bite-Sized Action Steps

One of the major purposes of deliberately setting a reach-out goal is to stimulate a shift in paradigms during the development of the action plan. Team creativity and the participation of every team member will result in an innovative action plan. After a team has completed each of the above structured goal-setting steps, it should develop the action plan, including the intermediate milestones.

One marketing group set the stretch goal of having a new product planned in half the time it normally took. That stretch goal forced the team to come up with a breakthrough action plan for achieving the goal. The plan represented a total departure from how previous products had been planned and developed. The group was successful with the plan, achieved the goal, and made millions of dollars for the company because its product beat the competition to the market.

Great achievements are accomplished in little steps. All team members should be involved in brainstorming small action steps. Team members then volunteer for those steps that fit their expertise and available time. Using frequently assigned bite-sized action steps results in greater performance than assigning major steps, which may require large amounts of time to complete. Part of human nature is to delay working on a task until it is close to the due date. Using the team to brainstorm and sequence the action steps results in the rapid development of a complete plan with a high degree of team ownership.

An action plan can help take a goal that appears totally overwhelming and make it seem feasible. When the team first considers the feasibility of achieving a goal, team members may be discouraged and disheartened. After the team creates an action plan, especially when it has deliberately created the first few steps to be easily implemented, the whole plan becomes doable. Initial milestones and action steps should be easy to complete in order to build in success for the plan and to create early momentum for its achievement. The team uses the plan to coordinate all of the little action steps taken on by the individual team members.

HOW TEAM GOAL SETTING FITS WITH THE OTHER COMPONENTS OF STRUCTURED TEAMWORK

Team goal setting is the focus for all of the other activities of the team. Team roles and responsibilities are set to achieve team goals. The team goals provide the compass for all team decisions that must be made. The team selects problems to work on according to how likely it is their solution will help the team achieve its goals. A major purpose of team meetings is to review progress on team goals. If the team is disappointed with its progress in achieving its goals, it uses team problem solving or work process improvement to overcome obstacles to goal attainment. Team meetings have goals themselves in order to create the structure needed for productive meetings. A major skill step of conflict management is to establish shared goals between the individuals who are having the conflict. In turn, conflict management skills are used to set the team goals when team members disagree about goals and priorities.

CONCLUSION

The Structured Teamwork processes for team goal setting really do work. The steps discussed above combine the best methods from the finest research on goal setting and team creativity. Team members should be involved in developing aligned, creative, challenging, specific, and time-based goals and the corresponding team measures and action steps. When they are, focus, commitment, and high performance result.

BREAKTHROUGH POINTS

- Goal setting is a key ingredient of team development and improved performance.
- Unstructured work groups that have not set their goals can spend half of their project time getting oriented.
- Teams should develop their goals early, usually immediately after the team mission.

- For improved work performance, team goal setting should be aligned and focused, creative, challenging and reach-out, specific, time based, measurable, and composed of small action steps.

12

CHAPTER

Roles and Responsibilities and Team Organization

TEAM ROLES AND RESPONSIBILITIES OPERATIONALIZE EMPOWERMENT

As teams form, an assumption often emerges that everything must be done as a group. This assumption is incorrect. The team comes together at regularly scheduled times to communicate and coordinate activities. However, most of the work is done as each person performs his or her individual roles and responsibilities. Everyone needs to understand how his or her role contributes to the desired business results.

In one company, a research study found that explaining to team members how the team and each team member's individual role influenced business results improved both motivation and performance on the company's assembly line. The team members set measurable goals relative to their expected roles. Productivity and quality improvement increased $1,000 per week compared to prior team goal-setting and role development efforts.[1]

Goal clarity and understanding how the individual's role supports organizational goals are two factors related to job satisfaction and reduced employee turnover.[2] A major source of job conflict and stress is not having a clear understanding of one's role in the organization. Only when everyone on the team understands his or her current role(s) and responsibilities is it possible for the team to participate in empowerment and other types of job redesign.

An implicit assumption of teamwork is shared management. Usually the focus of decision making is on managers. In any organization pursuing employee involvement and empowerment, the objective is to increase the decision-making authority of people "at the point of attack." As team members acquire Structured Teamwork skills, it is possible for them to take on the tasks of self-management. Changing job roles and responsibilities allows this to happen.

Team roles and responsibilities describe the tasks and decisions that are both unique and shared for each member of the team. The descriptions are developed through the involvement of the whole team. There are three kinds of tasks shared by team members: Structured Teamwork tasks, work responsibilities/tasks of the specific work area, and administrative self-management tasks. These will be discussed in the next three sections.

Structured Teamwork Responsibilities of Team Members

One set of team member responsibilities that promotes breakthrough performance is team ground rules and norms. Generating ground rules and norms provides the opportunity for team members to make explicit their highest values about how people should be treated at work. A *ground rule* is a predetermined behavior that every team member agrees to follow all of the time. In baseball, agreed-to ground rules determine how the game will be played. For example, if the ball goes under the ballpark fence and therefore out of the park, according to the rules of the game it is a "ground rule double" instead of a home run. A business example of a frequently adopted team ground rule is "No personal attacks."

A *norm* is a behavioral expectation that team members agree to adhere to most of the time, for example, "Be on time to team meetings." It is a valued behavior that the team wants to practice but recognizes is not always possible to achieve. Having clear ground rules and norms helps the team establish and maintain a high ethical base and idealism.

People need ground rules and norms for behavior. A 1991 survey of 5,700 Americans found that 91 percent of those surveyed admitted to lying at home and at work.[3] Almost 50 percent said they call in sick to work when they are not sick, and most admitted to goofing off at work for about seven hours a week. The most amazing part of the study is that the people surveyed stated they want to do the right thing. Team ground rules and norms create a framework of behavioral modeling, support, and consequences that allows individuals to behave responsibly.

At the beginning of an empowerment consulting project, managers and supervisors often tell me there is no way they will give their workers increased self-management. They state, "How can we trust our workers to manage their own work schedule and work quality when they falsely call in sick or hide from work during the day?" The answer: When the team members set the rules, they follow them!

Most organizations have informal ground rules and norms, which may or may not support quality. After interviewing hundreds of team members, I have found that, at the beginning of Structured Teamwork training, only about 20 percent of the members of a team believe in doing a high-quality job and satisfying customers. These 20 percent realize that high quality is the key to their own job security and future financial benefits. In the assessment interviews, they complain about fellow team members who do not follow good work procedures and do sloppy work. Through the team ground rules and norms process, these individuals influence the whole team to set a ground rule or norm to do high-quality work. As a result of this ground rule or norm, the team members emphasize quality in their goal setting and decision making, which in turn actually increases work quality.

Without explicitly developing ground rules and norms, team members may inadvertently offend each other. For example, one team member's personal norm about work deadlines may be that if the work is completed late but close to the deadline, it is OK. Another team member's view may be that if the deadline is Friday at 1:00 P.M., then the work should be completed by that exact time. A third team member may feel that the work should be done *before* the deadline so that if something goes wrong at the last minute, there is a margin of safety. When differences appear in the absence of explicit team-set ground rules and norms, team members may inadvertently hurt one another's feelings. These minor offenses can result in reduced communication.[4] Reduced communication leads to decreased cooperation and coordination.

The executive management committee of one Fortune 100 company had the bad habit of being late to meetings. In one of their first

Structured Teamwork sessions, the committee members set being on time for meetings as a ground rule. Two weeks later, one of the vice presidents was standing in the hallway talking to a group of managers and supervisors when he looked down at his watch. He asked the group to please excuse him because the management committee had a meeting that was about to start and he had to be there on time. He explained that it was a new team ground rule to be on time for meetings.

Within two hours, the news traveled throughout the company's 30-story building that the vice presidents were starting their meetings on time. As a result, several divisions and many other teams adopted the same ground rule, and meetings everywhere began to start on time. In addition, there was an increased urgency and awareness about how everyone used their time. People started completing assignments on time. Individuals walked a little faster in the hallways between offices.

The difficult part of developing team ground rules and norms is helping the team make its ground rules and norms as specific as possible. Almost every team sets a ground rule to respect each other. But a good ground rule must be an observable behavior. To transform an abstract idea into an observable behavior, the Structured Teamwork facilitator will ask the team to specifically describe the behavior it wants to see. In this case, the observable behavior of respect the team wanted was for people's ideas to be listened to without interruption or criticism. To listen fully and patiently is probably the hardest behavior to learn for the brilliant and experienced manager who thinks he or she knows what the employee is saying. But patiently hearing out others' ideas and concerns exemplifies respect for the team. Ground rules and norms should be as specific and measurable as possible in order to ensure their achievement.

Many frontline work teams set a ground rule that "everyone on the team is equal." This rule includes equipment operators, supervisors, managers, engineers—anyone. Frontline teams experience a burst of energy and release from frustration when they feel that their ideas and concerns are just as valid as their managers'. Managers do not appear to lose power or respect from such a team ground rule. However, the employees feel they have gained respect and confidence in their own ideas. As companies ask their employees to identify the areas of work in which they want to be empowered, managers are surprised that many of the decisions and tasks are ones that workers supposedly already have the authority to do. Managers wonder why their workers are not aware of or do not use the decision-making authority they already have. One reason is that many teams and individual workers lack self-confidence. A norm or ground rule stating that everyone's ideas in meetings are of equal value is a powerful confidence-builder, especially when people practice it.

In addition to agreeing to follow team ground rules and norms, every team member agrees to assume other Structured Teamwork roles, including participating in the development of goals and action plans, solving problems in and out of meetings, making decisions, managing conflicts, improving work processes, and supporting the team mission. Also, team members rotate performing certain necessary team meeting roles such as meeting leader, meeting minutes recorder, and meeting timekeeper. Team members should be taught the corresponding skills in all of the above areas so that their participation will be effective in those roles.

Work Responsibilities of the Work Area

The cover story in the September 1994 issue of *Fortune* magazine questioned whether there was such a thing as a job anymore. In the article, "The End of the Job," William Bridges predicted that in the future, employees' roles will break out from the rigid confines of a job description to become more dynamic and focused on the work that needs to be done, whatever that may be.[5] In the "post-job" organization, workers will be assigned to project teams, and their responsibilities and tasks will change with the needs of the project. Structured team roles and responsibilities for the work itself are different from traditional job descriptions. Some of the distinguishing elements are displayed in Figure 12–1.

As can be seen from Figure 12–1, Structured Teamwork approaches the organization of work in a flexible and dynamic fashion. Traditional job responsibilities are concerned only with job tasks and the knowledge to perform those tasks. In contrast, team members are concerned with achieving team goals to assist the organization in achieving breakthroughs in business results. Roles and responsibilities connect the work with desired goals. Because work goals change, roles and responsibilities must be flexible. Government laws and human resource policies may still require job descriptions, but most team-based companies write the job descriptions broadly enough to allow the team to specifically create the needed roles and responsibilities as new team goals are set.

Every job responsibility is not shared with every other team member. There are still unique responsibilities based on training and

FIGURE 12–1

Traditional Job Descriptions versus Structured Team Roles and
Responsibilities

Factor	Job Descriptions	Team Roles and Responsibilities
Process for developing	Low involvement of team; human resources department and management develop	High involvement of team; the team members develop in the context of team mission and goals
Stability	High—job descriptions are used, without revision, for years	Low—team roles and responsibilities are continuously revised as empowerment, new training, and work processes change
Job flexibility	Low—"one person, one job"	High—significant cross-training and sharing of tasks
Specialization	Job description determines specialization	Interests, ability, experience, and desire to learn new tasks determine areas of specialization
Continuous empowerment process	Occurs when individuals are promoted to a new job	Job boundaries expand as individuals and the team demonstrate competence with the authority they now have
Coordination	Mainly coordinate with one's boss	Coordinate internally with all team members; coordinate with customers and suppliers
Purpose	To communicate to an individual his or her work duties	To identify the key roles to achieve the current goals
When developed	Once every 3–10 years	Every time new goals are developed (not new target levels for old goals, but new goals themselves)

work area requirements. Still, there is more backup and overlap than in non-team-based organizations. For example, one of the most valuable team members in a manufacturing facility is the maintenance technician. His or her unique responsibility is to keep major pieces of equipment running. In facilities that are implementing teamwork, the maintenance technician has a number of responsibilities that can be shared. For example, the maintenance technician can teach machine operators how to do much of the preventive maintenance and simple troubleshooting that otherwise would fall solely on the maintenance technician's shoulders.

Empowerment and Self-Management Responsibilities

The first two parts of the team roles and responsibilities training are mandatory to accomplish team breakthrough. The following responsibilities are gradually transferred from the supervisor to the work team:

- Provide technical training.
- Coach fellow team members.
- Measure and manage quality.
- Create schedules using input from management.
- Assist in purchasing new equipment.
- Assist in work layouts.
- Measure important team goals: productivity, cycle time, and so on.
- Select new team members.
- Record attendance and tardiness.
- Schedule vacations.

These responsibilities can be clustered into coordinator roles that are rotated among team members. The most frequently used coordinator roles in manufacturing organizations are the following:

Quality: Measure and communicate quality performance.

Training: Maintain training records, schedule training, provide training to new team members.

Administrative: Maintain attendance records, coordinate and schedule vacations.

Safety: Attend organizationwide safety training, provide safety training, observe and report safety infractions.

Productivity: Schedule daily work, measure and report team productivity.

Financial or cost: Measure and report costs, coordinate budgets, approve expenditures.

Organizations that develop and use coordinator roles to relieve the supervisor sometimes call this the *star model,* because there are five or six points on the star corresponding to the number of roles that must be rotated. Organizations fail, however, when they try to legislate from the top down what configuration the star model will be. The model works significantly better when the team members themselves create and agree to the coordinator roles that are needed to best achieve their team mission and goals.

Supervisors or team facilitators must also have their roles defined by the team. The role of the supervisor or facilitator requires a bigger presence on teams where the work tasks and daily jobs are more unpredictable. A study of group performance in five large banks in the southern United States found that the more unpredictable the work, the greater the need for a variety of skill sets and high teamwork and communication on the team to achieve high performance.[6]

HOW TEAM ROLES AND RESPONSIBILITIES SUPPORT BREAKTHROUGH

A Structured Teamwork approach to roles and responsibilities supports cross-training and multiple roles for each team member. Teams in any work environment can achieve performance improvements through a team approach to their roles and responsibilities. David Pelz and Frank Andrews's research on 1,311 scientists and engineers found that job flexibility and variety increased performance: the more areas of specialization and the greater the variety of functions, the higher the performance rate.[7] Performance was measured by output of reports, output of papers or patents, judged contribution, and judged usefulness of the employee.

Job rotation and job flexibility are proven ingredients to productivity improvement in manufacturing organizations.[8] A key ingredient of successful start-up companies is that the team members wear multiple hats. A ground rule of one successful start-up company that went from zero sales to $50 million in five years was that everyone wore three hats. Each person performed, in effect, what would be three different roles in a larger company. For example, one manager was responsible for designing new products, marketing to one major customer, and managing the engineers. Large organizations lose that feeling of excitement and challenge by creating overspecialized and inflexible job roles.

As described above, the star model of self-management takes the tasks of the supervisor and divides them into five or six part-time coordinator roles shared among the team members. Care must be taken to transfer important and useful supervisory tasks. Since the supervisor role in many organizations has been filled with bureaucratic and non-value-added tasks, dividing those up and giving them to the team coordinators is foolish. When team members assume roles that focus on value-added technical, self-management administrative, and Structured Teamwork tasks, the team will achieve breakthrough results.

HOW TO DEVELOP TEAM ROLES AND RESPONSIBILITIES

The how-to steps correspond to the major areas of team roles and responsibilities. First is the development of team ground rules and norms, followed by team-generated roles and responsibilities and organization-directed job redesign.

Team Ground Rules and Norms

One of the first Structured Teamwork tasks is for the team to develop its ground rules and norms. Each team member participates in identifying what behaviors, if practiced by the team members, would result in great business results. After all of the possible ground rules and norms are listed, the team as a whole decides which ground rules and norms it will adopt and live by. The decision must be by consensus—everyone on the team must agree to follow the behaviors. Teams should have between 5 and 15 total ground rules and norms at one time. More than 15 is too hard to keep track of and follow. To reduce the list, teams can eliminate ground rules and norms they already follow consistently.

Many times the discussion gets quite lively, especially on teams where there is a long history of conflict and poor teamwork. This discussion is one activity the team cannot do by itself. A neutral facilitator is needed, and the more negative the past experience of the team, the more important it is that the facilitator be well-trained and experienced.

After the ground rules and norms are developed, they should be posted or placed in everyone's team notebook. At the beginning of team training or team meetings, the team members should review their team ground rules and norms and select one they think they need to practice throughout the training or the meeting. Later, at the end of the meeting, the members can evaluate how well they followed the ground rule or norm. Also at the end of team meetings, the team can consider the goals that need to be accomplished before the next meeting and select which ground rule or norm they should focus on that will assist in the goals being met.

The most difficult part of using team ground rules and norms is to determine what the team will do when an individual violates the ground rule or repeatedly violates the norm. Team members are uncomfortable challenging their peers. I was training an executive management team that had agreed to a ground rule to be on time for meetings. The day after the ground rules were developed, one of the key executives did not show up on time for the start of the training. The team talked about how one team member would have to confront the tardy executive when he finally showed up. I began the training without him, and the executive eventually came in about an hour late.

As he took his seat, the designated team member first asked, "How are you doing, Bob?" Bob replied in a hoarse voice, "Not too good. I was up most of the night sick." The team member then said, "We missed you at the start of the meeting, but we are glad you are here now." The team member spoke with warmth and concern but did not back off from the gentle reminder about the meeting start time, even though the individual had a good excuse. Most of the time all that is needed is a reminder to follow the ground rule or norm. Every team member is responsible for the ground rules and norms being followed.

Some teams take off like a rocket ship after they develop their ground rules and norms. Other teams will not take them seriously. Later, when these teams start having major difficulties in performance and teamwork, the problems can almost always be traced back to not following the ground rules and norms. When a team is having performance problems, I have learned to first check its ground rules and norms. Have they been established and communicated? Are they being followed? Are they still appropriate?

The next two sections are divided into what the team can do on its own and what the organization and its leadership must be involved in. Every team must determine its own roles and responsibilities, whether a management team, a project team, or a natural work group team. Other approaches are appropriate when an organization wants to implement job redesign and/or self-managed teamwork.

Team-Generated Roles and Responsibilities

Improved teamwork and breakthrough performance occur when the team is involved in developing the roles and responsibilities for everyone on the team. Team members who perform identical roles and responsibilities work together to develop a first draft of their description. Individuals on the team who have unique roles and responsibilities, like the supervisor or engineer, write down what they feel those roles and responsibilities are. Responsibilities must be described as specifically as possible, with strong action words. An example of a role description is below.

Role: <u>Administrative Assistant</u>

Responsibilities:

1. Type materials/products.

2. Manage files/documents.

3. Coordinate work that consultants bring in (typing, etc.).

4. Maintain equipment.

5. Maintain supportive and efficient supplier interface.

6. Distribute marketing materials.

7. Get office supplies.

8. Answer telephones.

9. File.

10. Use computer skills to keep computer system working properly.

11. Keep office neatly organized.

12. Proficiently produce graphics, tables, and columns.

13. Coordinate temporary employees when needed.

The second stage of the process is for the team to review every role and responsibility description and to modify them so that everyone can support every other person's roles and responsibilities. Some teams have roles with significant past conflict, and therefore the agreement stage can be emotional and heated. Teams do best installing this component of Structured Teamwork after they have learned team conflict management skills.

For example, in one company that was studied, one-on-one role clarification meetings between supervisors and their subordinates did not have a significant improvement on stress, physical symptoms, or time lost due to illness.[9] The whole team must be involved in role clarification for there to be significant impact. The supervisor or team facilitator must be perceived as a member of the team who also has a valuable role to play, and the team must understand and support the supervisor's role. Therefore, at the same time the team is agreeing to everyone else's roles and responsibilities, the supervisor or facilitator's role must also be agreed upon.

For high-performance teamwork to occur, the supervisor or team facilitator must allow each team member to have ownership of his or her role. The supervisor must promote the involvement of the team members in any role or responsibility changes.

A responsibility matrix or table is a useful tool to summarize those responsibilities that should be shared by more than one team member. The matrix also clarifies who has primary responsibility and who has backup duties for each key task. The responsibility matrix is developed by listing the team members down the left-hand side of the table and the job responsibilities across the top of the table. The job responsibilities that should be considered include work tasks, Structured Teamwork tasks, and self-management tasks (star model).

The letter P is put in the column next to the name of the person who has primary responsibility for the task. An S is put next to the names of people who may share in performing part of the task or are backups for performing the task. Sometimes on teams, each team member, over time, will present a problem to be solved or will have primary responsibility for customer satisfaction. In these cases, a P/S is used. If a task is performed as a team, then all people receive an S. See the example in Figure 12–2. As with written role and responsibility descriptions, the key success factor is to have the entire team develop the responsibility matrix.

Figure 12–2 shows how many tasks are shared even though one person has primary responsibility. The person in the primary responsibility role makes sure the task is completed and coordinates obtaining additional resources if the work demands exceed the resources.

FIGURE 12–2

Sample Responsibility Matrix

	Problem Solving/Process Improvement	Research	Marketing	Continuous Communication and Team Meetings	Budget and Finance	Hiring	New Product Development	Word Processing
Administrative assistant	P/S			S	S	S	S	P
Business manager	P/S			S	P	S		S
Marketing manager	P/S	S	P	S	S	S	S	S
Operations manager	P/S	S	S	P	S	P	P	S
Research coordinator	P/S	P	S	S	S	S	S	S

P = Primary responsibility; S = Shared responsibility.

Organization-Directed Job Redesign

There were a plethora of job redesign programs in the 1970s and 1980s under the names of "job enrichment" and "improving the quality of work life." Those programs reaped very mixed results, with many failures in terms of improving work performance. Only 3 of 28 studies reported totally favorable results.[10]

Employee involvement is a critical factor in successful job redesign. Experienced employees should be involved in the redesign of their work areas.[11] Studies indicate that when advanced manufacturing technology is installed, it fails to meet management's expectations 50 to 70 percent of the time. Examples of failures include 40 percent–plus downtime on expensive robotic equipment. Such failure can often be linked to how much the affected employees were or were not involved in the required job redesign.[12]

Just doing job redesign without teamwork training and team involvement does not produce the desired performance improvements. In fact, existing teamwork can unravel if the workers whose jobs are being redesigned are not involved in the job redesign. In contrast, if C^5 teamwork is in place when job redesign efforts are initiated, and if the team members themselves are involved, great business results occur.

Job redesign requires linking the newly developed responsibilities to the team's work goals, which in turn are aligned to the organization's business goals. Setting and using business and manufacturing goals to plan where and how to redesign work tasks helps deliver rapid and significant benefits. Without goal measurement and feedback, as without employee involvement, job redesign *fails* to improve performance![13]

Organizational job redesign also requires significant time and money. A systematic plan with several phases should be used.[14] Initial phases should be constructed to provide enough payback in business results to fund future phases. Initial phases of job redesign that have focused on training and developing the natural work group into a high-performance team have delivered excellent business results. The team is then able to effectively and efficiently contribute to further aspects of job redesign.[15]

The availability of high-quality training is a major critical factor in the success of job redesign. Both teamwork skills and technical skills training are necessary for improved business results.[16] Machine-specific training should be delivered just-in-time to small natural work groups (with two to eight employees) by their engineer, supervisor, or maintenance technician in the context of improving business results and corresponding work processes and specifications. This method is low in cost, is easy to implement and administer, has high learner retention and application, and achieves or exceeds the desired business results, in contrast with very slow and cumbersome top-down approaches.

Job redesign naturally occurs whenever new equipment is installed or new work methods must be implemented.[17] Unfortunately, whether it is a new computer work station for a design engineer or a new robotic-based manufacturing tool, the team is usually not involved in the selection, planning, and training. As a result, most new equipment is slow to deliver the significant benefits that pay for its acquisition costs.

One area of job redesign that has consistently obtained exceptional business results is the delegation of supervisory tasks such as planning, scheduling, assigning, work productivity, and quality to trained work teams.[18] Developing team roles and responsibilities identifies and eliminates duplication of work between team members, which can result in improved productivity. An even richer gold mine of savings can be found by eliminating the duplication of managerial work (meetings, decision approvals, goal reviews, etc.) as one goes up and down the management chain of command. Consequently, organizations are realizing reduced costs and improved productivity from self-managed teamwork and reduced levels of management.

A major teamwork tool that can assist teams in the structured implementation of empowerment and increased self-management is the decision-making matrix. An example of a decision-making matrix from a manufacturing organization is presented in Figure 12–3. Within the matrix, the S (for start) indicates which level of the organization has the current authority to make the decisions. As can be seen, prior to the shift in roles and responsibilities, Level 4 (the supervisor) has the majority of decision-making authority. The target levels of empowerment and job redesign are indicated with a T (for target level). Most of the targeted levels in the example are Level 2 (the team) and Level 1 (the individual team member).

The team represented in Figure 12–3 required approximately two years of cross-training and development by the supervisor and the team itself to reach the targeted levels. The team implemented those areas of redesigned decision making that had the highest leverage on achieving the team's priority work goals. The team set new records for productivity and quality improvement every month!

Most organizations attempt to implement both technical and empowerment types of major job redesign without either a structured process or a teamwork foundation. As a result, those organizations do not even come close to breakthrough. Instead, the managers' skepticism for employee involvement and job redesign increases.

This common negative experience contrasts with that of the ecstatic vice president I met with recently whose three divisions had all set new records of performance despite major obstacles that in the past had created a downturn in all performance measures. His organizations had implemented major job redesign using Structured Teamwork. Over 100 natural work groups simultaneously implemented redesigned job roles as part of each group's team goals to improve their work performance. The usual employee resistance was minimal because the teams were involved in *how* to install the new roles and saw how the job redesign helped them reach their team goals.

FIGURE 12–3

Decision-Making Matrix

Decisions	Decision Level (S = Start, T = Target)*				
	5	4	3	2	1
When to do equipment maintenance		S			► T
Scheduling work		S	► T		
Request for equipment replacement	S			► T	
Cycle time improvement		S	► T		
Materials, supplies, tools coordination		S			► T
Vacation schedules		S	► T		
Request for short delivery date		S			► T
Meeting scheduler		S	► T		
Quality problem recorder			S		► T
Work methods/specifications coordination			S		► T
Monitor attendance		S		► T	
Administer overtime		S	► T		
Maintenance chance requests		S			► T
Making training assignments		S		► T	
Conducting equipment training		S			► T
Resolve material shortages		S	► T		
Layout changes		S	► T		

*Decision Levels: Level 5, manager decides; Level 4, supervisor decides; Level 3, specialist decides (quality, maintenance, etc.); Level 2, team decides; Level 1, individual team member/members decide(s).

HOW TEAM ROLES AND RESPONSIBILITIES FIT WITH THE OTHER COMPONENTS OF STRUCTURED TEAMWORK

Team roles and responsibilities are created by the team to achieve the team's mission and goals. The actual development of the written roles and responsibilities involves the use of team communication, team creativity, and conflict management skills. A major source of team conflict is role ambiguity.[19] Make the roles and responsibilities clear, and a major source of team conflict is eliminated. Team roles and responsibilities clarify who has primary responsibility for key work processes that must be improved. In essence, many of the Structured Teamwork components are used to create the team roles and responsibilities, and roles and responsibilities activities interact with other teamwork components such as goal setting, problem setting, and work process improvement.

CONCLUSION

Developing roles and responsibilities as a team provides a solid base of self-confidence, knowledge of job expectations of self and others, and knowledge of who to go to for assistance. It also allows for the quick and effective implementation of new equipment and other product line changes while reducing role and task redundancies. Major job redesigns that involve team members, use structured procedures, and are linked to organizational goals are successful. Clearly defined roles and responsibilities in a teamwork-based and empowered environment lead to breakthrough teamwork.

BREAKTHROUGH POINTS

- A major source of job conflict and stress is not having a clear understanding of one's role in the organization.
- Generating ground rules and norms provides the opportunity for team members to make explicit their highest values.
- The team must specifically describe the behavior it wants to see in order to generate great business results.
- Structured team roles and responsibilities for the work itself are different from traditional job descriptions.

- Teams should have at least 5 but no more than 15 ground rules and norms at any one time.
- The whole team must be involved in role clarification, after the team has learned conflict management skills.

CHAPTER

Team Problem Solving

CONTINUOUS BREAKTHROUGH PROCESSES

Creating continuous breakthroughs requires a series of important processes. Chapters 13, 14, and 15 describe the latest research and process steps for team problem solving, team decision making, and work process improvement. Effective and frequent use of these processes by teams creates continuous breakthroughs. As with all the other components of Structured Teamwork, team creativity skills are essential to the success of these processes; without creativity, only mediocre improvements are identified and implemented.

One of the first areas of participative management training that Motorola provided to its manufacturing equipment operators back in 1981 was an eight-hour team problem-solving course. A manager at one of the company's southwestern U.S. locations was totally against the training. He believed it would reduce the monthly production by 5 percent in July because the operators would lose 5 percent of their production time to the training. He was baffled in August when he saw that the operators had broken their best month's production record, despite the time spent in training! The team problem-solving skills were put to immediate use to solve frequently occurring problems in the work area that normally held back productivity.

Team problem solving can be used effectively in team meetings when problems are identified. It also has tremendous application in real time as problems occur in the workplace. A 3M engineer, Phillip Bolea, described how a major problem occurred with an early prototype of one of 3M's laser printers during a demonstration to the Japanese joint venture engineers. Phillip was ready to box the printer up when the three Japanese engineers began talking very fast and pointing at it. After several minutes, Phillip asked for a translation. The engineers were identifying as many ideas as possible for why the printer was not working. They then tried out their various fixes. The solution that fixed the printer was one of the most improbable ideas.

Similar opportunities abound in every organization. Unfortunately, most organizations miss such opportunities because they do not follow certain research-based guidelines. A major obstacle is that the team members have not learned how to solve problems together.

IDENTIFY AND SOLVE PROBLEMS INSIDE YOUR OWN BOUNDARIES

We are all good at identifying problems—if the problems are someone else's responsibility. We normally call such behavior griping or complaining. A harder task is to be open and admit the problems at work in which we may play a role. I call this process identifying the problems inside the fence of your own yard's boundaries. My colleagues and I always kick off team problem-solving training by asking the team to identify current problems in their work area. Typically, one-half to two-thirds of the list of problems the team generates are someone else's responsibility. Often these types of problems were assigned to quality circles and took months to solve.

Teams achieve momentum for breakthrough by learning to identify problems they can solve for themselves. After team members begin to work on problems inside their own boundaries, they are able to achieve quick results because there are no delays for approval to implement the solutions. Rapidly implemented solutions in turn immediately influence the team's goals. Everyone on the team gets excited. Management gets excited. As a result, the team and individual team members, on their own, take on other problems inside their boundaries. A feedback loop now exists that promotes continuous performance improvements through rapid team problem solving.

Some people mistakenly believe that team problem solving revolves around difficulties related to how the team members get along with each other. However, while relationship problems are the responsibility of the team, team members initially use the problem-solving process to overcome obstacles that may prevent the team from achieving its work and business goals. Solving problems that interfere with the team's goals can bring the team members closer together and resolve many relationship issues. Because team relationship problems involve strong feelings, those issues are better handled using the team conflict management skills.

LET THE TEAM BE THE HERO

A major U.S. semiconductor organization went through a whole round of teamwork training and problem-solving training. In the summer of 1991, the company had a major quality problem that caused the factory to be shut down for four weeks. Every manager, including the plant manager, tried to be the hero in terms of solving the problem. No teamwork occurred in meetings, and there was no real creative brainstorming. Everyone tried to solve the problem individually. The problem-solving tools were thrown out the window. Needless to say, the problem did not get resolved quickly.

Managers and executives are often great fire fighters. We all like to jump in the middle and help when our employees have a crisis. Unfortunately, this behavior destroys the work team's momentum and constant improvement loop described above. Managers and executives need to be reminded to "identify and solve the problems inside their own fence or boundary." Organizations that can do this have the most successful long-term business results.

It is easy for executives to help solve operational and tactical problems. Much more difficult is preventing and solving strategic problems outside the organization with customers, suppliers, competitors, and the government. The executives and managers should pay attention to the harder, more abstract strategic problems and let the line team members be the hero for their own problems. The manager can be the hero for the problems the team members cannot solve on their own, after they have asked for help.

FACTS ARE FRIENDLY

Gather facts to solve problems. Don't guess. Stay close to the important facts of your business. Facts are friendly. A new surprising fact can make your day. Factual data are especially important in problem solving. For example, one of the manufacturing teams my company worked with was trying to increase the number of computer chips processed during a shift. The team members were upset because their production of chips for customers was lower than expected. The team guessed that the engineers were putting in practice chips to be used for scientific experiments rather than counted toward production numbers. Instead of immediately brainstorming solutions to this particular problem, the team decided to collect actual data. To their surprise, only 13 percent of the practice chips had been ordered by engineering. The operators were running three times more than that as test chips to be sure the equipment was set up right—a problem the operators could easily solve. The correct data assisted the team in solving the right problem. If the team members had proceeded on what they assumed the problem was, they would not have solved the most important part of the problem.

STRUCTURED PROBLEM SOLVING

The most important research finding regarding team problem solving is that teams need to use a structured process.[1] Groups that follow an organized approach to structuring the problem-solving process produce more effective solutions. Interestingly enough, the research implies that it makes almost no difference how many steps are used and what they are. Teams just need to use an agreed-upon problem-solving methodology every time.

The problem-solving steps should be few in number so they can be easily remembered. I used to teach the best, most perfect 13-step team problem-solving model in the world. The only problem was that no one could remember the steps, including me. Teams need a user-friendly model that can be applied anywhere: the boardroom, the office area, the manufacturing floor, the field, the construction site, the cockpit. Having the fewest number of steps means including only the essential elements of effective problem solving. The six-step model in Figure 13–1 is based on a synthesis of problem solving and teamwork research.

Using the problem-solving steps promotes the best possible solution(s) to the problem. The six-step model demonstrates that some

FIGURE 13–1

The Six-Step Model

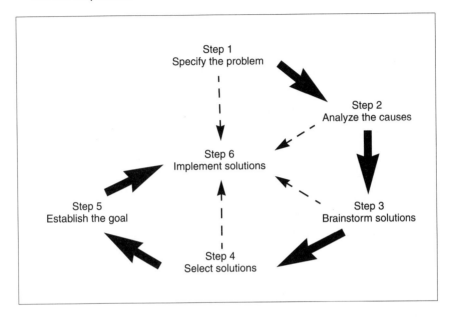

problems can be "solved" using only the first or first and second steps and then going immediately to Step 6. Some teams have found that when Steps 1 and 2 are done properly, the needed solutions are self-evident. Although team members always start at the same first step, the flexibility to jump to action in Step 6 provides a powerful model. Some tough problems require all six steps for solution breakthrough. Team members need a step-by-step methodology to reduce the uncertainty and manage the emotions of work problems.

Organizations need systematic processes to solve problems. I have observed many management team meetings in which no process was used to solve problems. Free-ranging conversations roamed around generalities of the problem and possible solutions over months of meetings. In contrast, a trained team can solve a problem in two or three team meetings.

Part of the delay in solving problems is due to the obstacles executives face in getting their solutions accepted and implemented by the organization. Usually more than one person does the same job. The individual who sees the problem and fixes it alone needs to get support from the others for his or her solution. Creativity and problem-solving skills training can result in improving team members' openness to new ideas.[2] Additionally, training in problem solving has improved various teams' performance on complex problems.[3]

Step 1: Specify the Problem

Performance Resources, Inc., has synthesized research from over 300 control-group studies on how to most effectively solve various interpersonal, small-group, and individual problems. Being specific when identifying or describing the problem is the most effective first step; that is, defining the problem in terms of symptoms, using factual data. The basic questions to answer in specifying the problem are: What is the problem? When did it start? Where is it occurring? When is it occurring? and What appears to happen before the problem occurs? All help specify the problem.

Teams achieve terrific insights by asking the *not* version of each of the key questions. For example, knowing when a problem is not occurring, but possibly could have occurred, raises an interesting question. What is the differece between the problem situation and the OK situation? For example, one manufacturing facility was having major quality problems in one of its work areas. Management thought the team members were getting lazy. When the team specified the quality problem, it found that it had not occurred until the Christmas factory-cleaning shutdown. In the next phase of problem solving, identifying the causes, the problem was traced to the way the equipment had been restarted after the shutdown. The team shut the machine down, restarted it using a different start-up procedure, and the machine was fixed. Identifying comparable situations where the problem is not happening is a fun and creative way to specify problems.

Specifying a problem narrows the target focus that a solution must hit. There are three major advantages. First, the more specifically the problem is defined, the more likely it is that it will be solved. Second, a narrowly defined problem will require less time and other resources to solve. And third, the more specific the problem definition, the less likely it is that the team will make the situation worse by implementing a solution for an overgeneralized problem.

For example, unintended negative results occur every day in business when managers impose strict work rules on everyone due to the misbehavior of a few individuals. If one or two employees do not come back from their morning break on time, a manager may "solve" the problem by requiring all employees to punch in and out on the time clock before and after breaks. This solution actually creates new problems. The good workers feel demeaned and unfairly treated. A long line grows at the time clock. Clocking in and out reduces the feeling of relaxation that is the whole purpose of a break. The manager would have solved the problem more effectively by specifying exactly who has the problem and under what circumstances.

Breakthrough results with any problem are more likely to occur if the entire team is involved in specifying the problem. A team can narrow the problem focus in 30 minutes or less. An individual might require a week because he or she may not have all of the information necessary. Using the team to specify the problem increases the likelihood that someone will identify a piece of information that suggests a solution that can be put immediately into action. My personal observation is that about 20 percent of the time, teams can discover excellent self-evident solutions through specifying the problem. In these cases, the team immediately can skip down to Step 6, implementing the solution.

Most problems, unfortunately, need more work to crack the puzzle. The next step prepares the way for solving those tougher problems.

Step 2: Analyze the Causes

Even in the first step of specifying the problem, we were dealing with symptoms versus causes of problems. Specifying the problem narrows the symptoms to the most specific one. Though this exercise can sometimes lead directly to a solution (especially in simple problems), more often the team will need to determine the causes of the problem and address the causes if the problem is to be solved. Team members benefit significantly from being trained in how to identify and analyze the causes of problems.

Most of us do not naturally think about the causes of problems. One organization I helped had 20 problem-solving teams. Each team brainstormed solutions as Step 1 in the problem-solving process. When the executive realized that the solutions the teams were working on were not connected to "root causes," he wanted to disband the teams. He was right! Teams achieve breakthrough solutions to problems only when they analyze and address the underlying causes of the problems they face.

Team creativity using a fishbone chart works great in expanding a list of possible causes to the problem. Figure 13–2 is an example of a fishbone chart that one team created to identify the causes of the following problem in a manufacturing facility: Operators do not update information on the computer data-logging system. From a list of major cause categories, they selected four the team thought would most likely result in identifying the most related causes of the problem. They thought the causes of the problem would fall under the categories of equipment, people, training, and work process. The team used structured brainstorming to identify specific causes for each category. As Figure 13–2 shows, the team discovered many possible causes of the problem. Some were causes they could easily address, while others would require assistance from someone outside the team.

After identifying the causes of a problem using a fishbone diagram, the team selects the most frequent, costly, or critical causes on which to collect data to verify that they are, indeed, causes. Data collection can range from simple approaches, such as counting attributes associated with the problem, to more complex approaches, such as using statistical process control charts and designed control-group experiments. A designed experiment can be valuable because the team can simultaneously verify or eliminate many potential causes of the problem. All of the analyzed causes should be displayed on a Pareto chart, which lists the causes from left to right in quantifiable order of importance. Figure 13–3 is an example of a Pareto chart.

FIGURE 13–2

Fishbone Diagram

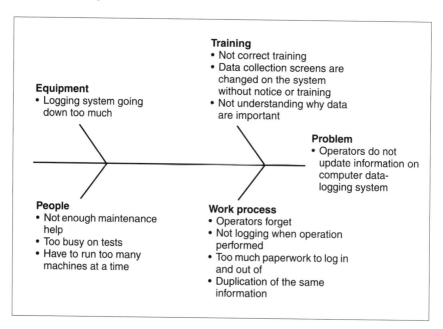

An effective method of narrowing causes, the Pareto chart is attributed to J. M. Juran, who is recognized by Japanese businesspeople as one of the main American consultants responsible for the success of the Japanese quality revolution. Juran introduced the business world to the Pareto principle, which states that when most things in business and industry are listed in order of importance, there are a vital few that are the most important. (This principle comes from Italian economist Vilfredo Pareto, who observed that usually a few people control most of the wealth of a city.) This is also called the 80/20 rule. For example, 80 percent of a company's revenue may be attributed to only 20 percent of its customers. Sometimes there can be as many as 500 other small customers accounting for the other 20 percent of the business. Juran termed these the "trivial many." A team can easily be overwhelmed with all the causes to a problem and not know where to begin. The Pareto chart provides an easy way to select the most important cause on which to work.

For example, in one high-technology computer chip factory, a team was experiencing a high number of quality rejects and rework. One of the major causes of the rework was due to machine performance. At the team meeting that addressed the rework problem, the data were presented using the Pareto chart in Figure 13–3. The team members had counted the number of quality defects per 1,000 units

FIGURE 13–3

Pareto Chart

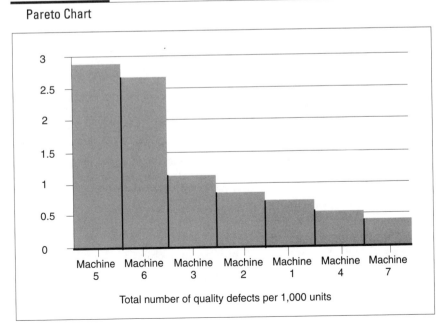

Total number of quality defects per 1,000 units

produced. On the chart, the machine that required the most rework was represented by the highest bar, placed directly next to the y axis of the graph. Machines that required less rework were placed, in order from most to least, on the chart. The Pareto chart clearly shows that machines 5 and 6 were causing the most quality defects. Creating a Pareto chart is important because it can help prioritize the causes of an overall problem the team is solving.

Cause analysis sometimes includes identifying the cause of a cause. The above team experienced this. As the rework data by machine was displayed using the Pareto chart, one team member shouted out, "Those are the machines on 'Congestion Alley,' where everyone bumps the machines because there is so little space!" When the team eliminated the machine bumping, the quality rejects significantly decreased.

"Romig's Pareto rule for problem solving": Focus on the vital few causes first; the savings that are created will pay for working on the subsequent, less important causes.

Prioritizing by Pareto chart has at least two uses. First, depending on the team's resources, the members can work simultaneously through several causes. Most self-managed work teams, however, do not have that much time. Instead, the causes are placed in priority order for the next step, brainstorming solutions. The team will tackle the highest priority cause first and work it through the next four steps of structured problem solving to resolution. They must save the Pareto chart of causes and work on the second most important cause later. This requirement is especially true if the problem continues to negatively affect the team's ability to reach its goals. By first handling the cause(s) of the problem that are the most pervasive, teams create resources from the improved results, which can be used to resolve the next most important cause. In fact, this leads to "Romig's Pareto rule for problem solving": Focus on the vital few causes first; the savings that are created will pay for working on the subsequent, less important causes.

By following this rule, Motorola was able to pay for solving the quality problems of its computer chips. Despite what may have been written, quality is *not* totally free. Motorola work teams wanted to improve the quality of their microcomputer chips as rapidly as possible. Using Pareto charts, the teams identified and worked first on the causes of defects that were the most frequent. Eliminating those major defects freed up time that the team had previously spent on their rework and scrap. Additional money was created because there were more computer chips passing electronic and field tests and thus sold to customers. The additional time and money allowed Motorola teams to go back and work on the next most frequent cause. This methodical process was repeated for all quality defects so that Motorola has an unheard-of quality of less than one defective part per million.

As teams use Pareto charts, an additional benefit accrues: using Pareto charts teaches Pareto thinking. Individuals are taught that when time is limited, look for the few most important factors and deal with them, rather than try to be exhaustive. Pareto thinking teaches team members how to set priorities whenever there are limited resources—which is most of the time.

When a team analyzes all of the causes of work or business problems, some causes are identified that are outside the team's boundaries. A team can easily summarize its work on the first two steps of problem solving and send the summary with a cover memo to the individual or team that has responsibility for that cause. The team then proceeds to handle the major causes that are within its own boundaries. Four work teams at E-Systems achieved $1.5 million in savings in six months while going through Structured Teamwork training partly because, while the teams solved problems inside their boundaries, a cross-level steering team addressed causes outside the teams' boundaries.

Step 3: Brainstorm Solutions

Solutions that result in spectacular performance breakthroughs are ones that solve a major cause of the problem or that address several causes simultaneously. The two key steps to creating breakthrough solutions are the following:

1. Focus the brainstorming on the major causes of the problem.
2. Use team creativity and structured brainstorming skills to identify a high number of solutions.

The first step is fundamental but often ignored. I have seen teams systematically go through specifying the problem and analyzing the causes and then jump to brainstorming preconceived solutions that in no way link up to any of the major causes of the problem. As a result, very weak solutions are considered and ultimately implemented. Solutions must match the causes under consideration.

The research-based methods for team creativity previously discussed are especially effective at this stage of team problem solving. Structured brainstorming involves every team member actively writing down and suggesting solutions in a rapid-fire manner. Team members can use structured brainstorming to obtain a higher quantity and quality of problem solutions. The structured brainstorming method follows these key steps:

- Participants write down solutions individually first.
- Participants share one solution at a time.
- Each shared solution is written down.
- "Wild ideas" are encouraged.
- Piggybacking on solutions and freewheeling are encouraged between turns and after all solutions are listed.
- All ideas are viewed positively.

An example of how structured brainstorming can benefit a company occurred recently at a trucking firm. Every morning at 8:00 A.M., trucks were lined up to get propane. The drivers wanted the fill-up job completed as fast as possible so they could get on the road. Even though the pumpers worked as fast as they could, the truckers complained that it took too long. They hated waiting so long. They hated starting late. The truck drivers were mad.

Now, if someone wanted a quick solution, and saw the truck drivers were angry, that person might teach a program on anger management. Maybe that person could teach them how to relax. But even if the truck drivers learned how to deal with their anger they would still have the problem of having to wait for their trucks to fill up with propane.

As it happened, however, one of the managers wanted to get to the cause of the fill-up problem. He called a meeting of everyone involved in the problem and asked them to help him discover the cause. It seemed obvious that there were far too many trucks, and far too few pumps. Now that the cause was known, they could find a solution.

During the creative brainstorming of solutions, one of the workers noticed that there was one extra hose at each pump whose purpose was to provide a vent. The technology of trucks had changed, however, and the vents were no longer used. What about using the vent hoses to transfer propane to waiting trucks?

The idea worked! No longer were the truck drivers upset by long waits. The cause of the problem had been identified and a useful solution created through the use of a structured process.

Team members should remember that when they are developing creative solutions, a noncritical and accepting environment is important. Even one's own internal mental environment is important. It is vital to replace negative, critical self-talk with positive affirmations like "Any idea is okay" and "The more ideas, the better."

Usually team members create the great solutions during this brainstorming step. When a team cannot solve the problem on its own, individuals not on the team can be involved. Donald Pelz has done more research on the productivity of engineers and scientists than any other individual. In one set of studies, he found that the most productive scientists were those who went outside the team for information and solutions to solving problems.[4] For organizational problems, I have seen management teams create extended teams that include people from across a variety of levels of the organization to help develop creative solutions.

To prevent people from being negative, a systematic process must be used that separates expanding the alternatives from evaluating the ideas. Consequently, the next step, selecting solutions, is separated from the divergent creativity phase of problem solving.

Step 4: Select Solutions

The objective of this step is to select the solutions for implementation. The emphasis is on the plural, solutions. Successful teams pursue *multiple solutions* simultaneously, when possible. There are three main avenues teams use to identify what solutions to put into an implementation plan from the long list of solutions that were brainstormed.

The first method is for the whole team to use team decision-making skills, which will be described in Chapter 14. The skill steps involve narrowing the list to the best two to five solutions. A quick way to find the top solutions is to combine solutions that are related and then give every team member three to five votes. The solutions that receive the most votes can then be discussed to pick the top two to five solutions.

Then comes the most important step, especially when the team must select from solutions that will require considerable time and/or money to implement. Team members should identify the positive and negative consequences of alternative choices. Research by Randy

Hirokawa and others suggests that groups reach higher quality decisions if they identify the pros and cons of possible action.[5] The improvement in decision making is by a whole magnitude of increased performance and results. A group that makes a poor choice has usually not thought about all of the negative consequences of a decision and may have misjudged the positive outcome of a choice.

Teams, after training, can complete a pro/con analysis of solution alternatives in 30 minutes or less! One team member facilitates the pro/con analysis using the structured brainstorming process. Data are collected and included as needed. Many times, the best choice becomes obvious after the pro/con analysis.

The computer chip manufacturing team with the problem of a high amount of rework created by people bumping the machines narrowed the solutions to two major choices. Option 1: Hang warning signs from the ceiling and train everyone in the area not to bump the machines. Option 2: Move the equipment. Everyone on the 11-person team except the supervisor, the equipment maintenance technician, and one operator voted for Option 2, to move the equipment. The supervisor knew that moving the machines would be very expensive and time-consuming, and that equipment availability would be cut. Rather than arguing about the alternatives for hours, one of the team members facilitated a pro/con analysis. A summary of the analysis is presented in Figure 13–4.

After the pro/con analysis, every team member agreed that the best solution was Option 1, to use signs and training to reduce the machine bumping. The solution was implemented and rework decreased to almost zero. The team pro/con analysis process not only ensures that a good solution is selected but also unites the team in support of whichever solution is selected.

The second avenue that teams can use to select solutions is to select most of the solutions that are on the list of brainstormed solutions and put them in an action plan. This works well when none of the solutions require a huge expenditure of money or team members' time. If there is not a huge impact on resources, the team does not need to do the pro/con analysis. I have observed management teams become especially adept at combining a variety of alternatives and creating an action plan using most of the solutions.

The third method is to delegate to a subteam of two or three individuals the task of narrowing the solutions, conducting the pro/con analysis, and bringing the results back to the team. This method saves team meeting time and works well in mature teams that have high trust and mutual support. A drawback is that beginning teams

FIGURE 13–4

Reducing Errors in Machines: Alternative Solutions

Alternative 1: Don't Bump Machine		Alternative 2: Move Machine	
Pro	Con	Pro	Con
1. Fewer defects	1. People will forget	1. No one can bump	1. No available space
2. Less money		2. Fewer defects	2. Will cost money
3. Can immediately implement		3. More room	3. May cause particle problem
			4. No production while moving
			5. Could damage machine

express a reluctance to implement the solution when the time comes. People on the team are more likely to resist the implementation it they do not feel ownership for the solution since they were not involved in creating it. Team participation in selecting the solutions creates the ownership that leads to action.

Step 5: Establish the Goal

After the team has selected its solutions, it must establish the goals and goal measurements for the action plan that will be created in Step 6. Developing the goals and how they will be measured improves the work results teams can obtain when they use team problem solving.[6] Establishing a goal clarifies in every team member's mind what the team is trying to accomplish. Examples of goals that teams have set in relation to problems they were working on are shown in Figure 13–5.

The goal measurements are the indicators that communicate how the team is performing on the goal. Research on behavioral problems indicates that measuring goal achievement regularly creates a constancy of attention and action that supports improvement.

FIGURE 13–5

Examples of Goals

Specific Problem	Cause(s)	Goal(s)
Example 1: 15% rework for a product because of "quality" problems.	The lack of written standards for determining defects is causing cosmetic problems to be identified as defects.	We want clear written standards and *models* to communicate frequently identified defects by September 1.
Example 2: Wafers are not passing inspections.	High particle counts.	Wafers to pass inspections with a particle count less than the level identified in the specification by June 30.

The entire team should participate in setting team goals and measurements. Ownership is important for the goals. Team creativity and involvement are often required to develop feasible methods to measure the achievement of the goal. Having developed the goal, the team is well positioned to develop an action plan.

Step 6: Implement Solutions

Action is the most important part of problem solving. There are excellent analytical managers and engineers who have superb problem-solving skills, with one exception: pushing solutions to action. Failure to act is what I call analysis paralysis. Team involvement in problem solving creates momentum for action through individuals on the team who are action oriented and who will voice their impatience if implementation is delayed too long. The previous step of setting the goal helps create acceleration and action.

During this step, the team consolidates the solutions that have been selected and identifies other actions that may be required to achieve the solutions. To implement the solution, the team identifies who will do what and by when, as well as the nature and source of resources needed to implement the solution. Then the team performs the necessary follow-up and verifies that the objective has been obtained by measuring the goal.

At Advanced Micro Devices, three operators and an engineer from one work area participated with another team in the Structured Teamwork training program. During the training, they achieved considerable success in solving several problems related to production and reducing costs. The supervisor decided that he wanted to quickly have some other problems solved that involved a larger team. The supervisor asked the operators to be a part of that team and work with the team in problem solving. The operators said they would not do problem solving with the team until the team went through the Structured Teamwork program. They said it would be a total waste of time. Without the team skills and without the creativity the skills engender, the whole activity would be a waste of time. The team believed the operators' position and pressured the organization to get Structured Teamwork training started in their part of the organization. The result, of course, was that the entire team was trained and went on to solve many problems. Their ability to solve problems helped create great business results in their area of the facility.

THE RELATIONSHIP OF TEAM PROBLEM SOLVING TO THE OTHER COMPONENTS OF STRUCTURED TEAMWORK

Team communication skills are especially helpful in Step 1 of problem solving, specifying the problem. We have seen how team creativity is used to brainstorm both the causes of the problem (Step 2) and the solutions (Step 3). Team decision-making skills are used in Step 4 to select solutions. Team goal setting and measuring are used in Step 5. Team creativity is useful again in the last step (Step 6) to brainstorm an action plan to achieve the goal and implement the solutions.

In addition, developing a team mission statement helps improve problem-solving effectiveness.[7] Team mission statement development can capture the team members' idealism, which is a strong motivating force to solve problems that may be barriers to achieving the mission. Also, team mission development clarifies what is inside and what is outside the team's boundaries. The mission statement identifies which problems team members are responsible for.

Team problem solving has been used effectively to solve major work process problems.[8] Creative problem-solving skills training is a success ingredient in implementing continuous improvement, of which work process improvement is a key.[9] Team problem-solving skills were successfully used as part of a job enrichment/redesign program and the development of new team roles and responsibilities.[10] Team problem-solving skills are also a major part of Step 4 in conflict management. A major purpose of team meetings is to solve important problems that are selected by team members.

BREAKTHROUGH POINTS

- Teams should first identify problems they can solve themselves.
- Teams should be the hero.
- Teams should gather sufficient data before attempting to solve a problem.
- Problems can be best solved by following a structured, six-step model that involves specifying the problem, analyzing the cause, brainstorming solutions, selecting solutions, establishing the goal, and developing the appropriate action to implement the solutions.
- By focusing on the vital few causes first, the savings that are created will pay for working on the subsequent, less important causes.

14

Team Decision Making

One of the major criticisms of teamwork is that it takes too long for a group to make a decision. For most teams, this negative view is justified. Without training and the use of a structured decision-making process, teams waste time in unproductive and disorganized activity as they make decisions. One study found that 20 percent of the untrained team's time is spent on such disorganized activity for each decision.[1] My personal observations are that a much higher percentage, from 50 to 75 percent of the time, is wasted. In addition, the decisions that are reached may not be the best ones.

Untold numbers of teams have been established without explicit training in team decision-making skills. At best, during the teamwork training, there was a team-building simulation or game to decide how to survive in the desert or on the moon. Research, however, has found that team-building activities by themselves are not powerful enough to teach the decision-making skills necessary for effective decision making.[2] Simulations can be used for practice after the team has acquired the skills.

Team decision-making skills and structured approaches are critically important for breakthrough teamwork. The key to breakthrough teamwork includes the *implementation* of solutions, decisions, and work process changes. Effective implementation requires consideration of the following questions:

- How rapidly can the solution, decision, or work process change be implemented?
- How effective will the implementation be?
- How disciplined will the implementation be?

Everyone in the organization has great ideas every day. The challenge is selecting the best ones and implementing them effectively. Team decision-making skills provide the methodology for preventing decision gridlock and for quickly moving the best ideas to action.

Effective decision making lies at the heart of empowered and self-managed teams. One measure of empowerment is the percentage of daily decisions the team and individual team members can make versus the percentage of decisions that must be delayed because someone outside the immediate work area is required to make the decision.

In order to make good decisions, of course, teams and individuals must have the necessary skills. Let's look at what has been learned from the best research available about developing decision-making skills in over 400 teams.

Team decision making is a carefully designed process for developing and selecting the best alternatives among a variety of choices. Good team decision making includes a structure that the team agrees to follow. When teams are taught decision-making skills and use them to make decisions in their work areas, business results improve substantially. For example, one study showed that participation in decisions related to improving the work group's performance resulted in increased productivity and reduced costs for hospital employees.[3]

Team decision making is a skill people use both inside and outside of meetings. For example, imagine that two team members are working together and must choose among several approaches to meet a customer's unique request. Those two individuals can immediately drop into the structured decision-making format and use it to make the best choice.

WHY TEAM DECISION MAKING IS ABSOLUTELY ESSENTIAL IN TODAY'S FAST-PACED BUSINESS ENVIRONMENT

Team decision making = Increased knowledge + Increased learning + Increased commitment

That team decision making equals increased knowledge is evident from the old adage "Two heads are better than one." Early in its march to world-class quality, Motorola relocated its manufacturing engineers as close as possible to the manufacturing operators and assemblers. Motorola managers found that having engineers confer with the operators *prior* to process or equipment changes always resulted in better decisions. The engineers brought one type of knowledge to the decision, and the operators presented practical information based on their experience. Also, it was easier for operators to consult with the engineers on decisions for which the operators were responsible. The relocation was an effective way to provide increased knowledge and facts for team decisions.

When a manager makes an individual decision for a course of action and then tells the team what he or she wishes to have happen, there is little awareness and learning by the team members about what is needed, why it is desired, and how it should be done. In contrast, when team members are involved in making decisions, their learning increases as various facts are discussed during the decision-making process. The facts are remembered and learning occurs when individuals mentally do something with the information, like weigh it carefully to make an important decision. The same facts could be presented by the manager when he or she tells the team about a decision that has already been made, but they would most likely be ignored or quickly forgotten.

During World War II, the citizens of the United States made many personal sacrifices as fuel, food, and other necessities were rationed. The U.S. government encouraged people to change their eating habits to consume foods that were nutritious but unpopular. Kurt Lewin, a brilliant psychologist, found that people were 10 times as likely to change their eating behavior if they were involved in discussing the changes and making a group decision versus hearing a lecture about changing their habits and making an individual decision.[4]

Including team members in decision making improves their commitment to the decision. When all team members are committed, astounding results will follow. A hospital work group discovered that when all team members were involved in making the decision, there was a 50 percent improvement in productivity of the work group as a whole.[5] In a classic study, Lester Coch and John French found that involvement in planning major work changes reduced resistance to the changes and increased productivity.[6] Involving people in important decisions produces results!

WHEN TO USE TEAM DECISION MAKING—NOT ALL THE TIME

The decisions that will involve the whole team must be carefully selected. There is flat out not enough time for a work team to make every decision as a team. Certain decisions must be made by individual team members based on their roles and responsibilities. Individuals can also huddle for subteam decision making.

Potential decisions to be made by the whole team should be brainstormed and then ranked in priority order. Priority should be given to decisions that meet the following criteria:

- The decision is important to achieving the team's goals.
- The decision and/or project is one whose implementation will involve most team members.
- The decision requires equally shared information from most or all team members.
- The decision is one that most team members are interested in making as a team.

Ralph Elsnear, the vice president responsible for Motorola's Participative Management Program at its inception, used the term *line of sight*. He believed that most people were both motivated and capable of making good decisions on matters that they could see and personally experience as they went about their day's work. Line-of-sight decisions include changing the equipment or tools one uses, modifying work procedures, and setting productivity and quality target goals. Frontline workers can contribute suggestions regarding their own work and maybe a little about their supervisor's work, but they may have little interest in being involved in such "out-of-sight" decisions as how to refinance the company's debt or how to defend conflicting product lawsuits. The line-of-sight rule of thumb allowed Motorola teams and individuals to meaningfully contribute their thinking on countless decisions.

I have discovered certain teamwork structures that should always involve team decisions:

- Team mission.
- Team values, ground rules, and norms.
- Team goals.

- Measures of team goals. ·
- Team meeting format.
- Team member roles and responsibilities.
- Implementation of any major change in the work area.

Most of the team members trained in the Structured Teamwork methodology have improved work performance by being involved in their team's decisions in the above areas.

Despite the above emphasis on involvement, however, removing individual responsibility and decision making is not good Structured Teamwork. Having every decision made by the whole team will take forever and will kill individual initiative. Groupthink is not high-performance teamwork. Therefore, the team must distinguish between those decisions individuals should make and those the team should make.

Because time is at a premium, every organization needs the most efficient and effective methodologies possible for team decision making. The better and faster teams can make decisions, the more opportunity they will have to make work and business improvements.

HOW TEAMS CAN MAKE EFFECTIVE TEAM DECISIONS

The most important step in successful team decision making is to use a structured approach. Structured group processes improve decision making.[7] Figure 14–1 presents key factors that favorably influence team decisions. Structured group interaction is significantly more productive than unstructured interaction. The group's decisions are more effective. In addition, there is greater implementation of the decisions: 60 percent implementation for structured groups versus 40 percent implementation for groups using unstructured discussion of the alternatives.[8] Unfortunately, unstructured discussion of alternatives still predominates in work decision making from the executive boardroom to the shop and office floor.

A major factor of success in team decision making is the participants' knowledge of the topic in question. Consequently, participative decision making with inexperienced employees is difficult. This factor also explains why it is difficult to involve people in decisions related to new equipment or methods when the employees have no knowledge of the potential improvements.

In a summary of over 200 studies related to participative decision making, Edwin Locke and his coauthor, David Schweiger, concluded that the main factor that influenced the effectiveness of participative decision making was subordinates' knowledge.[9] At first

FIGURE 14–1

Factors That Influence Effective Team Decisions

- Team uses a structured approach to making team decisions.
- Team members have some knowledge of the issue on which the decision is being made.
- For decisions with mutually exclusive alternatives, a pro/con analysis is conducted.
- Team uses a reach-out, idealistic goal as the North Star for its decision making.
- One team member facilitates the team's decision-making process.
- Team participates on an ongoing basis in work decisions versus participating only once in a while on special projects.
- Full participation of all employees in a work area is required rather than voluntary.

look, this conclusion appears very reasonable. If you involve employees in helping to make a decision in which they have some knowledge, a better decision will result than if the employees have not been involved. The better decision will lead to increased productivity or quality. Sounds good, right?

There is at least one major obstacle—management's generally low perception and expectation of what employees know. Let's take an example: the layout of equipment and work areas in an office or a factory floor. Who should be involved in deciding what goes where? The easy answer is the managers and the engineers. Few organizations ask for the ideas of the workers who will actually use the work area and who may have 5 to 25 years of daily experience working in various layouts. The advantage of the structured team decision-making processes is that there are methods for eliciting the best ideas of the employees *as well as* engineers and management in an efficient and organized manner.

Much has been written about how knowledge is the only thing to consider in participative decision making. This may be true when the decision is about whether or not to implement something new and different. The "whether" and "what" decisions require management. An example in manufacturing is whether to implement a just-in-time inventory and production system. One goal of just-in-time is to replace huge warehouses of stockpiled parts with an automated parts ordering and management system that acquires the parts in the shortest lead time possible. The decision for *whether* an organization should implement such a system is a management decision. The implementation decisions related to *how* to set up the just-in-time inventory and production system, on the other hand, would benefit greatly from the involvement of all the employees who will utilize the system.

An example comes from one of the manufacturing facilities where my firm and I have consulted. Without involving the workers, the managers and engineers installed a system that was expected to reduce product manufacturing cycle time from 15 days to 8 days. Initially, the system did reduce cycle time, to 10 days. After the engineers and managers left and put their attention elsewhere, however, the cycle time crept back up to 12 days, then 13 days, and finally back to the original level. The engineers and managers reacted by criticizing the employees for being lazy and resistant to change.

When we arrived to begin the installation of Structured Teamwork, we asked the shop workers about their resistance to the just-in-time system. They stated that they were not resistant to the ideas of just-in-time; they just thought that the managers and engineers were not listening to their concerns and suggestions. As we began training in the Structured Teamwork process, the concerns of the employees were addressed, both for the employee team and the steering team that included engineers and managers. As a result, in 12 months there was a cycle time decrease from 15 days to 5 days. The team beat the best estimate that management had envisioned! Also, instead of a gradual drift back up, there was continual improvement by the team to reduce the cycle time. In fact, it eventually decreased to less than three days. This further reduction occurred after the engineers and managers went on to other projects. The team stayed involved in measuring the results and aiming to do even better.

One team member should facilitate the team decision-making process to be sure the team sticks to the disciplined decision-making approach. When this occurs, the team makes better decisions.[10] One of the most respected researchers on group decision making, Randy Hirokawa of the University of Iowa, was amazed to learn that I was training teams in how to facilitate their own decision making. He observed that this approach could put facilitators and consultants out of work in terms of facilitating decision-making meetings.

Participative decision making and empowerment are most effective when practiced on an ongoing basis rather than on short-term projects. Informal, long-term participation in the work group results in higher satisfaction and productivity than the short-term or formal decision making that is typical of quality circles.[11] Occasional participation in decision making does *not* improve team performance. A research study of a retail chain, for example, found that having salespeople participate in only one decision for how to approach customers did not by itself improve store sales.[12]

Early in the implementation of its Participative Management Program, Motorola had the choice of making the program either voluntary or mandatory, and having a representative sample of employees involved or encouraging full participation. The decision that Motorola leaders made, and that research supported, was for full participation.

Other recent research has also supported the full participation decision. One study found that positive changes due to participation were significantly more substantial for direct participants than for employees who were, in effect, only bystanders.[13] Union members who were directly involved in participation groups had more positive attitudes about participation than indirect participants and no-participation employees at a comparison site. The lesson? Get every employee involved, not just selected employees.

STRUCTURED TEAM DECISION MAKING

By now, you should be convinced that everyone on a team should be involved in making certain decisions. But how do they do it? The next section will show you how teams can do each of the five steps of structured team decision making presented in Figure 14–2.

Step 1: Set Goal and Measurement Criteria

Randy Hirokawa's latest research on team decision making determined that teams that set a goal first and kept the goal in front of them as they proceeded through the decision-making process made better

---

FIGURE 14–2

Structured Team Decision-Making Steps

1. Set goal and measurement criteria.
2. Expand alternatives.
3. Narrow alternatives.
4. Do pro/con analysis.
5. Reach consensus on best alternative.

decisions than groups that did not remain focused on their goals.[14] Teams can expand and select alternatives better if they have the goal identified. When a goal is set in Structured Teamwork, it is developed first with words and then with numbers or other measurable criteria against which success can be assessed. Teams that refer back to the goal that the decision will help reach are better able to manage conflict during the heat of debate. For goals regarding equipment, personnel, and new facilities, teams can develop from 5 to 25 separate measurement criteria.

Teams can make significant errors when making decisions. A major error identified by management consultant Jerry B. Harvey is known as the Abilene paradox. Harvey identified the error when he was visiting his parents in Coleman, Texas, during an unusually hot August weekend. One afternoon when the family had nothing to do, someone suggested that a drive to Abilene for dinner might be in order. Without much discussion, the family piled into the non-air-conditioned car for the long, hot, dusty trip to Abilene. When they arrived back home after driving 120 miles to eat an uninspiring meal, Harvey's mother disgustedly remarked to his father that she hoped the trip had made him happy. Mr. Harvey replied that he had not wanted to go, he thought she did. It finally came out that no one had really wanted to go to Abilene. Everyone had just quietly gone along because they thought someone else wanted to go.[15]

The Abilene paradox occurs in groups when members repress their feelings about a decision because they assume that everyone else is enthusiastically in favor. The group assumes that silence means support. Many work decisions fall prey to the Abilene paradox. When I was training an executive team and described the Abilene paradox, everyone immediately identified one of their current projects, the construction of a new office building, as possibly the result of such a decision. They were on course to build a new multimillion-dollar office building that no one on the team thought was needed. The executive team decided right then and there in the training to neither fund nor construct the new building. A year or two later, their decision was totally vindicated as the projected need for new office space never materialized.

Setting a goal, especially an idealistic, reach-out goal, will prevent teams from falling prey to the Abilene paradox. The team's discussion regarding what goal everyone will support can guard against the nonsupported decision occurring at the end of the decision-making process. The amount of time a team spends on this step can vary from five minutes for workplace decisions to several hours for developing goals and criteria for new equipment. After the team has set its goal, the members are ready to proceed to Step 2.

Step 2: Expand Alternatives

There is a way to handle a major error that work teams sometimes make: quickly jumping to one solution. Teams that develop many creative alternatives make more effective decisions than teams that consider only a few options and do not expand options.[16] Team creativity and the structured brainstorming method, presented in Chapter 6, allow teams to develop a variety of alternatives rapidly. Teams begin by having the members individually write their own alternatives and then rapidly collecting and listing each alternative. Teams should be encouraged to come up with wild ideas, because the wild ideas stimulate team creativity. Using more creative alternatives can increase team effectiveness by anywhere from 2 to 10 times. Expanding a list of decision alternatives is called *divergent creativity*. This type of creative decision making is a key characteristic of effective teams.

Generally, teams complete Step 2 in 10 to 30 minutes, depending on how many team members participate and how many alternatives are needed. Sometimes teams will decide to implement most of the options because the options are not mutually exclusive. In this case, the team can stop here and develop an action plan using all of the alternatives generated. Most of the time, however, teams need to go to the next step—to develop a shorter and more manageable list of choices. This step requires a different type of creativity, called *convergent creativity*.

Step 3: Narrow Alternatives

Convergent creativity occurs as team members combine different alternatives that overlap or that are similar. A team can easily consolidate alternatives that are exactly alike, especially if they are worded the same. When combining alternatives, beware of the trap of creating a few overgeneralized alternatives that hide a lot of good and different specific alternatives under the general heading. Sometimes teams misplace their best alternatives when they narrow the list to a few general categories. One way to handle this problem is to identify major alternatives as the broad choices while keeping the other specific alternatives as action steps that in fact will be implemented if a particular related broad choice is selected.

After combining similar alternatives, a team may still have a long list of choices that it wants to narrow. Most teams use the multi-voting technique to narrow alternatives because it can be done rapidly. Before voting, the team should identify at least one creative alternative and discuss its advantages. This discussion serves to create a more open-minded consideration of the alternatives rather than a consideration based on a narrow range of approaches.

During multivoting, all team members vote on the alternatives they think would best achieve their goal. The team may wish to develop other criteria to consider, such as cost or time. Team members write down the numbers that correspond to their favorite alternatives on a sheet of paper. Each team member should have a number of votes equal to approximately one-fourth of the total number of alternatives on the list. For example, if there are 20 alternatives on the list, each team member gets five votes.

After all the team members have silently completed their selections, the votes should be tallied. Team members may vote by a show of hands as each item number is called out. The alternatives receiving the most votes are the ones the team should consider implementing or carrying to the next step. The team should spend a few minutes reflecting on the top choices to ensure that the team members can all agree that the best alternatives have been chosen.

If these alternatives can be simultaneously implemented and are not mutually exclusive, the team has completed the decision-making phase and can proceed to developing an action plan. Unfortunately, there is usually not enough time or money to implement all of the alternatives. Most of the time, the team must select one alternative: one new employee, one type of software, one new supplier, or one new piece of equipment. Step 4 has proven useful for performing this task.

Step 4: Conduct Pro/Con Analysis

> The best way ever devised for seeking the truth . . . is advocacy, presenting the pros and cons . . . and digging down deep into the facts.
>
> *Harold S. Geneen, former CEO, ITT*

Harold Geneen was known for his large, highly interactive, and sometimes emotional strategic business planning and review meetings. The above quote presents two of the most important research findings related to team decision making. Factual data are necessary in order to select from competing alternatives. Early in his research, Randy

Hirokawa identified the importance of using data and challenging assumptions as teams made decisions.[17]

The second major research finding is that teams that use pro/con analysis make more effective decisions than control groups that do not use pro/con analysis.[18] Team pro/con analysis is the decision-making method of listing the anticipated positive outcomes and negative consequences of each alternative a team is considering. The pros and cons examine the effects of each alternative using the measurement criteria developed in Step 1. Conducting a pro/con analysis of the major alternatives significantly improves the quality of the decision-making process.

Pro/con analysis can assist teams in becoming more empowered. In 1991, corporate management at AMD was highly involved in the business planning of the Personal Computer Division (PCD). They were involved because the PCD had the most profitable product in AMD history, the Am386® microprocessor. The problem with corporate involvement was that the PCD employees themselves sometimes felt disempowered, demoralized, and demotivated.

The documented pro/con analysis of several alternatives made it less likely that corporate management would overrule the PCD decisions. Prior to conducting pro/con analyses, corporate managers frequently generated alternatives that the PCD marketing management team had come up with but had rejected after an unstructured pro/con analysis. Sometimes, after pro/con analysis, the team came up with decisions that were more in line with corporate direction.

Irving Janis invented the term *groupthink* for a process in which a group uncritically agrees to only one course of action.[19] Part of the group's process is to pay attention only to the data that support the team's apparent consensus. The concept of groupthink is used to explain why executive teams and other work teams sometimes make poor decisions. The space shuttle *Challenger* disaster has been described as an example of groupthink where management considered the pros without considering the cons of their decision to launch the shuttle in near-freezing weather. Team pro/con analysis is one tool for eliminating, or at least reducing, the negative influence of groupthink. When every member of the team identifies data that supports the pros and cons for each alternative, groupthink is prevented.

Two structured approaches similar to pro/con analysis, dialectical inquiry and devil's advocacy, have also proved more effective than the usual method of unstructured discussion of alternatives that are either recommended by one of the managers on the team or by an expert. The dialectical inquiry method requires the identification of the assumptions in the predominant alternative or plan and the development of a counterplan based on the exact opposite of each assumption. A structured debate then weighs the relative merits of the plan and the counterplan. The devil's advocacy approach requires one or more individuals to develop a critique of the prevailing alternative or plan. Both devil's advocacy and dialectical inquiry result in more participation by team members and provide more structure than the usual method of open discussion of recommendations. They also result in more effective team decisions.[20]

A third variation of the pro/con analysis is the adverse consequences method. If a decision is a make-or-break decision, the adverse consequences approach to pro/con analysis should be used. The pros and cons should be identified for each alternative as was described earlier. However, the cons should undergo an additional assessment. Figure 14–3 lists and demonstrates the steps for how to perform an adverse consequences assessment. The example demonstrates that the likelihood of the first consequence of mechanical failure during the launch of the space shuttle *Challenger* had a score of 3. Although not a certainty to happen, some of the tests had revealed the possibility of mechanical failure of the O-ring. The seriousness score for this consequence is a 5, the highest rating possible. The two weights multiplied give the total risk score of 15.

Negative publicity from the press was certain to occur if the launch was postponed (likelihood score of 5), but the seriousness was low, with only a possible delay in future funding (seriousness score of 1).

The total scores at the bottom show a 150 percent greater risk for launching than for postponing. As it happened, however, the launch went on as scheduled. The mechanical failure did occur and *was* catastrophic, with the loss of the crew's life and a two-year setback for the space shuttle program itself. This tragedy might have been averted if the members of the launch team at NASA had better managed the risks of their decision making. Certainly it shows how crucial risk analysis can be in making important decisions.

Step 5: Reach Consensus

The last step of team decision making is to select the alternatives that everyone can support. Have you ever been part of a group that made a decision and later, out in the hall, you heard people say that they were not going to support that decision? Every day in the workplace group decisions are made that group members actively undermine, after the decision was supposedly made. When trying to decide which

FIGURE 14–3

Adverse Consequences Method

A. How likely is the consequence?
   Rate from 0 (unlikely) to 5 (highly likely).
B. How serious would the consequence be if it occurred?
   Rate from 0 (doesn't matter) to 5 (catastrophe).
C. Multiply seriousness by likelihood.
D. Total the "con" scores for each option (indicates magnitude of risk).

Negative Consequence	Alternative A Launch Space Shuttle Challenger in Freezing Weather		Alternative B Postpone Launch	
	Likelihood × Seriousness	Product	Likelihood × Seriousness	Product
Mechanical failure during launch (e.g., frozen O-ring)	3 X 5 =	15	0 X 5 =	0
Negative publicity from press	0 X 1 =	0	5 X 1 =	5
Inconvenience to crew	0 X 1 =	0	5 X 1 =	5
Unknown element of launching in freezing weather	5 X 2 =	10	0 X 2 =	0
Total		25		10

decisions teams should make by consensus, consider this rule of thumb: Ask yourself, "What type of decisions are the team members actively opposing during implementation?" These decisions are the ones on which teams should reach consensus.

Some difficulty exists with teams because of a misunderstanding about the definition of consensus. Some people think consensus means majority rules. If a team of 10 people has 6 people in favor of alternative A and only 4 people in favor of alternative B, then "majority rules" dictates that alternative A wins, and too bad about the people favoring alternative B. This scenario is exactly why disgruntled team members walk out of a meeting and do not support alternative A.

On the other hand, consensus is sometimes misunderstood as being unanimous support by all team members of one alternative, for example, alternative A. Though this is ideal, it almost never happens. Hours of discussion are necessary for teams to achieve a unanimous vote. Consensus does not mean a unanimous vote or majority rules. Instead, consensus is when everyone on the team can support and live with the selected alternative. Typically, teams have two or three alternatives and must, because of limited resources, select only one of them. Let's say the team had a six-to-four vote in favor of alternative A. After the pro/con analysis, the vote is eight to two. During Step 5, the team members who are against alternative A voice their concerns. Usually the team then modifies the alternative in some way to address the concerns. Eventually, the two individuals state that even though alternative A was not their favorite choice, they can live with it and support its implementation.

> **Consensus is when everyone on the team can support and live with the selected alternative.**

One self-managed team had completed the first four steps of effective team decision making. The members had developed a goal for an important decision, expanded alternatives, narrowed alternatives, and conducted a pro/con analysis. During Step 5, achieve consensus, everyone agreed to one of the alternatives except the supervisor, who was an equal member of the team. After much discussion, the supervisor stated that he could live with the alternative if the team would share the responsibility with him if there were bad results. The team thought for a few minutes and decided that the supervisor was right, that the negative consequences were too serious. The team selected a different alternative. All the members, including the supervisor, felt they could support the new alternative. The supervisor demonstrated excellent empowerment by teaching the concept that increased decision-making power results in increased responsibility for the consequences.

The following steps help teams reach consensus:

1. Use more data and generate new alternatives, if needed. The importance of using data and challenging assumptions has been identified as a valuable step in achieving consensus.[21]

2. Use the principle of the "grain of truth." I have found that most disagreements on different alternatives have some truth

in each position. Sometimes the grains of truth in each position can be identified and combined into a new alternative.
This principle is a major value of the pro/con analysis, particularly if the pro/con analysis itself does not result in a preferred alternative. The best pro aspects of each alternative can
be combined into a new alternative.

Consensus decision making is important for overall policy decisions and team priority setting, but it is not necessary for every decision. Too much consensus destroys individual initiative and
inspiration. Individual team members should be allowed to make
decisions within the scope of their team-defined roles and responsibilities. Using a systematic decision-making process is more important
than who makes the decision. Also, because reaching consensus is difficult when the group does not have the expertise to make the decision, consensus decision making should not be used if there is a single
expert inside or outside the group who can make the specific decision.
There are additional methods teams use to achieve consensus for a
special set of decisions, described below.

HOW TO MAKE DECISIONS RELATED TO DISCONTINUOUS CHANGES/NEW PARADIGMS

There is a category of decisions over which teams labor, usually with
little success. These decisions are related to what Jack Orsburn calls
"discontinuous changes."[22] Most decisions that teams make are continuous change decisions. Examples include whether to buy a replace-
ment piece of equipment, hire a new employee, open a new store
location, or try to get a new preferred customer. These decisions are
extensions and continuations of previous decisions made by the same
team or other teams or individuals in the organization. The five-step
team decision-making model presented above usually results in good
decisions of the continuous change type.

On the other hand, teams seem to spin around in a circle when
they try to make a major decision related to a discontinuous change.
Discontinuous change decisions are related to major changes the
organization has never before come close to considering or making.
Examples of discontinuous change decisions are getting into a
whole new product line or area of service, and acquiring another
company and trying to merge two different company cultures. Usually,

discontinuous changes are proposed by a visionary executive in the organization and represent changing paradigms or mindsets of how to view the business. If discontinuous change decisions can be promptly and successfully executed, such changes promote spectacular business results.

Decisions that are related to discontinuous changes, however, require some additional methods to help ensure success. One of the best documented studies of how to rapidly make discontinuous change decisions is Kathleen Eisenhardt's study of decision making in fast-growing Silicon Valley computer companies.[23] Eight microcomputer companies were studied to determine how their executive teams make effective, rapid decisions in the high-velocity microcomputer industry. The following characteristics describe the decision-making processes of the most effective and quickest teams in the study:

1. Real-time information is available and constantly consulted, including extensive current information about the firm's operations and competitive environment. The teams measure and report everything, and keep up with the information on a daily basis.

2. The executives interact continually through face-to-face communication, electronic mail, and weekly staff meetings.

3. The team creates large numbers of alternatives that are considered simultaneously.

4. Information and ideas are sought from all team members, and from the firm's most experienced executives. If no experienced executive exists in the organization, a consultant may be called in to fill the role. The experienced executive or consultant acts as a sounding board for ideas, does not have hidden agendas, and has past experience in the areas in which change is needed.

5. The teams use consensus with qualification. This is a two-step process. First, the team attempts to reach consensus as a group, involving everyone. If this agreement is reached, the decision is made. If the group cannot come to a consensus, the CEO and perhaps the relevant vice president make the choice, using input from the whole team.

6. The final strategic decision is integrated with other major decisions and tactical plans and often includes plans for execution

and a worst-case plan. Usually several decisions are made at the same time, due to the linkages between decisions.

The use of these strategies increased sales growth by a factor between 25 and 100 percent per quarter for one of the electronic firms, and in a second firm, by 500 percent in the two years following the study.

Additional methods that may be used to successfully implement discontinuous change decisions are to reduce uncertainty, minimize risk, support participation and creativity, go and view firsthand somewhere else, pilot, and bring the skill set inside the organization. Two methods that repeatedly succeed in unfreezing a struggling team are to pilot the change and to go somewhere else and view where the change has already been implemented. In the 1950s, managers and engineers from Japan made extensive visits for observation to U.S. automobile and electronic companies as they considered how to enter those industries. In fact, the management of Toyota has recently acknowledged the company's extensive use of methods learned from its early visits to the Ford Motor Company.

Many teams get stuck and are afraid of the risks of discontinuous changes. Developing a pilot or trial implementation is the fastest way to try the change and obtain firsthand experience and data about the change. I have seen teams waste time trying to anticipate every worst-case scenario. I have observed other teams that conduct a pro/con analysis, plan a limited-size pilot, and quickly move to implementation. For organizational development changes, the use of pilots has long been documented as one of the most important ingredients in successful change.

LINKAGE TO OTHER TEAMWORK COMPONENTS

Studies on decision making identify close links to other teamwork components like goal setting, roles and responsibilities, communication, creativity, and conflict resolution. Linda Neider found that participative problem solving and participative decision making combined with financial incentives and goal measurement showed significant improvement in sales.[24] Another study found that team decision making improved productivity when it was combined with new, expanded work roles and responsibilities for each team member.[25] When the decision-making process uses applicable teamwork components, its effectiveness increases.

CONCLUSION

Timely decision making is a critical element of business success. Structured team decision making allows many alternatives to be generated in a short amount of time using the team creativity methods. The alternatives can quickly be narrowed with a minimum of discussion. After the narrowing, there can be check steps to be sure that none of the best alternatives were mistakenly eliminated. The pro/con analysis can also be completed quickly in the team meeting using everyone's ideas. The steps of listening to and trying to combine the advantages of the different points of view help ensure a speedy and successful implementation. Any disadvantage to the time it takes a team to make a team decision is offset by the reduced time and increased effectiveness during the implementation and action stages.

BREAKTHROUGH POINTS

- Team decision making generates better decisions than individual decision making because the team as a whole is a greater pool of knowledge and team members generally have a higher commitment to decisions they participate in.

- Although not all decisions should be made by teams, teams should reach a consensus when (1) the decision is important to the team's goals, (2) many team members will be involved in the implementation, (3) shared information is required, and (4) most team members are interested.

- Effective team decisions occur when everyone participates, there is ongoing participation, one team member serves as a facilitator, a reach-out goal is set, a pro/con analysis is implemented, team members are knowledgeable about the subject, and a structured approach is used.

- Teams should use a structured approach to decision making that involves setting goal and measurement criteria, expanding alternatives, narrowing alternatives, conducting a pro/con analysis, and reaching a consensus on the best alternative.

- In making decisions related to discontinuous changes or new paradigms, the best decisions are made with constantly updated real-time information, continual executive interaction, large numbers of alternatives, wide-ranging consultation with team members and other experienced individuals, qualified consensus, and strategic integration.

15 CHAPTER

Work Process Improvement

Everyone knows that when problems occur at work, they must be solved. What about the times when there are no problems—can the quality, cost, and productivity of work be improved just to get better? This is the premise behind work process improvement and continuous improvement.

All work is composed of work processes. A restaurant's major processes are ordering and storing the food, advertising, preparing the dining room, taking the customer's order, cooking and serving the food, and receiving the money. Most industries have major work processes in the areas of marketing, product development, manufacturing, sales, finance, and human relations.

If you desire to improve the results of the work, improve the work processes. The dominant Western idea prior to 1985 was that major performance improvement occurred through restructuring and reorganizing people. The Japanese model of continuous improvement or *kaizen*, on the other hand, centers on improving work processes and work flow.

Work process improvement is about training teams and individuals to improve performance by doing their own industrial engineering.

Workers hate the industrial engineer with his clipboard and stop-watch because he is so disconnected from the work and the workers. Structured Teamwork trains teams or work groups in the spirit and methodology of industrial engineering. As a result, individuals gain major new insights and knowledge about their jobs and how to do them better.

Customer satisfaction for both products and services depends on three elements, which are the major areas for work process improvement:

Cycle time, which is the amount of time required to produce and deliver a good or to provide a service.

Productivity and cost, which means delivering more of the product or service at a reduced cost.

Quality improvement, which results in a more reliable and higher quality product or service.

Work process improvement directly affects these three drivers of customer satisfaction (see Figure 15–1). Ford Motor Company, for example, simultaneously addressed all three areas of customer satisfaction as it developed and manufactured its highly successful car, the Ford Taurus.

Chapter 5 presented the ultimate team as one that embodies the five characteristics of communication, cooperation, coordination,

FIGURE 15–1

Major Drivers of Customer Satisfaction

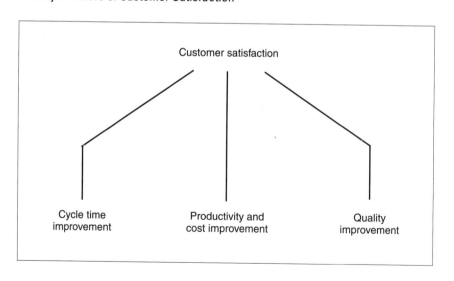

creative breakthrough, and continuous breakthrough—a C^5 team. One way to assess whether a team is a C^5 team is to ask whether the team is working to improve one or more of its major work processes. A C^5 team always has at least one continuous improvement project on which it is working. The team also has a method for always selecting those work processes that most directly contribute to the achievement of the team's mission and goals.

Work process improvement is a key factor in helping companies obtain spectacular business results from their quality improvement or total quality management program. On-time delivery improved from 75 percent to 92 percent between 1987 and 1990 at Wallace Co., Inc. in Houston, Texas, after the company implemented a total quality management program that emphasized teamwork and work process improvement. Sales increased 69 percent, from $52 million to $90 million, in three years. Company absenteeism decreased 50 percent, to half the industry average. The workers enjoyed coming to work because the red tape and non-value-added parts of their jobs were continually eliminated. To cap off Wallace's successes, the company won the Malcolm Baldrige National Quality Award in 1991.

Knowledge teams have experienced similar successes. When the Paul Revere Insurance Company instituted work process improvement, one of the quality teams reorganized the underwriting and issue departments. The departments were transformed from production lines to departmental teams. Each team coordinated everything involved in insurance underwriting for a specific group of field offices. This change allowed a customer to deal with only one team versus many different departments.

Customer service improved, and there was a $134,000 annual cost savings. The team members' morale also improved because they were able to see how the different parts of the work processes fit together to satisfy the customer. Work quality and customer satisfaction both increased.

HOW WORK PROCESS IMPROVEMENT
SUPPORTS BREAKTHROUGH

If we compare work teams with sports teams, we see that work processes are the work team's plays, which together form the team's playbook. Work processes may be called procedures, work methods, policies, or job specifications. They are the step-by-step methods for how a product is created or a service is delivered. The improvement of work processes can be based on improving quality, productivity, cost, cycle time, or all of the above.

Amoco Canada's first employee involvement director, Stan Wenger, discovered that some work process improvements achieved at or above 1,000 percent improvements. These 10× improvements are similar to the goals of Michael Hammer's work reengineering methodology. Using work process improvement to achieve 1,000 percent improvements is real breakthrough.

The famous economist Ludwig von Mises argues in his book *Bureaucracy* that the reason private industry will always be able provide any service or product cheaper than any government program is that the government program is hampered by its inflexibility.[1] Work process improvement is concerned with business and industry's ability to change policies and procedures that provide the company's competitive advantage. Companies that continually evaluate and improve their key work and business processes are able to increase productivity and customer satisfaction.

Work process improvement was the heart of the Hewlett-Packard Signal Division's spectacular business improvement. The two main interventions were process improvement project teams and the direct participation of the division's managers. Work process improvements by two teams resulted in a 30 percent decrease in assembly time for microwave oscillators and a 66 percent reduction in testing time of one line of circuit boards. This 1,800-employee organization's combined efforts increased revenue per employee by over 40 percent![2]

One of the usual methods of conducting work process improvement is to develop a flowchart of the steps and decisions involved in doing a piece of work. Geary Rummler, a consultant who assisted Motorola in its march to breakthrough performance, has developed a unique form of process improvement. It involves examining work processes that are performed and managed across different functional organizations. Great business results can occur when improvements are made across organizational boundaries. Rummler has termed this type of process improvement "managing the white space." In organization charts, the white space is the space between the vertical lines and boxes with job titles or people's names inside them. The white space represents the need for different functional organizations to better communicate and coordinate their activities.

To achieve breakthrough results from work process improvement absolutely requires the cooperation and creativity that the Structured Teamwork methodology establishes. The requirement for

FIGURE 15–2

Quality and Work Process Improvement with Structured Teamwork

	Without Structured Teamwork	With Structured Teamwork
Trust and openness	Individuals are defensive and argumentative. The problem areas identified are usually in another work area.	Individuals share problems they are having with a process. The team is open to any change that will help improve results.
Creativity and risk taking	Only very small changes are proposed ("rearranging the deck chairs on the *Titanic* as it sank").	Breakthrough creativity is encouraged. Everything is questioned, including whether the process is needed at all.
Implementation of improvements	Process improvement suggestions are attacked. Momentum is lost. Implementation is time consuming.	There is high support during rapid implementation. The spirit of continuous improvement lives!
Results	Very small gains in a short time, or 2–3 years required for major gains.	25% to 400% improvement within 6 months.

breakthrough process improvement is that more than one individual be involved in the process improvement effort. The most significant process improvements involve individuals who share job responsibilities or individuals who pass work to different members of their team. Therefore, a group is required to be involved in the process improvement for the successful implementation of the process because more than one person will be affected by the improved process. Effective group process improvement requires teamwork, and the most effective teamwork approach uses Structured Teamwork methods (see Fig. 15–2).

Without Structured Teamwork, individuals in a group discuss the work process and associated problems in an unstructured fashion. The meeting process takes a lot of time, only one or two ideas or solutions are approached, there is no systematic examination of what the problems and the causes of the problems are, and there is no priority setting of the most important problems that the process improvement should address. Most likely a structured approach to examining the question, "Who are the customers whom the processes are designed to serve and what are their quality requirements?" will be absent, which is an absolute requirement for effective process improvement.

As an outcome of unstructured process improvement, an individual may get a new piece of equipment that he or she wanted or some work that no one ever liked may be eliminated. But the real issue is, Has the process been improved? And has it been improved in a way that positively affects business results or customer satisfaction?

Structured Teamwork is required for process improvement because the discussions around improving work are so emotional. Process improvement gets right at the heart of individuals' daily work and their daily lines of sight in terms of how their offices are arranged and how their work flows to and from them. The emotions are very high regarding any change. The need for control over change is so high that openness to brainstorming in an unstructured way is nonexistent. People stop listening to each other and stop being supportive when they're discussing process improvements.

If a manager attempts to do process improvement in a team without Structured Teamwork, the emotional outbursts and defensiveness could be so destructive that individuals end up not speaking to each other for weeks after the meeting. The energy and emotions of these discussions on process improvement need to be carefully managed by the team as a whole—hence the need for Structured Teamwork processes.

Team communication and conflict management skills make it possible to discuss the emotion-laden issues rationally and not only manage the conflict but get a breakthrough resolution. Team goal setting around the process improvement increases the likelihood of great results.[3] Having measurable goals focuses the team's process improvement activities.

In fact, organizations should set companywide goals for all of the improvements they wish to achieve. Team creativity skills are absolutely essential. Otherwise, only very trivial changes are made.

HOW TO DO TEAM WORK PROCESS IMPROVEMENT

The customers' needs and wants should be the focus of work process improvement. Otherwise, workers may improve a process to make their jobs easier but create a horrible result for the customer. Examples come to mind from bureaucratic government services with long lines and lots of forms to fill out, where the work process has been organized to make the job easy for the government employee and the customer pays the price. The Xerox Corporation has been one of the best companies at keeping the customer's needs at the center of its quality and work process improvement activities. The company has used a multifaceted intervention that includes the following:

- Creating teams.
- Providing extensive training and education.
- Applying total quality concepts to senior management.
- Training people to know what the customer wants.
- Communicating the need for change with all of the employees.
- Recruiting people who will accept challenges.
- Opening channels of communication through expanding types of communication vehicles and removing communication barriers.
- Recognizing team and employee contributions.

Xerox also makes sure that work teams make decisions about task assignments and work methods, are responsible for a whole product or service, and have shared objectives.

The results of such an approach include saved costs, increased market share, and happier employees. Teamwork reaches across functions and increases communication, which has, for example, reduced the time of providing pricing documents from two weeks to four days!

The following six-step approach can help your organization achieve results similar to those of Xerox, Ford, Motorola, and other leaders in achieving customer satisfaction:

1. Select a work process to improve that will achieve break-through business results.
2. Form a team that includes representatives of each major step of the work process.
3. Set a measurable improvement goal.
4. Flowchart the process.
5. Use team creativity.
6. Analyze the process and implement improvements.

Step 1: Select a Work Process to Improve That Will Achieve Breakthrough Business Results

The steps of structured work process improvement require time and resources. The team should improve work processes that will provide an immediate payback in improvements in team performance. When a team sets its goals, whether quarterly or annually, the team should also identify the most valuable work processes to improve. When the team reviews results on its team goals, the work process improvements that have been pursued should also be evaluated. In this manner, work process improvement is aligned to the team's business goals.

Many times teams are in a situation where they need dramatic improvements in business results to help save their company. The team should identify potential areas for high-leverage improvements using the following four forms of waste categorized by W. Edwards Deming: wasted business opportunities, wasted time and talent, wasted material and equipment, and wasted money resources.[4] The team can then categorize the waste as high-dollar or low-dollar, and as fast or slow, to achieve the desired return. Ideally, teams in a crisis mode should concentrate on high-dollar, fast-return process improvement projects.

Step 2: Form a Team That Includes Representatives of Each Major Step of the Work Process

Rapid process improvements occur when all of the departments that have a role in the work process are involved in its streamlining. As you may recall from Chapter 4, Amoco Canada, like most oil companies, uses independent contractors for most of its oil field drilling. At one time, the Amoco Canada drilling manager and many of his key subordinates felt they were spending way too much time setting up contractors on the master contract. The process required 12 calendar weeks and four hours of Amoco personnel time. The manager and his subordinates knew they had to be represented on the team to attempt to improve the process. Wisely, they also included one of the company lawyers and a policies and procedures expert from administrative services, as well as one of the workers who did the paperwork. In a short time, the team developed a new process for setting up master service contracts for new contractors. The new process took only two weeks and required 95 minutes of personnel time. Even more incredibly, they were able to implement the new process within one week of finalizing it.

Two elements made this possible. First, the new policy and procedures did not require a lengthy review and critique by the legal and administrative services departments. Those departments had been represented on the team. Without their involvement, the final approval process might have taken months of negotiating. The members of the legal department might not have supported the changes because they may have felt threatened that someone else was taking over their turf. Without their inclusion, the time required to fight for the approvals would have been tremendous. The other built-in success factor was the inclusion of one of the workers. Not only did he provide insight into real-world problems during the process improvement, but his involvement made it natural for him to support its immediate implementation.

If most product innovations come from customers, why wouldn't some of the best ideas for process improvement come from the customers of a process? Why not interview the customers or have them participate on the process improvement team? ABB Coral Springs invited customers to participate on electrical relay system design teams; they loved it and assisted in increasing the quality of the relay system and reducing the cycle time to produce it. Ford Motor Company had customers participate on teams with the new-car designers as part of the Taurus development project.

Step 3: Set a Measurable Improvement Goal

For each process the team has determined to improve, the team should develop a specific, measurable goal. The structured team goal-setting methodology includes the step of setting a reach-out target for the process improvement goal. Many companies, especially during desperate business times, embark on quality improvement with only a "do your best" type of goal. The results are usually disappointing. Real breakthrough results occur when the team sets a specific, measurable stretch goal for improvement.

The most important element in work process improvement goal setting is to address the customers' requirements. Motorola has discovered that its customers want high-quality products, and they want them fast. In the early 1990s, Motorola publicly announced its intention of reducing the defect rate on everything it manufactured to 34 parts per million (or 99.999997 percent defect free). The company labeled this goal Six Sigma Quality and had reached 5.4 sigma (40 parts per million) by 1992. More recently, all work units of Motorola set quality improvement and cycle time reduction goals every year. Some areas have the stretch goal to improve the quality and reliability of their products by 1,000 percent every two years. That is a reach-out goal!

Step 4: Flowchart the Process

After the team has set its customer-based process improvement goal, the team members should get better acquainted with all of the steps in the current work process. I have never seen a more powerful learning experience than when a group of workers and their manager identify all of the steps required to produce a product or service in their area of responsibility.

Mark Henry, one of my colleagues, was training an oil well drilling team in work process improvement. When Mark got to the step of flowcharting the existing process, the manager of the group argued that the step would be a waste of time. He said he had been involved in drilling oil wells for 20 years and there was nothing he could learn from doing this activity. Mark, in his tactful way, asked the manager to humor him and just play along with the activity.

Mark used a method of having everyone write on small sticky notes the major steps they took as they drilled oil wells. The manager furiously filled up many notes. However, after the entire team's notes were displayed across the room in a start-to-finish flowchart, the manager was very quiet and still. He then apologized to Mark and the team as he continued to stare at the flowchart. Inadvertently, all the team members except the manager had written their steps with black felt-tip pens. He had used a red ink pen. What he was staring at were all of the important steps the team had identified that were in between his steps in red writing. The manager who thought he knew everything discovered that he didn't!

Everyone who participates in team flowcharting of the work process learns something valuable. The flowchart describes the current state of the process, which is then available for the team to simplify and improve.

Step 5: Use Team Creativity

Team creativity, in which major assumptions are questioned, is required for work process improvement. Having a stretch goal for improvement encourages breakthrough creativity. During Structured

Teamwork training on work process improvement, the participants play a paradigm creativity game as a team. They must perform an activity as fast as possible and still maintain the game's quality requirements. After the team has achieved its best performance, the participants are told that other teams have actually done the same tasks in one-fourth the time. There is no way the team can improve its performance that much by doing the task the same way. Doing the old tasks more rapidly will never achieve a 400 percent improvement.

The team must be creative. It must break out of the current model or paradigm of how the steps of the game are done. In fact, the team members must start with a blank sheet of paper and use one another's creative ideas as stimulators for new ideas. As the members apply the team creativity skills, they are able to achieve breakthrough performance.

Their experience in the game can be transferred to using creativity to eliminate steps in the work process in order to improve customer satisfaction. This blank-sheet-of-paper creativity is what was used by the Ford Motor Company to reduce the number of steps in its procurement and accounts payable work process. The numerous steps of processing purchase orders and invoices were reduced to three basic steps: (1) as ordered parts arrive at the Ford plant's receiving docks, they are checked against what was ordered; (2) if the received parts match the ordered parts, the dockworker enters that into the computer; and (3) the computer generates and mails the check.

Unless creativity is used, there can be no breakthrough improvements in the work process and results. Without creativity, the time spent by the team does not even provide a payback equal to the amount of time invested.

Step 6: Analyze the Process and Implement Improvements

At Asea Brown Boveri (ABB), a breakthrough occurred using Structured Teamwork to help install a new computer and software system. The old order-entry system took eight weeks. Management thought a new computer system could improve that performance. As the ABB team members began to design the software system, they decided to use Structured Teamwork to improve the work processes to be automated. The members decided that rather than automating the current cumbersome eight-week manual system, they would first reduce the number of steps and automate a new and improved work process.

Ironically, the outside computer consultants were initially resistant to this approach. They said it would slow the overall computer installation process.

The team completed a flowchart of all the steps in the current system, did some creative elimination of a few major steps in the process, and began analyzing each remaining step in the process. The main analytical steps were to quantify the time and personnel required for each step and determine the degree to which the step was value-added. The main criteria for whether a step was value-added was whether or not it assisted in providing something the customer wanted. In other words, if a customer was sent a bill for each step with an explanation of how that step added value, would the customer be willing to pay for it?

All five Cs of Structured Teamwork (communication, cooperation, coordination, creative breakthrough, and continuous breakthrough) were required by the team to openly and successfully analyze each of the steps in the old order-entry system. As a result of the process improvement effort, the ABB team successfully installed a system that decreased order-entry time from eight weeks to two days!

INSTILL WORK PROCESS IMPROVEMENT AS AN ORGANIZATIONAL STRUCTURE

Work process improvement creates an attitude of improvement. Everything can be improved. In one company, everyone got into the act. The corporate attorneys used to hinder and delay joint ventures that the company needed for faster market penetration of its products. After adopting the continuous improvement methodology, the lawyers began to look at their jobs as critical for making the joint ventures succeed, which now includes rapidly providing legal opinions and solutions. In every meeting, there is an attitude of "We can improve anything."

Companies have bosses to do performance evaluations of their subordinates. These days, we are starting to have employees evaluate their bosses. What we really need, however, is to bring bosses and employees together to evaluate the *work!* There are not enough regularly scheduled opportunities for employees to evaluate their work and work processes. Almost 70 percent of 11,000 workers surveyed stated that the way the work is performed and designed is not evaluated frequently enough to continually improve productivity.[5]

Work process improvement can become an integral part of any company by having a steering team develop guidelines for how people in the organization can rapidly develop and implement improvements, *both in teams and as individuals.*

The guidelines could help everyone understand how they can make suggestions for improvements. Work process improvement, as a structure, would include all of the management or engineering approvals that are required for each of the different types of process improvements. A streamlined path would be created for some types of work process improvements so they could be implemented within 48 hours. Adopting such an approach would create a corporate atmosphere that says improvement suggestions do make a difference.

CONCLUSION

The presence or absence of Structured Teamwork makes a profound difference in the results and capability of an organization's quality and work process improvement activities. Without teamwork, an attempted quality improvement activity can result in zero productivity improvement! A considerable amount of time can be spent flowcharting and analyzing how the work is done, yet without teamwork no real improvements may be discovered—or if they are, they are not implemented.

BREAKTHROUGH POINTS

- Work process improvement is about training teams and individuals to improve performance by doing their own industrial engineering.
- Customer satisfaction and work process improvement share three areas of concern: cycle time, productivity and cost, and quality improvement.
- Since groups of workers must resolve complicated and emotional issues to achieve work process improvement, Structured Teamwork is the most effective methodology because it establishes a framework that promotes trust, openness, creativity, risk taking, and the implementation of improvements.
- Structured Teamwork uses a six-step approach to work process improvement that involves selecting a work process to

improve that will achieve breakthrough business results, forming a team that includes representatives of each major step of the work process, setting a measurable goal, flowcharting the process, using breakthrough creativity, analyzing the process, and implementing improvements.

Part Three of this book will describe how leaders can promote breakthrough teamwork.

THREE

EMPOWERING THE BREAKTHROUGH ORGANIZATION

16

CHAPTER

Breakthrough Teamwork Synergizes the Disconnected Organization

THE DISCONNECTED ORGANIZATION

Most organizations are disconnected. Every major corporation is comprised of many smaller organizations: one for each geographic location, one for each division, one for each major product or service, and sometimes one for each major function (sales, marketing, research, operations, finance, human resources, etc.). These separate organizations are usually detached from each other psychologically as well as operationally and geographically.

The disconnected organization is depicted in Figure 16–1. At the top of each organization is the visionary executive. The defining characteristic that qualifies men and women for this position is their ability to see changes and trends in business and to predict how their organizations must adapt to be successful. This characteristic is, literally, vision. Many times the trends that executives see represent windows of opportunity to significantly improve or expand the business. Like all windows, these can close quickly and unexpectedly.

Visionary executives are disconnected from the rest of their organization by the very characteristic that qualifies them for the executive

FIGURE 16-1

The Disconnected Organization

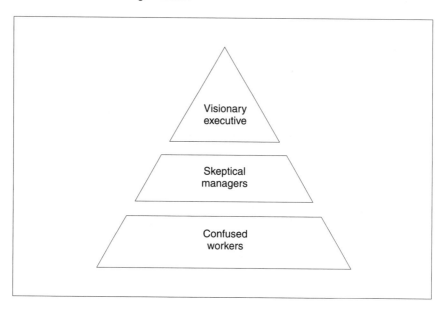

role: the ability to see in business what others do not perceive. As the executive first begins communicating his or her vision to others in the organization, there is often disbelief, resistance, and anger. Many of the managers who report directly to the executive respond with skepticism and animosity. Their attitude is, "Hey, leave me alone! I've been doing a great job achieving the goals that have been set in the past. Why do you want to change everything?" The managers even have trouble comprehending what the executive is talking about.

Depending on how much urgency the executive feels about the necessity for the change, he or she will push, and sometimes push hard. The skeptical managers are frustrated because they see what is in front of them today and do not understand the tomorrow that the executive is trying to reach. Their differences can deepen, and too often someone gets hurt. I know personally of two occasions where manager and executive conflicts resulted in the managers having heart attacks, one fatal. That little white space between the visionary executive and the skeptical manager can seem as wide as the Grand Canyon. Not successfully bridging the chasm can be fatal to the organization and can be just as dangerous to the people involved.

There is also white space that separates the skeptical managers from the confused workers. The workers are often confused because they feel caught between the visionary executive's direction for what is needed to achieve the future and the skeptical managers' demands for results in the present. With many of the changes the visionary executive desires to pursue, an interesting irony unfolds. Since they are closer to the customer, the workers sometimes recognize the validity of the executive's position more readily than their bosses, the skeptical managers, do. Such perceptions only increase the workers' confusion because they do not understand why their managers do not see the necessity for the changes. The workers can end up feeling torn between following the direction of the managers who review their performance and sign their payroll time sheet and the executive leader whose vision they respect and support.

Part of the disconnectedness is a difference in business languages. Executives and managers speak the language of money and financial results. Workers speak the language of work—equipment, job tasks, work processes, and daily work results. Executives know the business results they need. They usually do not know how to get those results through the workers and the work system. Workers, on the other hand, do not know how to get management to see the major barriers that are interfering with their ability to obtain improved work performance. Trying to communicate across the white space of a disconnected organization is like trying to communicate across a deep chasm via one-way carrier pigeons.

If they allow it, executives can become far removed from the work and work systems. Part of the validity of Tom Peters's observation that some successful companies encourage their executives to "manage by wandering around" (MBWA) is that this activity helps them keep in contact with the teams and individual contributors who perform the work that customers pay for.[1] In the disconnected organization, employees are isolated from other employees, from management, and from the work system as a whole.

Often another ironic result occurs when organizations use internal or external organizational development consultants to help fix the organization. The organizational consultants often believe that the higher up in the organization they work, the greater the positive impact they will have. So they spend almost all of their time with the executive and the managers and become imbued with that view of the world. They, like the executives and managers, lose touch with the workers, which prevents connectedness from occurring throughout the company. Perhaps it is evident why the following organizational development research conclusion is so important: Breakthrough team-work requires credibility and close interaction with all levels of the organization. If the organizational consultants hope to bring the dis-connected organization together, they must be successfully engaged with all levels of the organization.

> **Breakthrough teamwork requires credibility and close interaction with all levels of the organization.**

In the face of increasing global com-petition for every product and service, one scenario has unfolded countless times in an array of disconnected organizations: the executives push one visionary strate-gic initiative after another. You have heard their names: participative manage-ment, quality circles, employee involve-ment, total quality management, cus-tomer satisfaction, and so on. The execu-tives' vision prompted these initiatives because they saw the need for break-through teamwork and great business results. The sad fact is, however, that no one, not even visionary exec-utives and motivated workers, can achieve breakthrough teamwork in a disconnected organization.

The disconnected organization must be brought together if breakthrough teamwork is to be even a remote possibility. Break-through teamwork involves bridging the canyons that separate execu-tives, managers, and workers. The C^5 organization has proved that it can reconnect the organization, thus allowing rapidly achieved break-through results today and laying the groundwork for unimaginable breakthroughs tomorrow.

The visionary leader needs an engine to power his or her vision. Structured Teamwork empowers because it taps existing power. It's not just people who need power; organizations and leaders need power. Leaders need to be taught how to use the power that is lying at their feet ready to be tapped. This is true management empowerment. José Morais, a visionary Texas Instruments leader in Europe, told me, "For years, Texas Instruments has taught us quality tools. It's refresh-ing to see that they are now teaching us how to change our organiza-tions."

The C^5 organization can replace the disconnected organization, which is mired in conflict and inaction. Having a C^5 organization is the major requirement for any team to achieve and sustain Level 5, continuous breakthrough performance. The dramatic contrast of the disconnected organization versus the C^5 organization is presented in Figure 16–2.

Interactive, two-way communication typifies breakthrough teamwork communication (Level 1). The typical top-down communication leads nowhere. Executives of one company were shocked when the all-employee attitude survey revealed that employees felt uninformed of company goals, strategies, plans, or results. In the survey review meeting, the executives exclaimed, "How dare the employees accuse us of not communicating our goals? Every January, we *tell* them exactly what the year's goals are!" A meeting of several hundred employees in a large room is not real communication. Months after the January meeting, employees did not recall any of the material

FIGURE 16–2

The Disconnected Organization versus The C^5 Organization

Level	Disconnected Organization	C^5 Organization
1. Communication	■ Workers do not voluntarily talk about work or share problems. ■ Information flows from top down but not in reverse; few or no feedback loops. ■ Departments in the organization do not communicate—they are separate entities. ■ Communication is critical and nonsupportive. ■ Communication is good only within each stratum of the organization.	■ Problems are identified early and prevented. ■ Interactive communication with constant feedback is used. ■ All-way communication exists. ■ All communication is supportive of creative thought and risk taking. ■ Communication leads to action.
2. Cooperation	■ "Look out for number one" or "me first" attitude pervades. ■ Employees do not offer to assist others or ask for help. ■ Each part of the organization feels in competition with all others.	■ "All for one and one for all" attitude pervades. ■ Employees assist each other as need and opportunity arise. ■ Departments cooperate to solve problems, get work done, and communicate. ■ Everyone's role has overlap with at least one other role.

(continued)

The Disconnected Organization versus The C^5 Organization (concluded)

Level	Disconnected Organization	C^5 Organization
3. Coordination	■ Goals are set, but there is no support for the goals. ■ High conflict in roles exists. ■ Most meetings are ineffective. ■ Departments do not work together except in crisis. ■ Each department has its own separate goals. ■ Departments do not align their goals to the organizational goals.	■ A system of natural work group teams is in place to rapidly respond to problems. ■ The entire organization participates in the development of vision and goals. ■ All actions are aligned from the bottom to the top of the organization to achieve desired business results and values. ■ Departments and individuals plan how to reach goals and work together to reach them.
4. Creative breakthrough	■ Only certain people are expected to come up with creative ideas. ■ The executive's vision and most other creative ideas never break through the resistance barrier. ■ Individuals or teams sometimes achieve breakthroughs, but they are not shared and may not be recognized.	■ Everyone is expected to come up with creative ideas. ■ Teams rapidly implement vision and goals in a concerted fashion. ■ Teams achieve creative breakthroughs using the combined efforts of the team members.
5. Continuous breakthrough	■ Any contributor or team that continually has outstanding performance is subjected to attack or ostracism. ■ Managers are skeptical of change and actively resist even beneficial changes. ■ Continuous breakthroughs do not occur, or they are only in short-range, tactical areas.	■ Continuous breakthrough teams and individuals are applauded. ■ All teams repeatedly make continuous breakthroughs using Structured Teamwork. ■ Breakthroughs occur simultaneously in tactical and strategic goals.

presented. They would swear that the goals were never communicated to them.

There is profound research from the field of learning that relates to employee communication. Jean Piaget, the famous Swiss psychologist, discovered that the main way people learn new knowledge is to operate on the knowledge.[2] No, not surgical operation, but performing a mental activity with the new knowledge. Examples of valuable mental operations include asking questions, restating the information in one's own words, and using the information to perform a task. Two-way communication and other forms of discussion encourage longer-lasting retention of the knowledge. The more interaction using the new information, the more the information becomes a part of the person.

Bill Siegle and Jim Doran, two executives at Advanced Micro Devices' Sunnyvale Submicron Development Center, tried a new approach to the all-employee quarterly meeting. In this meeting, employees sat at round tables and interacted as small groups at different times during the meeting. The employees' ideas were incorporated into the quarterly planning. There were lots of good comments from the "troops." Bill and Jim vowed to never go back to the old meeting format. The new way was more energizing, fun, and productive. People incorporated the goals and strategies as their own. They were committed to the goals.

Communication in a C^5 organization leads to action. Communication of goals leads to the development of strategies and action plans. Communication about problems leads to those problems being solved. Communicating suggestions for work improvements leads to implementation now, not waiting for weeks while hierarchies of suggestion committees review the ideas. Collapsing the lag time between communication and action is a primary characteristic of a breakthrough organization.

The second level, cooperation, is different as an organization moves to breakthrough. Managers in most organizations are so busy competing with each other for resources and their next promotion that they cannot fathom offering to help. As a result, people, computers, other equipment, and supplies are duplicated because no one wants to cooperate and share.

Organizational cooperation has become the byword within Advanced Micro Devices' Wafer Fab Division. Gary Heerssen, the division vice president, promoted a vision of "seamless boundaries" and teamwork across the different departments, facilities, and locations. As a result, managers share equipment, people, personal time, and solutions to shared problems as fast as they are discovered. As this vision has been implemented, managers of similar functions have formed what they feel is an informal brotherhood.

The distinguishing characteristic of Level 3, coordination, is alignment. Everyone has heard of automobile wheel alignment. The car is fixed so that the wheels go exactly straight ahead. Organizational alignment occurs when all individual work energies are headed in the same direction. At the heart of strategic planning systems, the organizational goals are set by the corporate executives and passed to the head of each division. Each division manager sets goals that support the organizational goals. In turn, the division manager passes the goals down to his or her direct subordinates, who are supposed to set goals that support the achievement of the manager's goals. And so it goes until every individual has goals that support his or her boss's goals. This common approach to alignment creates an empty shell of conformity and compliance.

Contrast this to a strategic planning system that incorporates employees at all levels. In this scenario, managers at every level develop the organization's values and vision and mission, which are used as a framework to develop the goals that describe the most desired business outcomes. Then individuals from all levels of the organization develop creative strategies for how to achieve the goals. Work teams develop goals that support the selected strategies. Now there is not only goal alignment on paper, but alignment in action that produces results. This configuration accomplishes two functions concurrently: establishment of (1) what to do and (2) how to do it.

The people in disconnected organizations hold a false assumption about who can suggest creative ideas that may become the genesis of a breakthrough. In the spurious hierarchies of these kinds of organizations, people believe that only the product development engineer is allowed to be creative.

In the C^5 breakthrough organization, that kind of restricted environment disappears completely. The creativity of every engineer, technician, operator, and secretary is tapped. For instance, manufacturing engineers working with machine operators in one company increased profit $25 million through innovations in how products were manufactured. Manufacturing engineers working with natural work groups used their creativity to increase quality and productivity. A team of secretaries used the groups' creativity to significantly reduce supplies and equipment costs by coordinating across departments. Both product quality and delivery cycle time were also improved. The secretaries became so enthused they agreed to be ambassadors of their organization's teamwork and quality program. C^5 establishes vehicles for communication of ideas coupled with the positioning to take action. This enables small, seemingly insignificant ideas to create value.

C^5 is not just about improving communication, cooperation, and coordination among the team members. It's also about improving communication, cooperation, and coordination with the leader. Leaders need support and cooperation, too. In fact, when the leader and team support each other, they produce an incredibly powerful combination that no one can stop.

Continuous breakthrough, Level 5, is starkly different in the C^5 organization and the disconnected organization. In C^5 organizations, teams are supported and recognized for their accomplishments. The organization provides ways to break the barriers that teams confront (see Fig. 16–3).

Using all levels of C^5 and using Structured Teamwork tools and skills, continuous breakthroughs happen over and over again. The disconnected organization, on the other hand, lacks the ability to support continuous breakthroughs. Competition between parts of the organization and individuals becomes a barrier to sharing creative

FIGURE 16–3

C^5 Breakthrough

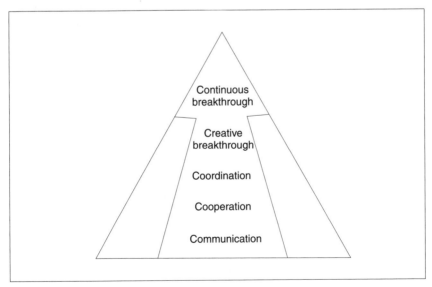

ideas and, in fact, tends to stifle the creativity and success of anyone other than the individual or part of the organization directly involved.

THE C⁵ ORGANIZATION HAS A CULTURE RESPONSIVE TO CHANGE

Nothing is static. The issues change. The customers change. The work changes. How people interact changes. The organization must choose to be either a breakthrough organization or a breakup organization. Breakup organizations are torn apart and sold off in pieces. The reason is that they already function as pieces. The resistance barrier of Level 4 in the disconnected organization is like trying to fly to the moon in a passenger airplane. It is impossible to break out of Earth's gravity. Employees and managers resist and procrastinate on changes and innovations they have not developed themselves or for which they do not see the purpose.

Top executives try to stay abreast of needed changes and ways to respond. For example, I was brought into an organization that was in major financial trouble. The top executives problem-solved and came up with a great list of solutions. But there were no rapid means to set the ideas in motion. The ripe ideas withered on the vine because there were no vehicles for coordinating efforts to move them into action. Disconnected organizations are unable to respond to needed changes.

Another major advantage of a C^5 organization is the ability of the organization to advance on strategic as well as short-range, tactical goals that meet the never-ending requirements for change. In the disconnected organization, a major excuse offered for not proceeding on the executive's vision is the perception voiced by managers that there is not enough time to work on strategic, long-range issues and still achieve daily and weekly productivity targets. In the C^5 organization, having time to work on the vision is part of the way business is done. Everyone knows that to continually achieve and exceed daily and weekly performance, certain strategic and fundamental improvements must also be simultaneously addressed.

There is no one magic answer for how they do it. It happens because breakthrough creativity is a way of life. The schedule and resource conflicts are addressed in the team environment using the best team creativity, problem-solving, conflict management, and work process improvement skills available. Daily, teams resolve the conflict of how to meet the productivity goals and still have time for training, team meetings, and work process improvement. Breakthrough teams create time by eliminating waste. They are committed to the continual success of their organization.

Breakthrough organizations look different from disconnected organizations. Not only do they generate constant improvements and corresponding great business results, but their organizational cultures are different. Terrence Deal and Allan Kennedy, in their book *Corporate Cultures*, present a usable definition of culture as "the way things are done around here."[3] I would amend this definition to "the way *important* things are done around here." How are people treated when management is all excited? What does management get excited about? What do workers get excited about? Deal and Kennedy propose that the early breakthrough successes of IBM, Procter & Gamble, and Johnson & Johnson occurred because each company's leader paid close attention to the development of his organization's culture, reinforcing important values. Thomas Watson, the founder of IBM, promoted the value of constructive, positive thinking throughout IBM by putting signs with the one word *think* in every office and conference room. The slogan was meant to generate a positive, creative, can-do attitude at all times.

When Tom Peters and Bob Waterman did their investigation to determine what distinguished the excellent companies from average or "so-so" companies, they discovered that it was organizational culture differences that mattered. The characteristics of excellent companies they listed are all attributes of organizational cultures:

1. *A bias for action.* The preference and ability to move fast.

2. *Close to the customer.* Best ideas come from the customer.

3. *Autonomy.* Promote autonomy on the shop floor. Allow project champions a long tether.

4. *Productivity through people.* Communicate respect for employee thinking.

5. *Hands-on, value-driven.* Promote the basic values and philosophy.

6. *Stick to the knitting.* Stay close to the businesses you know.

7. *Simple form, lean staff.* Small corporate staff.

8. *Simultaneous loose-tight.* Have loose autonomy, but insist on tight compliance to core values.[4]

Culture is composed of values and beliefs and how they are practiced. In *Corporate Cultures,* their 1982 study of 80 companies, Deal and Kennedy found that only one-third of the companies had a set of articulated beliefs.[5] The companies that had a written set of beliefs were divided into two groups. One group's written values emphasized financial goals. The second group had qualitative beliefs like improved customer service. It was the second group that had the most outstanding business results. Partially as a result of the work of Peters, Waterman, Deal, and Kennedy, every major corporation has developed written vision, mission, and values statements. Unfortunately, the anticipated great business results have not occurred most of the time.

The written beliefs have to be put into practice. Just stating them without demonstrating how to practice them increases the skepticism of managers and the confusion of the workforce. Organizations need Structured Teamwork to develop and instill the new C^5 culture. The coordinated action orientation of a C^5 culture makes it possible for vision, mission, and values to become real influences in the company. Breakthrough organizations' cultures look different because those organizations are able to direct and rapidly put into effect whatever action is needed to further their goals.

BEYOND TEAMWORK AS A FAD

The idea of teamwork has reached almost faddish proportions. Consequently, everyone says they are implementing teamwork, while only a few companies will make a serious attempt at it. Companies need to be hardheaded about this thing called teamwork. If properly done, a carefully nurtured teamwork program results in fantastic improvements in an organization that manages to get it right. In order to get it right, everyone in the organization has to be involved, a complete assessment has to be undertaken, and all the identified elements of breakthrough teamwork have to be attended to in a structured way.

The resulting cooperation, coordination, and creativity need to become part of the very fabric of business, industry, and, yes, even government. Organizations must not only instill these new behaviors throughout their various levels, they must regularly renew and refresh their teamwork structures to ensure the reality of continuous breakthrough. To do less is simply unacceptable. Learning how to do it better is what this book is all about. Choosing *not* to do it better is indeed a choice, but it is a choice fraught with graver perils today than ever before.

BREAKTHROUGH POINTS

- The disconnected organization prevents organizational breakthrough by separating visionary executives from skeptical managers from confused workers.
- The C^5 organization bridges the gaps of the disconnected organization to create a corporate culture that is responsive to change.
- To achieve organizational breakthrough using teams, a company must thoroughly commit itself to a structured approach.

Empowerment Accelerates Breakthrough Teamwork

EMPOWERMENT AS THE ENERGIZER TO BREAKTHROUGH

"Empowerment is not just a word. We live it!" So began a telephone conversation with Russ Frame, an ABB profit center manager. Customer orders at ABB now go directly to the teams, and they manage for themselves how to get the work done. They solve problems on the spot. The teams delegate to subteams work process improvement projects to improve quality, cycle time, and customer satisfaction. In 1993, a difficult year for the electrical relay business, Russ and his empowered teams achieved 120 percent of their financial objective! Russ observed, "As we were forced to continue to take out layers of management and support people, there is no way we could have continued to make the required cost improvements without the Structured Teamwork approach to empowerment."

Russ Frame graciously acknowledged the role Structured Teamwork and the Performance Resources, Inc., consultants played in his company's success. But who made the improvements at ABB? The workers and their managers working together did! At ABB, the ratio of supervisors to employees dropped from about 1 to 8, to 1 to 40.

Supervisors who did not retire were converted to engineering and other support positions, or promoted to manager positions with responsibility for 40 people. Besides being accountable for large numbers of workers, the supervisors accepted duties once done by former middle managers because whole layers of management between the firstline manager and the executive manager were gone.

These new managers were now required to assist their profit center manager with customers and external parts and equipment suppliers. How were they going to have time to coordinate the daily work for 40 or more people? As Russ remarked, there was no way—without the movement to a form of empowerment called self-managed teams. A self-managed team is a group of workers who manage their own communication, cooperation, coordination, creative breakthrough, and continuous breakthrough with minimal or no involvement of a manager or supervisor. In other words, an empowered team sets and achieves work goals and continually improves its work and business processes.

In 1994, the use of the term *empowerment* became a fad. Politicians discussed how citizens, especially the poor, should be empowered. Business executives talked about empowering the workforce. The word itself was often undefined. The connotation was that empowerment was good for everyone involved, but how? Let us begin this discussion with a definition of empowerment and an explanation of how it benefits the organization, the workers, and the managers (as well as a clarification of what empowerment does *not* include). See Figure 17–1.

Empowerment, as defined in Figure 17–1, is giving individuals increased authority to decide and implement decisions without checking with management. Representatives of one industrial company that asked for my help bragged that they had totally eliminated supervisors and had implemented a form of empowerment called autonomous self-managed work teams. Management at this midwestern plant was concerned because the workers were complaining that the plant management team overturned every decision they tried to make. My colleague Mark Henry and I conducted interviews, made observations, and administered a plantwide employee survey to determine the current status of teamwork and empowerment in the plant. The results showed that the workers were right. They had no power to make any real decisions related to their work processes or team performance. They could recommend suggestions through a fairly cumbersome and bureaucratic suggestion system. Though they did not have direct supervisors, the managers on the plant management team told

F I G U R E   17–1

What Is Empowerment?

Empowerment is a structured and planned process that increases employee decision-making authority and accountability.

Benefits to the Organization

- Improved business results such as reduced cycle time, reduced scrap, increased productivity, and customer satisfaction.
- Earlier and better communication of potential problems by employees.
- Reduced need for direct supervision.
- Increased intellectual and emotional commitment by all employees.
- Faster and better problem solving at the problem source.

Benefits to the Employees

- Having a voice in decisions that most directly affect them.
- Increased job knowledge and skills.
- Improved teamwork within the work group.
- A work environment that supports self-confidence.
- Individual and team recognition.

What Empowerment Is Not

- Total democracy.
- An equal say by everyone in all decisions.
- Having managers agree with or use all employee suggestions.

them weekly everything they were supposed to do. When Mark and I came into the situation, the teams were not pursuing significant business improvements. Their hour-long weekly team meetings were spent communicating to each other directions from the managers. Simply implementing "autonomous self-managed work teams" and eliminating supervisors does not achieve empowerment!

Notice that the definition in Figure 17–1 indicates that empowerment is a "structured and planned process." Empowerment has definite outcomes with a specific road map for how to improve business results. Some companies are critical of empowering employees through autonomous self-managed teams. Their criticism is justified if their experience with empowerment has consisted of announcing to their workers one Monday morning that they would not have supervisors anymore and would now manage their own work. This course of action is a "light-switch approach" to empowerment. The implication is that empowerment can be flicked on like a light switch. Of course, however, this approach to creating autonomous self-managed teams has never helped any organization achieve breakthrough. Team members must acquire the necessary information and decision-making skills to make good decisions. Contrast the light-switch approach with a structured approach that transmits the knowledge and skills to the employees "just-in-time" for them to use their increased decision-making authority to improve business results.

One benefit to a company implementing a structured empowerment process is increased employee self-confidence. Workers in countless organizations today are already empowered to make decisions on work problems they face, yet organizational survey data have revealed that one reason team members do not take the initiative to solve problems themselves or improve work procedures is that they do not have confidence in their ability. Increased self-confidence occurs as individuals and the team make decisions that actually improve work results. Management reinforces workers' confidence as the managers see the monetary benefits of decentralized decision making and problem solving. What occurs is an increased sense of pride in significantly contributing to a winning team.

EMPOWERMENT AS THE FOUNDATION OF ORGANIZATIONAL CAPABILITY

A pathfinding book called *Organizational Capability: Competing from the Inside Out* by Dave Ulrich and Dale Lake explains why empowerment and its associated predecessors are of interest to executives.[1] Ulrich and Lake present a powerful premise for business success in the future based on certain capabilities. Business organizations of the past have lived and died based on how well they managed and improved their financial capability, their marketing and sales capability, and their technological and operational capability.

These capabilities have been the fundamental ingredients of business success. Every executive is well aware of the necessity of financial capability and resources; money is required to make money. Nor can a company sell its products and services without marketing and sales prowess and resources. Technological capability is responsible for research and development, while operational capability is the heart of providing the products and services to customers. Ulrich and Lake demonstrate that equally important to the business enterprise of the future will be a fourth characteristic: organizational capability.

Organizational capability is how well the company manages and utilizes the resources of its people. In a global economy with instant communication and rapid transportation, no company can long hold a competitive advantage through marketing capability and technological capability alone. Competitors can easily find out any other company's marketing and technological innovations. Organizational capability, on the other hand, is less apparent and harder to rapidly reproduce.

For a business to achieve organizational capability, it must shift from the limiting attitude about workers that is prevalent in most corporations. The thinking about workers in most large corporations is one-dimensional: one job equals one person. The *first* paradigm shift away from one-dimensional thinking arose from the total quality management movement with the idea that workers could and should inspect the quality of their own work. At a minimum, the quality of the work of a group was inspected by a member of the work group instead of by quality inspectors at the very end when products were ready for shipping to customers. Workers were responsible for two "jobs": producing and inspecting quality.

The *second* shift away from one-dimensional thinking was the idea that workers could help their organizations survive if they were cross-trained in multiple jobs so that if work decreased in one area, employees could shift to another area where higher output was needed. Cross-training was a significant innovation that increased the organization's flexibility to rapidly respond to changes in what customers wanted. On production lines in manufacturing facilities throughout the world, bottlenecks occur at certain pieces of equipment. Organizations that have workers who are cross-trained on several pieces of equipment can quickly move workers to the equipment in need when a bottleneck is identified. Cross-training on multiple machines also allows the equipment to continue to work when the primary operator goes to lunch or takes a break. For expensive and critical pieces of machinery, this flexibility promotes increased equipment utilization and productivity.

The *third* shift away from one-job-equals-one-person thinking is the transfer to employees of the more difficult and technical job tasks that are currently being performed by individuals in different job grades. For example, equipment operators are being taught how to do maintenance and simple repairs on their equipment. In offices, drafters are being taught how to do simple engineering tasks, clerks are being trained in data analysis and interpretation, and secretaries are being taught report writing. Technical job enlargement requires an investment in training.

Empowerment and participative management are concerned with workers achieving the *fourth* dimension by performing management and supervisory tasks for themselves in their work areas. Currently, many organizations are improving business results by providing self-managed teamwork training and immediately implementing the fourth dimension of job enlargement. As each dimension is added and coordinated, that organization's internal capability is increased in ways that may not be present in its competitors.

Organizational capability must be strongly linked to customer satisfaction strategies in order to provide the highest benefit. At E-Systems in Salt Lake City, Utah, the customer, Boeing, wanted reduced costs every year. E-Systems increased its organizational capability by establishing self-managed work teams at the operating level and by implementing a cross-level, cross-function organizational steering team. The teams implemented aspects of all four types of job enlargement. The self-managed teams have met or exceeded Boeing's cost reduction requirements every year since they came into being using Structured Teamwork. Organizational capability is a competitive advantage at E-Systems in Salt Lake City. All of the various approaches to empowerment and participative management are designed to increase the power and potential of the organization to move rapidly and effectively to satisfy customers.

I have personally observed executives "get it" when organizational capability is described. They say yes to the concept. They get excited and share the concept in speeches to the employees, in lunches with the boss, and in staff meetings. When executives get sold on a major strategy, they want it implemented now! But just talking about organizational capability does not make it happen. A methodology for its rapid implementation has been missing. There are two key ingredients in systematically increasing organizational capability: teamwork and empowerment.

Ulrich and Lake have admonished, "Organizational capability, much like success in sports, requires teamwork."[2] Each dimension of job enlargement discussed above—quality inspection, cross-training, technical job enlargement, and empowerment itself—requires increased communication, cooperation, and coordination of all the workers involved just to get started. When teams develop work goals for themselves, they freely associate the need for cross-training with improving quality and productivity. As individuals learn the new tasks, creativity and the supportive work climate allow them to challenge how the work tasks are currently performed and to develop improved methods for how to do the work.

Just as teamwork is required to improve organizational capability, so is empowerment. The research on job redesign and job enlargement is clear on this point. Involve employees in planning the cross-training and enlargement of their own work, and significant business results occur. Do not involve the employees, and the whole job redesign effort is a waste of time. Empowerment is truly the foundation for increased organizational capability.

BREAKTHROUGH POINTS

- Empowerment is the driving force behind organizational breakthrough, but often it has not been properly defined.
- Empowerment means giving individuals increased authority within a structured environment to decide and implement decisions without checking with management.
- Empowerment produces benefits for both employees and the organization.

18 CHAPTER

Empowerment by Any Other Name Smells Just as Sweet

Empowerment as a desired ingredient of business and organizational success is not new. Only the use of the term *empowerment* is new. In the 1970s and early 1980s, the term in vogue was *participative management*. From 1987 to 1993, the popular term was *employee involvement*. As each concept became fashionable, organizations wanted to pursue it. Executives and managers felt it would benefit their organization. News magazines and television reported successes. Employee involvement was thought to be essential to any company's major shift to organizationwide quality improvement under the label total quality management (TQM). A survey of *Fortune* magazine's top 1,000 companies found that 70 percent of the companies responding indicated they were pursuing employee involvement to increase productivity and that 72 percent wanted to have it improve their quality.[1]

Companies like Motorola, Ford, and Xerox were selected in 1989 and 1990 to receive the Malcolm Baldrige National Quality Award as the leaders of quality in the United States. These same companies were also leaders in employee involvement. Xerox improved manufacturing quality by 90 percent while reducing manufacturing costs

companywide by 20 percent over a four-year time frame using participative management and employee involvement.

The same attraction has proved true for empowerment. Visionary executives believe that it can increase organizational capability.
Participative management, employee involvement, and empowerment are similar in their intent to involve the hearts and minds of people at work. The ultimate aims are to simultaneously improve
business performance and better meet the needs of employees.

The considerable similarity among the above three concepts
must be recognized because it demonstrates a continual quest in business to better utilize a company's human capital. The fact that every
five years a new fad appears that is very similar to a previous one
shows a basic drive in organizations to tap more effectively the
resources of their workforce.

THE EMPOWERMENT CONTINUUM

In addition to similarity of intent, all three concepts have used the
same six methods with varying levels of success. These methods are
depicted in Figure 18–1. I see the Empowerment Continuum as six
stages of gradually increasing authority and accountability. As organizations move from left to right on the continuum, there is more
involvement by employees in how their work is managed.

In the following sections, each of the six stages of empowerment
in Figure 18–1 will be described along with research conclusions on
how effective each method has been in achieving breakthrough teamwork. The research conclusions on the effectiveness of the different
empowerment methods may explain why frustration grows as organizations start and stop implementing participative management,
employee involvement, empowerment, or any other similar concept.

Stage 1: Employee Surveys and Focus Groups

In Stage 1, employee surveys and focus groups are used by managers
of organizations to gather data on the opinions of employees on problems and potential management actions. Surveys are most often used
once a year to gather data on employee attitudes and morale problems. The use of focus groups as an employee involvement and
empowerment technique was an idea borrowed from advertising. In
preparing the release of a new product, advertisers expose groups of
potential buyers to the product, for example, a new type of pizza. The

F I G U R E 18–1

The Empowerment Continuum

Low			→	↑	High
Stages of Empowerment					
Employee surveys and focus groups	Employee suggestion systems	Quality circles and problem solving groups	Participative decision making	Semiautonomous teams	Autonomous teams
Key Characteristics					
Managers and employees give their opinions	Ideas submitted; management decides	Groups formed to solve specific problems; managers approve solutions	Workers and managers work together on decisions; managers have final word	Self-managed team responsible for most decisions; team facilitator provides communication link to management and support groups	Self-managed team responsible for *all* decisions; individual team members provide links to management and support groups
Types of Empowerment					
Problem identification	Suggesting solutions to problems	Problem analysis and solution development	Goal setting and planning, problem solving	Goal setting, planning, and implementation including job redesign and work process improvements	Goal setting, planning, and implementation including job redesign and work process improvements

potential customers are then asked a series of structured questions regarding what they liked or did not like about the product. In business and industry, employees are brought together in focus groups to react to proposed changes such as new salary structures, communication methods, or job designs.

While they are valuable tools for collecting data, employee surveys and focus groups by themselves do *not* lead to improved work or organizational performance. When you really analyze the methods of focus groups or surveys regarding job redesign, for example, you see strong elements of centralized control. Management is in effect saying, "We and the engineers have developed this great new way for how *you* will do your work in the future, and now we want your opinion." A better approach, one supported by research, is to directly involve the employees in the job redesign at each key step of the planning. One way to improve the effectiveness of surveys and focus groups is to ask people to suggest improvements on whatever is being surveyed, not just to identify the problems with, for example, organizational communication or management information services. This step extends the participants' empowerment by asking them to suggest solutions as well as to identify problems.

Stage 2: Employee Suggestion Systems

Everyone has seen a box on the wall labeled Employee Suggestions. Suggestion systems are designed to encourage employees to submit ideas for how to improve any aspect of work or the work environment. Unfortunately, most suggestion systems are ineffective. Recently, companies have tried to link monetary rewards to either individual or group suggestions. However, research indicates that paying employees for suggestions has either no impact on work results or an impact that is significant for only two to three months at the beginning of the program. Most systems are slow to respond to the suggestions and to put the ideas into action. The best suggestion system I have seen was Motorola's, where management was required to respond to every suggestion within 48 hours. Even that system got bogged down, however, when a manager for a function had too many suggestions to review. Moreover, the written submission process did not allow for two-way dialogue on the suggestion. Organizations cannot achieve rapid breakthrough with cumbersome, bureaucratic suggestion systems alone.

The National Association of Suggestion Systems reported in one study that the average number of suggestions in U.S. companies was

1.7 ideas per 10 employees per year.[2] Compare that figure with the Paul Revere Insurance Company's results of four ideas per person using quality teams and participative management, two of the next stages on the empowerment continuum.[3] A technique for improving a suggestion system is to have individuals submit suggestions directly to the managers or individuals who are responsible for an improvement area versus to a centralized committee. If everyone knows the current goals of all functions and submits ideas in the context of promoting goal achievement for that function, the innovation barrier will be overcome more quickly.

Stage 3: Quality Circles and Problem-Solving Groups

In the early 1980s, a new form of employee empowerment called quality circles appeared on the American and European scenes. It was one of the many imported Japanese management techniques that became extremely popular, and some of the early results of its use were positive and encouraging. Many corporations implemented quality circles throughout their organizations worldwide. Gradually, further results filtered in: significant work and business improvements did not always happen. Often the quality circles took a long time to get any kind of result.

Of 29 hard-data studies of quality circles, only 5 reported unqualified work performance improvements. Ten of the studies had partially successful improvements in work or organizational factors such as performance appraisals, attendance, promotions, employee grievances, and safety accidents. The remaining 14 studies had comparison groups doing the same or better than the quality circle participants. Two of the studies that obtained positive results required 8 to 10 months of quality circle participation to achieve individual and organizational changes.[4]

An example of a quality circle (QC) study where there was no difference comes from an organization whose job is literally to make money—the U.S. Mint. The federal mint implemented quality circles using many of the agreed-upon standards of implementation: training the circle facilitators, using a QC steering team, allowing the groups to meet one hour a week, and obtaining management approval of QC recommendations. Many organizations implement quality circles composed of individuals from different work groups. This U.S. Mint study is unique because each quality circle was composed of individuals from the same work group. Another unique feature was that after the QC steering team approved recommendations made by a QC, they were sent back to that QC to be implemented. Unfortunately, the research comparing work groups that had QCs with those that did not have QCs generally found no significant work or organizational improvements in the quality circle work groups.[5]

As an empowerment method, quality circles do have a favorable impact—some of the time. One factor that might be inhibiting the success of quality circles is the lack of a clear definition and standards. In a 1992 study of quality circles, Brian De Sorbe found that even though they were called quality circles, many quality circles did not meet the majority of recognized and published standards of quality circles.[6] The definition of *quality circles* appears to be just as ambiguous as that of *teamwork* or *empowerment*.

Quality circles took off in fadlike fashion throughout the world. As happens with fads, the quality circles were often implemented without training or clear managerial sponsorship. Usually the quality circle considered problems for which management approval was required before the solution could be put in place. As a result, there were disconnects with management. Sometimes management would disapprove of the quality circle's recommendation. Other times management would get impatient with the group's progress and implement a solution without waiting for the quality circle's recommendation. After the above consequences occurred once, most employees lost their faith and trust in management and did not want to have anything to do with quality circles. Many executives and managers were exposed to both the promise of quality circles and their eventual demise for lack of results. The negative results of quality circles have reinforced manager skepticism toward employee empowerment in many organizations.

Some specific actions seem to make a positive impact on the results quality circles can make. In high-technology companies, for example, managerial sponsorship of quality circles and manager participation in management-member quality circles were found to be key ingredients of success, as shown in an extensive Silicon Valley study conducted by Bob Montgomery.[7]

Additionally, Hewlett-Packard recognized early that quality circles alone were not enough. One division implemented a three-day program in which the division manager and management team led the improvement effort by studying areas of company improvement for which they were responsible. This division of Hewlett-Packard achieved a 42 percent increase in revenue per employee!

The Paul Revere Insurance Company implemented an organizationwide program that achieved high success. The company required managers to be regular members of management problem-solving teams. All team members were given training, not just the quality circle facilitator, which is the usual scenario. Their results were $3.5 million in cost savings the first year and $7.5 million the second year.

In a three-year study of 47 quality circle teams, Tang and others found that management-initiated QCs solved problems faster than employee-initiated QCs.[8] They discovered that management-initiated QCs took an average of 83 days to solve their problems versus the 133 days that employee-initiated QCs required. Additionally, management-initiated QCs solved more problems than employee-initiated QCs: 3.7 versus 2.1, or almost double. The researchers also found that a smaller group of 6 to 11 participants had better performance than a larger group of 7 to 14.

The above findings lead us to the following conclusion: Quality circles and other types of problem-solving groups *can* make a significant difference if certain key success factors are followed:

1. Management initiates QCs and identifies the areas or topics on which they work.

2. Managers participate in management QCs to solve problems themselves.

3. All QC members receive training, not just the QC facilitator.

4. QC size is no larger than 11 members.

Stage 4: Participative Decision Making

The next stage of empowerment that has been utilized is participative decision making. In this method, a manager or supervisor asks the opinions of his or her subordinates before making a decision. Typical decisions include choosing which goals a group will pursue or which solutions should be implemented for a particular problem. A key feature of this type of decision making is that the manager or supervisor always makes the final choice.

In an early landmark study, employees at a hospital laundry were brought together to discuss potential work improvements during a weekly 30- to 40-minute meeting.[9] The supervisor planned and scheduled the meeting and had been taught how to listen and be positive about the workers' ideas. The employees shared the decision-making authority with their supervisor for how to implement various work process improvements. The supervisor retained the authority to influence which work improvement ideas were pursued. The results were a 50 percent increase in productivity and a 40 percent decrease in absenteeism within 12 months!

There are many areas of work in which participative decision making that includes a supervisor and the employees pays off with improved work performance. Figure 18–2, the Participative Decision Making Research Summary, provides a list of areas where employee participation has made significant business improvements, and areas in which employee participation has not made a significant positive difference or has been detrimental.

During the 1970s and 1980s, when managers selected one or two areas of work in which employees were allowed a say in the decision making, there were usually improved results. An important conclusion is that employees do *not* need to participate in every decision and

FIGURE 18–2

Participative Decision Making Research Summary

Functions Where Participative Decision Making Is Best	Functions Where Participative Decision Making Is Not Effective by Itself
1. In meetings or informal interactions with the manager or supervisor.	1. With inexperienced or new employees.
2. When developing suggestions for how to implement any management-initiated improvement.	2. In making final decisions regarding the delegating of work when individuals vary considerably in work ability.
3. In setting production goals or work unit goals.	3. In short-term task forces or representative committees.
4. In creative problem solving when individuals have been assigned hard, specific goals.	
5. When developing ways to reduce costs.	
6. When identifying how to measure and communicate goal achievement.	
7. When developing new plans, processes, or procedures for doing work.	
8. When developing ways to improve quality.	
9. When developing budgets.	

management function to feel participative.[10] This implies that the organization, manager, or supervisor can choose the areas for employee participation. A major condition for success is that the employee feels that he or she is making a valuable and real contribution toward the work group's goals.[11] Therefore, the supervisor or manager should select areas for participation that are high leverage and where the workers' knowledge and support are critical.

Goal setting as part of participative decision making is very important. One study showed that general employee participation in work improvement and personnel policy setting without specific goal setting did not result in superior productivity.[12] Goal setting as a part of any participation activity increases productivity. Therefore, the setting of specific goals during problem solving or work process improvement must be a major standard for participative decision making and the empowerment process as a whole.[13]

It has been found that involving all employees in a participative program is more effective than using representatives only.[14] It is not necessary, however, to have all employees involved in all aspects of the participative empowerment.[15] Group members can be spun off into short-term problem-solving groups or quality circles. However, in the weekly communication or staff meetings, the entire employee group can have an opportunity to participate in identifying problems, solving problems, setting goals, and other work unit management functions.[16]

A major study regarding how to motivate employees to participate reported that if employees find their initial attempts at participation accepted and used by management, they will be more motivated to continue participation activities.[17] If employees see the results of their participation actually utilized, there will be an increase in their desire to participate. With this in mind, managers and supervisors should select decisions for worker input where they can be sure that results of the participation will be used. For example, an employee brainstorming session on ways to reduce costs in the work unit is likely to result in several suggestions that can be immediately implemented.

Some managers and supervisors resist participative decision making, but the resistance can be overcome. Resistive managers will increase their use of employee participation in decision making when the decisions or goals are initially implemented on a trial or "pilot" basis.[18] Participative decision making that follows research-based guidelines sells itself after it is implemented, because it works. The following are the research-based guidelines for successful participative decision making:

1. The supervisor plans, schedules, and runs the meetings, being careful to listen to and support the ideas presented by the team members.

2. The supervisor retains the authority to influence which work improvement ideas are pursued.

3. Managers or supervisors make sure the functions of participative decision making are aligned with those that research says produce positive results.

4. Employees do not need to participate in every decision and management function to feel participative.

5. The supervisor or manager should select areas for participation that are high leverage and where the workers' knowledge and support are critical.

6. Goal setting is a necessary aspect of participation.

7. Involving all employees in a participative program is more effective than involving only volunteers or representatives.

8. Select decisions for worker input where supervisors can be sure that results of the participation will be used.

9. Resistive managers will increase their use of employee participation in decision making when the decisions or goals are initially implemented on a trial basis.

Stage 5: Semiautonomous Teams

A self-managed team is usually composed of 3 to 15 individuals who must work together to complete a segment of work. The difference between semiautonomous and autonomous self-managed teams is the presence of a team facilitator in semiautonomous teams. The primary role of the facilitator is to provide an interface and linkage communication function between the self-managed team, upper management, and support groups. The team facilitator may have different names, such as team advisor, team leader, coordinator, or even supervisor. No matter what the individual is called, there is a big difference between this role and the role of a traditional supervisor.

The team facilitator devotes significantly less time on day-to-day supervision than traditional supervisors spend, moving from between 60 percent and 80 percent to less than 10 percent of his or her time daily. The team and its individual members take over the supervisory tasks of setting and measuring daily work goals, solving problems, managing the quality of their work, and even arranging for the training of fellow team members. The team facilitator takes time, however, to listen and to understand issues that involve people or resources outside the team. He or she is a conduit of information from managers, suppliers, and customers back to the team. The facilitator also gives attention to training and coaching team members in how to perform teamwork and technical and administrative skills that the team assumed from the supervisor's former role.

As mentioned earlier, many organizations are moving to self-managed teams as a way to reduce the number of supervisors and middle managers in the organization. As a result, a team facilitator may have responsibility for between 15 and 45 people (one to five teams), whereas before there were two to four supervisors responsible for the same number of people. As organizations implement self-managed teams, many supervisors fear they will lose their job. This fear is not justified. Most of the time only the lowest-performing supervisors actually lose their jobs. The majority of supervisors are reassigned and trained either to be team facilitators or to provide direct contributions in developing new products and services.

Team facilitators are also different from supervisors in another respect. They use the additional time that is freed up to do work that is more upward and outward focused. They facilitate and contribute to improvements in work and business processes that result in greater customer satisfaction. The team facilitator also participates in major organizational process improvements such as new information systems. Many team facilitators take on the job duties of their managers, who in turn become more upward and outward focused to create an organization that is more responsive to customers and their needs. Turning over day-to-day management to a high-functioning, self-managed team allows every manager to contribute to breakthrough projects that will meet customer needs.

One difference between semiautonomous teams and participative decision making is that the teams take full responsibility for all of the management functions shown in the Participative Decision Making Research Summary (Fig. 18–2) all of the time, not just at the occasional instigation of the manager or supervisor. Having workers take ownership of management functions as well as the work itself is possible because of the following major principle: Management is a process, not a person.

Like any other business or work process, management processes can be significantly improved and reengineered. The process has always involved workers as well as people with a formal title such as supervisor or manager. Self-managed teamwork promotes the workers to a more active position in the management process.

Another major difference is that in participative decision making there are various degrees of weight that the employee group has in the decisions related to the work and work area. Usually the supervisor's opinion carries more weight than that of a worker. In a semiautonomous team, the team facilitator's role is dramatically different. He or she is an equal member of the team for team decisions. Team decisions are major decisions that require the creativity and involvement of every team member. Those decisions are made by team consensus. Recall from Chapter 14 that consensus decision making is not "majority rules," as occurs in most democratic processes. The precise definition of consensus is that everyone on the team can support the team's decision. *Everyone* includes the team facilitator. His or her viewpoint is equal to everyone else's, which means that he or she must be able to support the decisions, too.

> Management is a process, not a person.

What have been the results of semiautonomous teams? Newspapers and news magazines have reported spectacular successes as well as dramatic failures. Productivity and quality improvements from 40 percent to 250 percent have been reported. On the other hand, a 1992 best-practices survey of 580 organizations commissioned by the American Quality Foundation reported that self-managed teams had a negative impact for certain organizations.[19] To resolve that apparent contradiction, I reviewed every available documented study of self-managed teams. Unfortunately, most of the studies did not have control or comparison groups or measured worker attitudes only and did not assess work results. Figure 18–3 presents the findings of the eight hard-data studies I discovered.

Five of the eight studies obtained positive results. Each of the four semiautonomous team studies with negative results did not include team skills training as an implementation step. The self-managed teamwork program in the candy factory included training, but it was theoretical versus practical skills training. Looking back, it now seems obvious that management tasks *cannot* be turned over to workers successfully without training them in management skills such as

Results of Research on Semiautonomous Teams[20]

Work Setting	Key Methods	Results	Observations
Aluminum and titanium fabrication	Semiautonomous; team skills training; job redesign; technical training	Increased productivity; fewer workers needed; no union grievances; higher performance ratings	Job redesign not fully implemented; supervisors did performance evaluations
Aluminum and titanium cost estimating and engineering	Semiautonomous (supervisors were present); job redesign; voluntary weekly team meetings with consultants	Decreased effectiveness, accuracy, and cooperation with internal customers; major negative impact on company's business results	No teamwork training; no team goal setting; no technical training
Hourly workers	Semiautonomous; coordinators; elected team leaders	20% greater productivity than at similar plants	Coordinators coached individuals in self-observation and improvement
Union workers in a food processing plant with a new product line	Semiautonomous; team skills training for supervisors; team meetings; job redesign; job rotation; employee surveys	33% greater production volume; 8% less cost; 20% fewer employees needed	In a second operation, no team training provided to supervisors; results not as dramatically positive
Coal miners (Study one)	Semiautonomous; job-specific team skills training; team problem solving; job redesign	60% reduction in federal violations; increased productivity; decreased operating and maintenance costs; no difference in accidents and absences	Management initially resisted workers submitting requests for major barriers to be removed
Workers in candy factory	Semiautonomous (support manager with 1:40–70 manager-to-employee ratio); weekly team meetings; theoretical training on autonomous work groups; job redesign	Productivity was 5% to 10% worse than at comparison site; machine utilization was poor; reduced cost due to 4 to 5 fewer supervisors; labor turnover higher	No team skills training or self-management skills training; high amounts of conflict and stress reported in start-up, but no team conflict management training provided
Coal miners (Study two)	Semiautonomous; cross-training; gain sharing of increased profits	No difference in productivity, turnover, or union grievances	No team skills training
Bank processors and clerks in a stock transfer department	Semiautonomous; job redesign; survey data and employee interviews	No difference in productivity or motivation	No team skills training; no team goal setting; cross-training not implemented

goal setting, communication, decision making, and team problem solving.

In addition to providing team skills training, the effective programs involved the workers in the job redesign of their work area. Recall from Chapter 12 that job redesign is systematically examining how to change the work to improve quality, productivity, and cycle time. The research on job redesign itself has one major implementation standard—involve the employees whose job is being redesigned. Semiautonomous teams not only have involvement in job redesign, but the team members manage it and drive the activity to achieve priority work goals.

I worked with one manufacturing organization where the semiautonomous team obtained significant work improvements through continuous job redesign. Because of a major downturn in customer orders, management needed to restructure and lay off a percentage of the machine operators. The manufacturing managers felt bad because the workers had performed so well. Since the team managed everything else so well, management decided to put this problem to them. The team used its problem-solving and creativity skills to resolve this emotion-laden issue. One operator wanted to go back to school, two individuals wanted to work only part-time, and the team reduced other operating costs so that no one was forced to lose his or her job. Self-managed teams can make tough decisions, too.

The last stage on the empowerment continuum, autonomous teams, is perhaps the most controversial.

Stage 6: Autonomous Teams

The main distinguishing characteristic of autonomous teams is the absence of a supervisor or team facilitator. In the fully autonomous team, the workers run their own team meetings and work area without any participation from management. Most manufacturing organizations use a method called the star model to make this work. In this model, the five or more roles that a supervisor generally performs are divided up among the team members. Examples of roles, or points on the star, include training, quality, finance and cost control, human resources, production and work scheduling, engineering or work process improvement, and safety. Individuals on the team who hold these roles are called coordinators, facilitators, or officers.

Figure 18–4 contrasts the ways semiautonomous teams and autonomous teams relate to the world outside their team. Notice how

Ways Semiautonomous Teams versus Autonomous Teams Relate to the World Outside Their Team

Semiautonomous Team Linkages

Autonomous Team Linkages

Managers

Team facilitator

Team members

X
X
X
X
X
X
X

Manufacturing manager

Engineering manager

Productivity coordinator

Engineering coordinator

Human resources manager

Human resources coordinator

Finance coordinator

Finance manager

Quality coordinator

Quality manager

the interface and linkage functions of the team facilitator/supervisor are replaced with the star avenues in the autonomous team.

Many organizations have seen the value of the star model as a way to free up the team facilitator's time. So now even organizations that have semiautonomous teams are using limited star models, but they still have a team facilitator in a management interface and coordinator role. Figure 18–5 shows how the star roles stay generally inside the boundaries of the semiautonomous team with the team facilitator as the primary interface outside the team.

The six stages of the empowerment continuum have strengths and weaknesses. Ray Gumpert, the manager of Texas Instruments Semiconductor's worldwide training and organizational development group, has implemented an effective method for promoting empowerment. Each TI site management team is encouraged to study the continuum and select the stage of empowerment that overlaps best with promoting that site's current business strategies and goals. As a result, empowerment is not viewed as doing something extra and there is the perception that Ray's group is supporting site leaders versus directing.

FIGURE 18–5

Semiautonomous Star

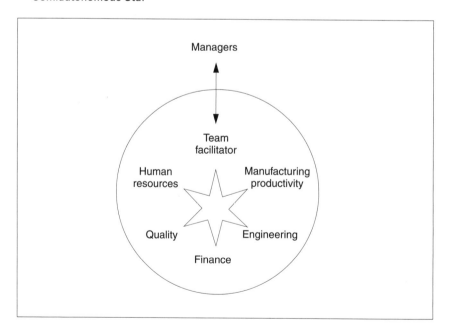

The question I am asked most frequently is, "Which is better, semiautonomous teams or autonomous teams?" Semiautonomous teams are successful if managers and workers are trained and there is a structured and gradual process for the transfer of decision-making responsibility. What about autonomous teams? This question is answered in Chapter 19.

BREAKTHROUGH POINTS

- Empowerment has been known by other names, such as participative management and employee involvement.
- The empowerment continuum provides a means of evaluating the level of employee empowerment within an organization.
- Employee surveys and focus groups represent the minimum level of employee empowerment.
- Employee suggestion systems are the next level but seldom produce significant results when used by themselves.
- Quality circles and problem-solving groups, the third level, can be effective with management leadership, manager participation, training for everyone, and membership limited to no more than eleven.
- Research indicates that the fourth level of empowerment, participative decision making, can be successful where supervisors run meetings, retain ultimate authority, select the areas for participation, and involve all employees in the process.
- The next level of empowerment, semiautonomous teams, which operate with a facilitator, has produced phenomenal results when properly implemented.
- The last level, autonomous teams, which operate without a facilitator, has generated substantial controversy. They will be discussed in Chapter 19.

19
CHAPTER

The Myth of the Autonomous Team— Let the Buyer Beware

Autonomous empowerment is a big temptation that is difficult for organizations to resist. Imagine no supervisors! The organization saves money by not having to pay salary and benefits to one whole layer of managers. Workers do not have to put up with bosses. As we proceed across the empowerment continuum, business results generally improve if certain success factors are followed. Thus, autonomous teams appear to be the ultimate in empowerment. Why not go for it?

Unfortunately, three critical problems face organizations that attempt autonomous empowerment. First, in spite of all of the publicity about "workers without bosses," I have not found a single hard-data comparison-group study of autonomous teamwork in my 1,200-study research database that indicates it is *effective*. The one study I do have clearly favors semiautonomous teams over autonomous teams.[1] This study was conducted in a high-technology research and development organization where most project teams were autonomous. Management noticed major problems due to the lack of coordination of facility, test, and support resources. Team coordinators were established in one part of the organization to coordinate each team's project with the use of tests and facilities. These teams, which became semiautonomous, completed 98 percent more research reports and worked on 51 percent more projects than the autonomous teams! Value is added when one person's role includes the interfacing and coordinating responsibility for a work group with the rest of the organization.

Many articles state that "autonomous" teams were established, and that they achieved great business results. In every case, however, the teams had someone called a supervisor or facilitator or manager who provided some aspect of coordination and upper-management linkage. The teams were called autonomous, but they were actually semiautonomous because of the presence of a supervisor, even though it was in a limited coordinator/linkage role. In some instances, the publications were written prior to the development of the term semiautonomous, and had that term been in existence at the time of writing, the authors would more than likely have used it.

The second problem with autonomous teams is their ominous lack of creative breakthroughs. I have never seen them achieve creative work breakthroughs or lead the way to breakthrough teamwork. In two firsthand experiences, the teams never had time to think about breakthrough. The workers in the autonomous teams spent all of their team meeting time hearing reports from coordinators for quality, productivity, human resources, and so on. The coordinators spent the team time communicating information from the managers of human resources, production, quality, accounting, safety, and so on. Consequently, little time was left for creative problem solving or continuous work process improvement. Autonomous teams do allow the supervisors to be replaced, but little opportunity then exists for the team to focus on major breakthroughs like job redesign. In meetings and in the workplace, there is not the creative problem solving and continuous improvement that occurs when one person coordinates, filters the communication, and performs the interfaces the team requires.

A major irony is that autonomous teams with no facilitator are less empowered in their team and individual responsibilities than semiautonomous teams. Organizations that have totally eliminated anything resembling a supervisor role keep a tight rein on team members who wish to make changes in work processes or job redesign. Improvement suggestions absorb huge amounts of time because the managers who need to approve them are swamped with managing their side of the team interface. Both of the autonomous team organizations described earlier decided on their own to bring the supervisors back and move to semiautonomous teams. Having one person spending a small amount of time interfacing with management and support organizations, versus having a variety of team members perform the interface function, promotes breakthrough teamwork.

The third and final difficulty with autonomous teams is that the anecdotal reports of their greatest successes are in very stable businesses where the work processes are not required to change often or rapidly. A company manufacturing pet food or some other type of commodity product or service that has few if any customer- or technology-driven changes may be candidates for autonomous teams. Businesses and industries requiring rapid continuous improvement like electronics or semiconductor manufacturing have difficulty with autonomous teams. They need the rapid dissemination and implementation of new direction, new products, and new processes to meet ever-changing consumer demands. These industries need an integrated picture of new requirements, and they need the unencumbered creativity and intellect of the team members for rapid implementation.

Based on these considerations, the following conclusions can be drawn:

- Autonomous teams (those with no supervisor or facilitator) are not effective in work systems, such as in semiconductor manufacturing, that undergo frequent changes.

- A facilitator/supervisor is required as a coordinator to ensure that the customer-driven changes are implemented rapidly and accurately.

MANAGERIAL CONCERNS ABOUT EMPOWERMENT

It was a poignant scene in the Amoco Canada building in downtown Calgary. Chairman and President T. Don Stacy was meeting with Stan Wenger, his newly appointed employee involvement coordinator for Amoco Canada Petroleum Company, Ltd. Stan was in the middle of a special one-on-one briefing for Don on the new employee involvement program. Don interrupted and exclaimed, "Stan, I support increased employee involvement, but how do we tell our managers to give up the power and authority they have spent their whole careers trying to obtain?"

Most managers strongly question giving up their power through employee involvement and teamwork programs. T. Don Stacy was more direct and honest in voicing these concerns than most. This is another example of the disconnected organization: the executive has a vision that will promote breakthrough teamwork, but his managers are skeptical. From presidents to frontline supervisors, there are strong concerns about relinquishing power to one's subordinates. Managers observe the current poor performance of their employees, and they remark, "There is no way I can give those people more responsibility. Things are out of control now. The power they do have they are misusing. If anything, I need to be more in control." The managers notice their workers taking long breaks, producing poor quality, and turning in late work. They also see that documentation and required reports are not done, and basic requirements are not followed. The managers are used to calling individuals and groups into their offices for disciplining. Some of the case studies describing the before-empowerment picture even depict instances of employee sabotage and major theft.

It appears inconceivable to further empower employees who are not behaving responsibly with the power they currently have, especially in the face of no teamwork structures or skills. In many situations, managers and supervisors use their authority to try to control the workers, with little success. Hence, managers facing a long list of poor-performance behaviors carry a view that workers are incompetent or just don't care.

Ironically, when a team is trained to develop team structures for self-management, including team goals, ground rules, roles, and responsibilities, management ends up achieving more control than it ever had without a structured empowerment program. Productivity and quality goals are more readily achieved. Tardiness and attendance problems are not as big an issue because the team is driving toward and achieving its important goals. The team uses peer pressure and conflict management to manage individual performance problems that interfere with team goals. The team elevates everyone's performance by the team's development and adoption of ground rules for what makes a good team member. Because the workers develop the expectations and structures for managing themselves, there is strong motivation to adhere to the teamwork structures. The adherence to the ground rules, team goals, and other structures is a powerful form of control: it is self-control.

An element that allows the team to use the new power and decision-making authority responsibly is the team's participation in Structured Teamwork skills training. Most dramatic failures of self-directed teamwork occur when worker teams are given decision-making authority with no training in team decision-making skills. Teams are given goal-setting authority with no training in goal setting and conflict management. As was described earlier, some organizations are trying to implement self-managed teamwork as if they are turning on a light switch. Flip. Click. Then management screams when they do not see any improvement. Unfortunately, empowerment does not work that way in business and industry. Individuals must be given team and management skills training first and then gradually be given more responsibility as they successfully exercise the authority they already have.

Managers need to focus directly on the team's work results and achievement of business goals. Many managers like to retain tight control for *how* the work is done. They remember how they used to do it, and they are comfortable with the work methods they used. Nothing could be more disempowering than overmanaging how the team's goals are achieved. Managers can save themselves stress and anxiety by participating *with* the team in setting the team goals and then standing back and watching the results. Most of the time the team will exceed any previous baseline measurement of performance. Managers must only ensure that the team is pointed in the right direction and working on the right goals. After that, they should stand back and look out!

CHOOSING THE STAGE OF EMPOWERMENT BEST FOR YOUR ORGANIZATION

Empowerment is one of the major requirements for breakthrough teamwork. The leaders of every organization must decide what stage of empowerment would best create additional thrust and acceleration for their current business priorities. One European organization I worked with selected semiautonomous teams as the major empowerment method to reduce costs and achieve greater productivity. The steering team, however, also wanted to use employee surveys and problem-solving groups occasionally. A combination approach may also be best for you and your organization.

Regardless of which stages of empowerment are selected, the success factors discussed earlier for each stage must be implemented. The structures for successful empowerment are presented in Figure 19–1. Each stage of empowerment has specific Structured Teamwork components that managers and workers must be trained in and that must be utilized for the empowerment to lead to improved business results and breakthrough teamwork. As can be seen, the further across the empowerment continuum an organization wishes to move, the more training and structures are required.

FIGURE 19–1

Structures for Successful Empowerment

Structured Teamwork Components	Low					High
	Employee Surveys and Focus Groups	Employee Suggestion Systems	Quality Circles and Problem Solving Groups	Participative Decision Making	Semiautonomous Teams	Autonomous Teams
1. Team creativity	X	X	X	X	X	X
2. Team communication	X	X	X	X	X	X
3. Team meetings			X	X	X	X
4. Conflict management				X	X	X
5. Team mission				X	X	X
6. Team goal setting			X	X	X	X
7. Team roles and responsibilities				X	X	X
8. Team problem solving		X	X	X	X	X
9. Team decision making			X	X	X	X
10. Work process improvement		X	X	X	X	X

BREAKTHROUGH POINTS

- No hard research exists to support the notion that autonomous teams produce great results.

- Autonomous teams fail to produce creative breakthroughs, suffer from a lack of real empowerment, and are successful only in stable businesses.

- Each organization must choose the level of empowerment that best fits its situation and train its members with the specific Structured Teamwork components necessary for that level of empowerment.

20 CHAPTER

From Breakthrough Teamwork to Organizational Breakthrough

Great team communication, cooperation, coordination, creative breakthrough, and continuous breakthrough generate C^5, the ultimate model for teamwork. Figure 20–1 identifies the required structures for attaining each level of C^5 teamwork. Team members must acquire and learn teamwork skills in order to be truly effective. Some early studies found that small groups and teams were not always superior to individuals in problem solving.[1] That line of research and conclusions caused some of the early skepticism about teamwork. The difficulty with those studies is that the teams studied were expected to perform in a superior fashion even though they had not received explicit training in team skills. No wonder they failed to perform as expected.

The 10 research-based components of Structured Teamwork serve as the core areas for team training and development. To achieve Level 1 in the C^5 model, teams must utilize key team communication skills, team meeting skills, and conflict management skills. Teamwork requires excellent communication. One reason most teams seem to take forever to do their work is that the members are not trained in team communication skills; therefore, they are unable to really hear the points of view and ideas of the other team members. Consequently, I

FIGURE 20-1

Requirements for C^5 Teamwork

Levels	Required Structures
Level 1: Communication	Team communication skills Team meetings Team conflict management
Level 2: Cooperation	Team creativity Team problem solving Team conflict management
Level 3: Coordination	Team creativity Team mission Team goal setting Roles and responsibilities Team decision making Team meetings
Level 4: Creative breakthrough	Team creativity Work process improvement Team conflict management Team problem solving Team goal setting
Level 5: Continuous breakthrough	A C^5 organization

begin the development of most teams with an evaluation of the communication skills and structures that already exist. For those who would argue that team development should start with team goal setting, I would respond that unless members already have excellent communication skills, a team will flounder even as goals are developed.

If the teamwork assessment of the team indicates that the team does not have or does not use good communication skills, then the skills must be developed. Executives and upper managers usually have good listening and speaking skills, but they do not always use their listening skills with fellow executives.

Once members of a team have demonstrated their communication skills, cooperation (Level 2 in the C^5 model) is developed, allowing for creative solutions to problems. Armed with their communication skills, team members are able to assist each other with their work and resolve conflicts between themselves.

After training in how to develop team mission statements, set goals, and define roles and responsibilities, cooperation leads to coordination, Level 3 in the C^5 model. Unnecessary duplication is eliminated. Decisions can be made and implemented. Job duties and actions are aligned to achieve the goals that the team has set.

With communication, cooperation, and coordination skills in hand, Level 4 in the C^5 model, creative breakthrough, can lead to major innovations. These innovations in how work is done or a problem is solved can result in significant cost savings and higher profits.

To reach the type of organization represented by Level 5 in the C^5 model, both the organization, its teams, and its employees must be fully empowered to generate continuous breakthroughs. Improvements are communicated rapidly throughout the organization. Rather than single, isolated innovations, major work process improvements and job redesign improvements are repeatedly achieved everywhere within the organization.

Clearly the 10 components of Structured Teamwork provide the skills that teams use to become successful. The components are firmly linked to the levels of the C^5 model. When they are learned and practiced, they enable teams to create breakthrough solutions to problems and improve processes that create ongoing organizational breakthroughs.

You will benefit from reading this book only if you *implement* the ideas that I am sharing with you. A successful program based on Structured Teamwork requires total commitment to all 10 components. A partial implementation and a halfhearted effort will not result in breakthrough but may lead to breakdown. In the global business race, Structured Teamwork can be the engine that powers you across the finish line, but only if you install it and turn it on.

NOTES

Chapter 1

1. The information in this figure was drawn from the following sources:

Albrecht, K. (1992). *The only thing that matters: Bringing the power of the customer into the center of your business* (p. 93). New York: HarperCollins.

Bowles, J. & Hammond, J. (1991). *Beyond quality: How 50 winning companies use continuous improvement.* New York: Putnam.

Collins, J. C., Porras, J. I. (1994). *Built to last: Successful habits of visionary companies.* New York: HarperCollins.

Crosby, P. B. (1979). *Quality is free: The art of making quality certain.* New York: McGraw-Hill.

Hammer, M., & Champy, J. (1993). *Reengineering the corporation: A manifesto for business revolution.* New York: HarperCollins.

Imai, M. (1986). *Kaizen: The key to Japan's competitive success.* New York: McGraw-Hill.

Juran, J. M. (1964). *Managerial breakthrough: A new concept of the manager's job.* New York: McGraw-Hill.

Juran, J. M. (1988). *Juran on planning for quality.* New York: Free Press.

Ouchi, W. (1981). *Theory Z: How American business can meet the Japanese challenge.* Reading, MA: Addison-Wesley.

Pascale, R. T., and Athos, A. G. (1981). *The art of Japanese management: Applications for American executives.* New York: Simon & Schuster.

Peters, T. J., & Austin, N. K. (1985). *A passion for excellence: The leadership difference.* New York: Random House.

Peters, T. J., & Waterman, R. H., Jr. (1982). *In search of excellence: Lessons from America's best-run companies.* New York: Harper & Row.

Senge, P. M. (1990). *The fifth discipline: The art and practice of the learning organization* (p. 10). New York: Doubleday.

Schonberger, R. J. (1982). *Japanese manufacturing techniques: Nine hidden lessons in simplicity.* New York: Free Press.

Schonberger, R. J. (1986). *World class manufacturing: The lessons of simplicity applied.* New York: Free Press.

Walton, M. (1986). *The Deming management method.* New York: Putnam.

2. The quotes in this figure were drawn from the following sources:

Albrecht, p. 93.

Bowles & Hammond, p. 97.

Collins & Porras, p. 228.

Hammer & Champy, p. 70.

Pascale & Athos, p. 55.

Peters & Waterman, p. 127.

Schonberger, p. 217.

Senge, p. 10.

Walton, p. 27.

Chapter 2

1. Blood, D. J., & Ferriss, S. J. (1993). Effects of background music on anxiety, satisfaction with communication, and productivity. *Psychological Reports, 72,* 171–177.

2. Lawrence, L. C., & Smith, P. C. (1955). Group decision and employee participation. *Journal of Applied Psychology, 39(5),* 334–337.

3. Mudrack, P. E. (1989). Group cohesiveness and productivity: A closer look. *Human Relations, 42(9),* 771–785.

Chapter 3

1. Buller, P. F. (1988, Summer). Long-term performance effects of goal setting and team building interventions in an underground silver mine. *Organization Development Journal,* 82–87.

2. The following are the hard-data studies from which this list was derived:
   Beckhard, R., & Lake, D. G. (1971). Short- and long-range effects of a team development effort. In H. Hornstein, B. Bunker, W. Burke, M. Grindes, & R. Lewicki (Eds.), *Social intervention: A behavioral science approach* (pp. 421–439). New York: Free Press.

   Bragg, J., & Andrews, I. (1973). Participative decision making: An experimental study in a hospital. *Journal of Applied Behavioral Science, 9(6),* 727–735.

   Buller, P. F. (1988, Summer). Long-term performance effects of goal setting and team building interventions in an underground silver mine. *Organization Development Journal,* 82–87.

   Buller, P. F., & Bell, C. H., Jr. (1986). Effects of team building and goal setting on productivity: A field experiment. *Academy of Management Journal, 29(2),* 305–328.

   Chaudron, D. G. (1992). Effects of team building on productivity: An interrupted time-series analysis. (Doctoral dissertation, United States International University). *Dissertation Abstracts International, 53(3),* 1635-B.

   Cohen, S. L., & Turney, J. R. (1978). Interviewing at the bottom: Organizational development with enlisted personnel in an Army work-setting. *Personnel Psychology, 31,* 715–730.

Doyle, S. X. (1990). Improving productivity and quality of working life: The U.S. experience. In H. C. Jain (Ed.), *Worker participation: Success and problems* (pp. 249–256). New York: Praeger.

Fiedler, F. E., Bell, C. H., Jr., Chemers, M. M., & Patrick, D. (1984). Increasing mine productivity and safety through management training and organization development: A comparative study. *Basic and Applied Social Psychology, 5(1)*, 1–18.

Hughes, R., Rosenbach, W., & Clover, W. (1983). Team development in an intact, ongoing work group: A quasi-field experiment. *Group and Organization Studies, 8(2)*, 161–186.

Krigsman, N., & O'Brien, R. M. (1987). Quality circles, feedback and reinforcement: An experimental comparison and behavioral analysis. In T. C. Mawhinney (Ed.), *Organizational behavior management and statistical process control* (pp. 67–82). New York: Haworth Press.

Lawrence, L. C., & Smith, P. C. (1955). Group decision and employee participation. *Journal of Applied Psychology, 39(5)*, 334–337.

Paul, C. F., & Gross, A. C. (1981). Increasing productivity and morale in a municipality: Effects of organization development. *Journal of Applied Behavioral Science, 17(1)*, 59–78.

Petty, M. M., Singleton, B., & Connell, D. W. (1992). An experimental evaluation of an organizational incentive plan in the electric utility industry. *Journal of Applied Psychology, 77(4)*, 427–436.

Pritchard, R. D., Jones, S. D., Roth, P. L., Stuebing, K. K., & Ekeberg, S. E. (1988). Effects of group feedback, goal setting, and incentives on organizational productivity. *Journal of Applied Psychology, 73(2)*, 337–358.

3. Nicholas, J. M. (1982). The comparative impact of organization development interventions on hard criteria measures. *Academy of Management Review, 7(4)*, 531–542.

4. Buchanan, P. C. (1969). Laboratory training and organization development. *Administrative Science Quarterly, 14(3)*, 466–480.

5. Mudrack, P. E. (1989). Group cohesiveness and productivity: A closer look. *Human Relations, 42(9)*, 771–785.

6. Smith, P. E. (1976). Management modeling training to improve morale and customer satisfaction. *Personnel Psychology, 29*, 351–359.

7. Delbecq, A. L., Van de Ven, A. H., & Gustafson, D. H. (1975). *Group techniques for program planning: A guide to nominal group and delphi processes.* Glenview, IL: Scott, Foresman.

8. Poole, M. S., & Roth, J. (1989). Decision development in small groups IV: A typology of group decision paths. *Human Communication Research, 15(3)*, 323–356.

9. Hirokawa, R. Y., & Rost, K. M. (1992). Effective group decision making in organizations: Field test of the vigilant interaction theory. *Management Communication Quarterly, 5(3)*, 267–288.

10. Cummings, T. G., & Molloy, E. S. (1977). *Improving productivity and the quality of work life.* New York: Praeger; Dobbs, M. F. (1978). *Organizational development interventions: A comparative study.* Doctoral dissertation, University of Southern California; Montgomery, R. N. (1989). *Group and program effectiveness in a quality circle program.* Doctoral dissertation, Fielding Institute.

11. Boss, R. W. (1983). Team building and the problem of regression: The personal management interview as an intervention. *Journal of Applied Behavioral Science, 19(1),* 67–83; Morton, R. B., & Wright, A. (1964). *A critical incidents evaluation of an organizational training laboratory.* Aerojet General Corporation (working paper); Pioneers in quality: Thirteen companies share their secrets to success in quality training. (1991, June), 11, 12. *Training and Development.*

Chapter 5

1. Katz, R., & Tushman, M. L. (1983). A longitudinal study of the effects of boundary spanning supervision on turnover and promotion in research and development. *Academy of Management Journal, 26(3),* 437–456.

2. Cheng, J. L. (1983). Interdependence and coordination in organizations: A role-system analysis. *Academy of Management Journal, 26(1),* 156–162.

Part Two, Part Opener

1. Burke, B., & Scalfano, D. (1990, January). Toward continuous improvement. *Training,* 75–79; Miles, C. A. (1986). *Differences in the impact of two management development programs.* Paper presented at Evaluation '86, American Evaluation Association, Kansas City, MO; Smith, P. E. (1976). Management modeling training to improve morale and customer satisfaction. *Personnel Psychology, 29,* 351–359.

Chapter 6

1. Eisenhardt, K. M. (1989). Making fast strategic decisions in high-velocity environments. *Academy of Management Journal, 32(3),* 543–576.

2. Basadur, M., Graen, G. B., & Green, S. G. (1982). Training in creative problem solving: Effects on ideation and problem finding and solving in an industrial research organization. *Organizational Behavior and Human Performance, 30,* 41–70; Basadur, M., Wakabayashi, M., & Takai, J. (1992). Training effects on the divergent thinking attitudes of Japanese managers. *International Journal of Intercultural Relations, 16(3),* 329–345; Gist, M. (1989). The influence of training method on self-efficacy and idea generation among managers. *Personnel Psychology, 42,* 787–805.

3. Basadur, Graen, & Green, 65; Fontenot, N. (1992). Effects of training in creativity and creative problem finding upon business people. *Journal of Social Psychology, 133(1),* 11–22.

4. Plunkett, D. J. (1990). The creative organization: An empirical investigation of the importance of participation in decision-making. *Journal of Creative Behavior, 24(2)*, 140–148.

5. Cohen, D., Whitmyre, J. W., & Funk, W. H. (1960). Effect of group cohesiveness and training upon creative thinking. *Journal of Applied Psychology, 44(5)*, 319–322.

6. Diehl, M., & Strobe, W. (1987). Productivity loss in brainstorming groups: Toward the solution of a riddle. *Journal of Personality and Social Psychology, 53(3)*, 497–509; Gist, M. (1989). The influence of training method on self-efficacy and idea generation among managers. *Personnel Psychology, 42*, 787–805.

7. Dunnette, M. D., Campbell, J., & Jaastad, K. (1963). The effect of group participation on brainstorming effectiveness for two industrial samples. *Journal of Applied Psychology, 47(1)*, 30–37.

8. Delbecq, A. L., Van de Ven, A. H., & Gustafson, D. H. (1975). *Group techniques for program planning: A guide to nominal group and delphi processes.* Glenview, IL: Scott, Foresman; Diehl & Strobe, 497.

9. De Bono, E. (1992). *Sur/Petition: Going beyond competition.* New York: HarperCollins, p. 37.

10. Nutt, P. C. (1976). Field experiments which compared the effectiveness of design methods. *Decision Sciences, 7*, 739–758.

11. Narramore, K. D. (1992). The use of focus groups for organizational research: The effects of moderated focus groups versus self-moderated focus groups on employee self-disclosure and idea generation. (Doctoral dissertation, California School of Professional Psychology—Los Angeles). *Dissertation Abstracts International, 53(7)*, 3822B. (University Microfilms No. AAC 9233736).

12. Diehl & Strobe.

13. Bouchard, T. J., Jr. (1972). Training, motivation, and personality as determinants of the effectiveness of brainstorming groups and individuals. *Journal of Applied Psychology, 56*, 324–331.

14. Diehl & Stroebe.

15. Creativity wears six hats: An interview with Edward De Bono. (1992). *Quality Digest, 12(5)*, 36–44.

16. Gist, 800.

Chapter 7

1. Pelz, D. C., & Andrews, F. M. (1966). *Scientists in organizations: Productive climates for research and development.* New York: John Wiley & Sons; Shapero, A. (1985). *Managing Professional People.* New York: Free Press.

2. Nichols, R. G., & Stevens, L. A. (1957). Listening to people. *Harvard Business Review, 35*, 85–92.

3. George, J. M., & Bettenhausen, K. (1990). Understanding prosocial behavior, sales performance, and turnover: A group-level analysis in a service context. *Journal of Applied Psychology, 75(6)*, 698–709.

4. Seabright, M. A., Levinthal, D. A., & Fichman, M. (1992). Role of individual attachments in the dissolution of interorganizational relationships. *Academy of Management Journal, 35(1)*, 122–160.

Chapter 8

1. Bragg, J., & Andrews, I. (1973). Participative decision making: An experimental study in a hospital. *Journal of Applied Behavioral Science, 9(6)*, 727–735.

2. Buller, P. F., & Bell, C. H., Jr. (1986). Effects of team building and goal setting on productivity: A field experiment. *Academy of Management Journal, 29(2)*, 305–328.

3. Frank., L. L., & Hackman, J. R. (1975). A failure of job enrichment: The case of the change that wasn't. *Journal of Applied Behavioral Science, 11*, 413–436.

4. Jackson, S. E. (1983). Participation in decision making as a strategy for reducing job-related strain. *Journal of Applied Psychology, 68(1)*, 3–19.

5. Krackhardt, D., McKenna, J., Porter, L. W., & Steers, R. M. (1981). Supervisory behavior and employee turnover: A field experiment. *Academy of Management Journal, 24(2)*, 249–259.

6. Poole, M. S. (1992). *Procedures for managing meetings: Social and technological innovation.* Paper prepared for 3M Meeting Management Institute Training and Development Research Center.

7. Lewin, K. (1950). Group decision and social change. In T. Newcomb & E. Hartley (Eds.), *Readings in Social Psychology* (pp. 459–473). New York: Holt.

8. White, S., Dittrich, J. E., & Lang, J. R. (1980). The effects of group decision making process and problem-situation complexity on implementation attempts. *Administrative Science Quarterly, 25*, 428–440.

9. Poole, 17–19.

10. Poole, M. S., & DeSanctis. G. (1990). Understanding the use of group decision support systems: The theory of adaptive structuration. In C. Steinfield & J. Fulk (Eds.), *Perspectives on Organizations and New Information Technology.* Newbury Park, CA: Sage.

11. Narramore, K. D. (1992). The use of focus groups for organizational research: The effects of moderated focus groups versus self-moderated focus groups on employee self-disclosure and idea generation. (Doctoral dissertation, California School of Professional Psychology—Los Angeles). *Dissertation Abstracts International, 53(7)*, 3822B. (University Microfilms No. AAC 9233736).

12. Cartwright, D., & Zander, A. (Eds.). (1968). *Group dynamics (3rd ed.).* New York: Harper & Row.

13. Rackham, N. (1978). *Models for explaining behavior.* England: Huthwaite Research Group.

Chapter 9

1. Maier, N. R. F. (1965). Acceptance and quality of solutions as related to leaders' attitudes toward disagreement in group problem solving. *Journal of Applied Behavioral Science, 1(4),* 373–386.

2. Rath & Strong, Inc. (1989, September). *Rath & Strong Climate Index.* Lexington, MA: Rath & Strong, Inc.

3. Burnaska, R. F. (1976). The effects of behavior modeling training upon managers' behaviors and employees' perceptions. *Personnel Psychology, 29(3),* 329–335; Goldstein, A., & Sorcher, M. (1974). *Changing supervisor behavior.* New York: Pergamon Press, pp. 70–82.

4. Anger, not impatience, linked to heart trouble. (1989, January 17). *Austin American-Statesman,* p. A1.

5. Barker, J., Tjosvold, D., & Andrews, R. I. (1988). Conflict approaches of effective and ineffective project managers: A field study in a matrix organization. *Journal of Management Studies, 25(2),* 167–178; Thamhain, H. J., & Wilemon, D. I. (1977). Leadership, conflict and program management effectiveness. *Sloan Management Review, 19(1),* 69–89.

6. Delbecq, A. L., Van de Ven, A. H., & Gustafson, D. H. (1975). *Group techniques for program planning: A guide to nominal group and delphi processes.* Glenview, IL: Scott, Foresman.

7. Baker, B. N., & Wilemon, D. L. (1977). Managing complex programs: A review of major research findings. *R&D Management, 8(1),* 23–28.

Chapter 10

1. Terkel, S. (1972). *Working: People talk about what they do all day and how they feel about it.* New York: Ballantine.

2. Frankl, V. E. (1959). *Man's search for meaning: An introduction to logotherapy.* New York: Washington Square Press.

3. Garfield, C. A. (1986). *Peak performers: The new heroes of American business.* New York: Morrow, p. 77.

4. Kotter, J. P., & Heskett, J. L. (1992). *Corporate culture and performance.* New York: Free Press.

5. Pearce, J. A., II, & David, F. (1987). Corporate mission statements: The bottom line. *Academy of Management Executive, 1(2),* 109–116.

6. Rastogi, R., & Pandey, J. (1987). The effect of organizational structure and personality characteristic on perceived need-satisfaction. *Indian Psychological Review, 32(2),* 13–18.

7. Holmes, T. H., & Rahe, R. H. (1967). The social readjustment rating scale. *Journal of Psychomatic Research, 11,* 213–218.

8. Maddi, S. R., & Kobasa, S. C. (1984). *The hardy executive: Health under stress.* Homewood, IL: Dow Jones-Irwin.

9. Katzenbach, J. R., & Smith, D. K. (1993). *The wisdom of teams: Creating the high-performance organization.* Boston: Harvard Business School Press.

Chapter 11

1. Bergen, S. A., & Pearson, A. W. (1983). Project management and innovation in the scientific instrument industry. *IEEE Transactions on Engineering Management, EM-30(4),* 194–199.

2. Gersick, C. J. G. (1988). Time and transition in work teams: Toward a new model of group development. *Academy of Management Journal, 31(1),* 9–41.

3. This claim is based on the following studies:

   Buller, P. F. (1988, Summer). Long term performance effects of goal setting and team building interventions in an underground silver mine. *Organization Development Journal,* 82–87.

   Petty, M. M., Singleton, B., & Connell, D. W. (1992). An experimental evaluation of an organizational incentive plan in the electric utility industry. *Journal of Applied Psychology, 77(4),* 427–436.

   Pritchard, R. D., Jones, S. D., Roth, P. L., Stuebing, K. K., & Ekeberg, S. E. (1988). Effects of group feedback, goal setting, and incentives on organizational productivity. *Journal of Applied Psychology, 73(2),* 337–358.

   Reimer, R. A. (1992). The effects of productivity, gain sharing, and employee involvement in the innovation process on job performance and organizational commitment. (Doctoral dissertation, California School of Professional Psychology–San Diego). *Dissertation Abstracts International, 53(2),* 1096-B.

4. Mento, A. J., Steel, R. P., & Karren, R. J. (1987). A meta-analytic study of the effects of goal setting on task performance: 1966–1984. *Organizational Behavior and Human Decision Processes, 39,* 52–83.

5. Latham, G. P., & Kinne, S. B., III. (1974). Improving job performance through training in goal setting. *Journal of Applied Psychology, 59(2),* 187–191.

6. Locke, Edwin, & Schweiger, D. M. (1979). Participation in decision-making: One more look. *Research in Organizational Behavior, 1,* 265–339.

7. Hardaker, M., & Ward, B. K. (1987, November/December). Getting things done: How to make a team work. *Harvard Business Review, 65,* 112–119.

8. Sherman, J. D. (1986). The relationship between factors in the work environment and turnover propensities among engineering and technical support personnel. *IEEE Transactions on Engineering Management, EM 33(2),* 72–78.

9. Locke, E. A., & Latham, G. *Goal setting: A motivational technique that works!* Englewood Cliffs, NJ: Prentice Hall, 1984.

10. Bassett, G. A. (1979). A study of the effects of task goal and schedule choice on work performance. *Organizational Behavior and Human Perfor-*

mance, 24(2), 202–227; Latham, G. P., Mitchell, T. R., & Dossett, D. L. (1978). Importance of participative goal setting and anticipated rewards on goal difficulty and job performance. *Journal of Applied Psychology, 63(2),* 163–171.

11. Locke & Latham.
12. Katzenbach, J. R., & Smith, D. K. (1993). *The wisdom of teams: Creating the high-performance organization.* Boston: Harvard Business School Press.
13. Koch, J. L. (1979). Effects of goal specificity and performance feedback to work groups on peer leadership, performance and attitudes. *Human Relations, 32(10),* 819–840.
14. Pritchard et al, 352.
15. Becker, L. J. (1978). Joint effect of feedback and goal setting on performance: A field study of residential energy conservation. *Journal of Applied Psychology, 63(4),* 428–433; Kim, J. S., & Hamner, W. C. (1976). Effect of performance feedback and goal setting on productivity and satisfaction in an organizational setting. *Journal of Applied Psychology, 61(1),* 48–57; Locke & Latham, Chapter 7.

Chapter 12

1. Sorcher, M. (Fall 1971). A behavior modification approach to supervisor training. *Professional Psychology, 2,* 401–402.
2. Sawyer, J. E. (1992). Goal and process clarity: Specification of multiple constructs of role ambiguity and a structural equation model of their antecedents and consequences. *Journal of Applied Psychology, 77(2),* 130–142.
3. Patterson, J., & Kim, P. (1991). *The day America told the truth.* New York: Prentice Hall.
4. Biddle, B. J., & Thomas, E. J. (Eds.). (1966). *Role theory: Concepts and research.* New York: John Wiley & Sons.
5. Bridges, W. (1994). The end of the job. *Fortune, Sept. 19, 1994, 130(6),* 62.
6. David, F. R., Randolph, W. A., & Pearce, J. A. (1989). Linking technology and structure to enhance group performance. *Journal of Applied Psychology, 74(2),* 233–241.
7. Pelz, D. C., & Andrews, F. M. (1966). *Scientists in organizations: Productive climates for research and development.* New York: John Wiley & Sons.
8. Cummings, T. G., & Molloy, E. S. (1977). *Improving productivity and the quality of work life.* New York: Praeger.
9. Schaubroeck, J., Daniel, C., Sime, W. E., & Ditman, D. (Spring 1993). A field experiment testing supervisory role clarification. *Personnel Psychology, 46(1),* 1–25.

10. Ondrack, D., & Evans, M. (1986). Job enrichment and job satisfaction in quality of working life and non-quality of working life work sites. *Human Relations, 39(9),* 871–889.

11. The Conference Board (1971). *Job design for motivation.* (Conference Board Report No. 515). New York: The Conference Board.

   Dulworth, M., Landen, D., & Usilaner, B. (1990). Employee involvement systems in U.S. corporations: Right objectives, wrong strategies. *National Productivity Review, 9(2),* 141–156.

   Guest, R. H. (1989). Team management under stress. *Across the Board, 26(5),* 30–35.

   Majchrzak, A. (1990). Effect of CAD on the jobs of drafters and engineers: A quantitative case study. *International Journal of Man-Machine Studies, 32,* 245–262.

   Walton, R. E. (1982). The Topeka work system: Optimistic visions, pessimistic hypotheses, and reality. In R. Zager & M. Rosow (Eds.), *The innovative organization* (pp. 260–287). New York: Pergamon Press.

12. Wall, T. D., Jackson, P. R., & Davis, K. (1992). Operator work design and robotics system performance: A serendipitous field study. *Journal of Applied Psychology, 77(3),* 353–362.

13. Ibid.; Cummings, T. G., & Srivastva, S. (1977). *Management of work: A sociotechnical systems approach.* San Diego, CA: University Associates; Frank & Hackman, 429.

14. Frank & Hackman, 434, 435.

15. Guest, 35; Walton.

16. Guest, 31, 32.

17. Ibid., 30–35.

18. Ford, R. N., & Gillette, M. B. (1969). A new approach to job motivation: Improving the work itself. In R. N. Ford, *Motivation through the work itself* (pp. 21–44). New York: American Management Association.

   Guest, 32.

   Nagamachi, M. (1973). *Job enrichment designs.* Tokyo: Daiamond-sha, p. 188.

   Wall, T. D., Jackson, P. R., & Davis, K. (1992). Operator work design and robotics system performance: A serendipitous field study. *Journal of Applied Psychology, 77(3),* 353–362.

19. Schaubroeck et al.

Chapter 13

1. Bayless, O. L. (1964). An alternative model for problem-solving discussion. *Journal of Applied Psychology, 48,* 175–179.

   Brilhart, J. K. (1966). An experimental comparison of three techniques for communicating a problem-solving pattern to members of a discussion group. *Speech Monographs, 33,* 168–177.

Gouran, D. S., Brown, C., & Henry, D. R. (March 1978). Behavioral correlates of perceptions of quality in decision-making discussions. *Communication Monographs, 45,* 51–63.

Parnes, S. J., & Meadow, A. (1960). Evaluation of persistence of effects produced by a creative problem-solving course. *Psychological Reports, 7,* 357–361.

Putnam, L. L. (1979). Preference for procedural order in task-oriented small groups. *Communication Monographs, 46,* 193–218.

2. Basadur, M., Graen, G. B., & Green, S. G. (1982). Training in creative problem solving: Effects on ideation and problem finding and solving in an industrial research organization. *Organizational Behavior and Human Performance, 30,* 41–70.

3. Fontenot, N. (1992). Effects of training in creativity and creative problem finding upon business people. *Journal of Social Psychology, 133(1),* 11–22.

4. Pelz, D. C. (1988). Creative tensions in the research and development climate. In R. Katz (Ed.), *Managing Professionals in Innovative Organizations: A Collection of Readings,* pp. 37–48. Cambridge, MA: Ballinger.

5. Hirokawa, R. Y. (1982). Consensus group decision-making, quality of decision, and group satisfaction: An attempt to sort "fact" from "fiction." *Central States Speech Journal, 33(2),* 407–415.

Hirokawa, R. Y. (1987). Why informed groups make faulty decisions: An investigation of possible interaction-based explanations. *Small Group Behavior, 18(1),* 3–29.

Hirokawa, R. Y., & Pace, R. (1983). A descriptive investigation of the possible communication-based reasons for effective and ineffective group decision making. *Communication Monographs, 50,* 363–379.

Hirokawa, R. Y., & Scheerhorn, D. R. (1986). Communication in faulty group decision-making. In R. Y. Hirokawa & M. S. Poole (Eds.), *Communication and group decision-making.* Beverly Hills: Sage.

6. Krigsman, N. (1983). Quality control circles and feedback: Effects on productivity and absenteeism. (Doctoral dissertation, Hofstra University). *Dissertation Abstracts International, 45(3),*1052–B; Krigsman, N., & O'Brien, R. M. (1987). Quality circles, feedback and reinforcement: An experimental comparison and behavioral analysis. In T. C. Mawhinney (Ed.), *Organizational Behavior Management and Statistical Process Control* (pp. 67–82). New York: Haworth Press.

7. Galagan, P. (1991). How Wallace changed its mind. *Training and Development Journal, 45,* 23–28.

8. Chaudron, D. G. (1992). Effects of team building on productivity: An interrupted time-series analysis. (Doctoral dissertation, United States International University). *Dissertation Abstracts International, 53(3),* 1635–B.

9. Burke, B., & Scalfano, D. (1990). Towards continuous improvement. *Training, 27*, 75–79.

10. Cohen, S. L., & Turney, J. R. (1978). Interviewing at the bottom: Organizational development with enlisted personnel in an Army work-setting. *Personnel Psychology, 31*, 715–730.

Chapter 14

1. Poole, M. S., & Roth, J. (1989). Decision development in small groups. IV: A typology of group decision paths. *Human Communication Research, 15(3)*, 323–356.

2. Warshauer, S. (1977). The effects of learning team-building process evaluation skills on decision-making ability. (Doctoral dissertation, University of Connecticut). *Dissertation Abstracts International, 38(8)*, 3964–B.

3. Bragg, J., & Andrews, I. (1973). Participative decision making: An experimental study in a hospital. *Journal of Applied Behavioral Science, 9(6)*, 727–735.

4. Lewin, K. (1950). Group decision and social change. In T. Newcomb & E. Hartley. (Eds.), *Readings in social psychology.* New York: Revised Edition.

5. Bragg & Andrews, 727–735.

6. Coch, L., & French, J. R. P., Jr. (1948). Overcoming resistance to change. *Human Resources, 1*, 512–532.

7. Poole & Roth; White, S., Dittrich, J. E., & Lang, J. R. (1980). The effects of group decision making process and problem-situation complexity on implementation attempts. *Administrative Science Quarterly, 25*, 428–440.

8. Vinokur, A., Burnstein, E., Sechrest, L., & Wortman, P. M. (1985). Group decision-making by experts: Field study of panels evaluating medical technologies. *Journal of Personality and Social Psychology, 49(1)*, 70–84.

9. Locke, E., & Schweiger, D. M. (1979). Participation in decision-making: One more look. In B. M. Staw & L. L. Cummings (Eds.), *Research in Organizational Behavior, Volume 1*, pp. 265–339. Greenwich, CT: Jai Press.

10. Vinokur et al.

11. Cotton, J. L., Vollrath, D. A., Froggatt, K. L., Lengnick-Hall, M. L., & Jennings, K. R. (1988). Employee participation: Diverse forms and different outcomes. *Academy of Management Review, 13(1)*, 8–22.

12. Neider, L. L. (1980). An experimental field investigation utilizing an expectancy theory view of participation. *Organizational Behavior and Human Performance, 26*, 425–442.

13. Macy, B. A., Peterson, M. F., & Norton, L. W. (1989). A test of participation theory in a work re-design field setting: Degree of participation and comparison site contrasts. *Human Relations, 42(12)*, 1095–1165.

14. Hirokawa, R. Y., & Rost, K. M. (1992). Effective group decision making in organizations: Field test of the vigilant interaction theory. *Management Communication Quarterly, 5(3)*, 267–288.

15. Harvey, J. B. (1990). *The Abilene paradox and other meditations on management.* San Diego, CA: Pfeiffer & Co.

16. Eisenhardt, K. M. (1989). Making fast strategic decisions in high-velocity environments. *Academy of Management Journal, 32(3),* 543–576.

17. Hirokawa, R. Y., & Pace, R. (1983). A descriptive investigation of the possible communication-based reasons for effective and ineffective group decision making. *Communication Monographs, 50,* 363–379.

18. Hirokawa & Rost, 283.

19. Janis, I. L., & Mann, L. (1977). *Decision making, a psychological analysis of conflict, choice, and commitment.* New York: Free Press.

20. Schwenk, C. R. (1990). Effects of devil's advocacy and dialectical inquiry on decision making: A meta-analysis. *Organizational Behavior and Human Decision Processes, 47,* 161–167.

21. Hirokawa, R. Y. (1987). Why informed groups make faulty decisions: An investigation of possible interaction-based explanations. *Small Group Behavior, 18(1),* 3–29; Hirokawa & Pace, 17, 26.

22. J. Orsburn (personal communication, May 1991).

23. Eisenhardt.

24. Neider, 439.

25. Sorcher, M. (1969). Motivation on the assembly line. *Personnel Administration, 32,* 40–48.

Chapter 15

1. Von Mises, L. *Bureaucracy.* (1969). New Rochelle, NY: Arlington House, 67, 68.

2. Senia, A. (1986, May). Hewlett-Packard's team approach beats back the competition. *Production, 98,* 89–91.

3. Buller, P. F., & Bell, C. H., Jr. (1986). Effects of team building and goal setting on productivity: A field experiment. *Academy of Management Journal, 29(2),* 305–328; Reimer, R. A. (1992). The effects of productivity gain sharing and employee involvement in the innovation process on job performance and organizational commitment. (Doctoral dissertation, California School of Professional Psychology–San Diego). *Dissertation Abstracts International, 53(2),* 1096–B.

4. Walton, M. (1986). *The Deming management method.* New York: Putnam, 26.

5. Rath & Strong, Inc. (1989, September). *Rath & Strong Climate Index.* Lexington, MA: Rath & Strong, Inc.

Chapter 16

1. Peters, T. J., & Waterman, R. H., Jr. (1982). *In search of excellence: Lessons from America's best-run companies.* New York: Harper & Row, 261.

2. Piaget, J. (1967). *Six psychological studies.* New York: Random House.

3. Deal, T. E., & Kennedy, A. A. (1982). *Corporate cultures: The rites and rituals of corporate life.* Reading, MA: Addison-Wesley.
4. Peters, 13–15.
5. Deal & Kennedy, 7.

Chapter 17

1. Ulrich, D., & Lake, D. (1990). *Organizational capability: Competing from the inside out.* New York: John Wiley & Sons.
2. Ibid., p. 40.

Chapter 18

1. Dulworth, M., Landen, D., & Usilaner, B. (1990). Employee involvement systems in U.S. corporations: Right objectives, wrong strategies. *National Productivity Review, 9(2),* 141–156.
2. Townsend, P. (1986). *Commit to quality.* New York: John Wiley & Sons.
3. Ibid.
4. Gunatilake, S. (1984). An exploratory study of quality circles and team building in two hospital settings. (Doctoral dissertation, University of Hawaii). *Dissertation Abstracts International, 45(6),* 1723B; Mohrman, S. A., & Novelli, L., Jr. (1985). Beyond testimonials: learning from a quality circles programme. *Journal of Occupational Behaviour, 6,* 93–110.
5. Steel, R. P., Jennings, K. R., & Lindsey, J. T. (1990). Quality circle problem solving and common cents: Evaluation study findings from a United States federal mint. *Journal of Applied Behavioral Science, 26(3),* 365–381.
6. De Sorbe, B. M. (1992). An exploration of the relationship among quality circle participation, job satisfaction, and organizational climate. (Doctoral dissertation, New York University). *Dissertation Abstracts International, 53(8),* 2616A. (University Microfilms No. AAC 9237747).
7. Montgomery, R. N. (1989). Group and program effectiveness in a quality circle program. Doctoral dissertation, Fielding Institute, 504.
8. Tang, T. L., Tollison, P. S., & Whiteside, H. D. (1987). The effect of quality circle initiation on motivation to attend quality circle meetings and on task performance. *Personnel Psychology, 40(4),* 799–814.
9. Bragg, J., & Andrews, I. (1973). Participative decision making: An experimental study in a hospital. *Journal of Applied Behavioral Science, 9(6),* 727–735.
10. French, J. R. P., Jr., Israel, J., & Ås, D. (1960). An experiment on participation in a Norwegian factory. *Human Relations, 13(1),* 3–19.
11. Sorcher, M. (1969). Motivation on the assembly line. *Personnel Administration, 32,* 40–48.

12. Morse, N., & Reimer, E. (1956). The experimental change of a major organizational variable. *Journal of Abnormal and Social Psychology, 52,* 120–129.

13. Kay, E., Meyer, H. H., & French, J. R. P., Jr. (1965). Effects of threat in a performance appraisal interview. *Journal of Applied Psychology, 49(5),* 311–317; Locke, E. A., Cartledge, N., & Koeppel, J. (1968). Motivational effects of knowledge of results: A goal-setting phenomenon? *Psychological Bulletin, 70(6),* 474–485.

14. Coch, L., & French, J. R. P., Jr. (1948). Overcoming resistance to change. *Human Resources, 1,* 512–532.

15. French et al., 18.

16. Macy, B. A., Peterson, M. F., & Norton, L. W. (1989). A test of participation theory in a work re-design field setting: Degree of participation and comparison site contrasts. *Human Relations, 42(12),* 1095–1165.

17. Negandhi, A. R. (1973). *Modern organizational theory: Contextual, environmental, and socio-cultural variables.* Kent, OH: Kent State University Press.

18. Rosen, B., & Jerdee, T. H. (1978). Effects of decision permanence on managerial willingness to use participation. *Academy of Management Journal, 21,* 722–725.

19. Ashley, S. (1992). U.S. quality improves but Japan still leads. (Study by Ernst & Young and American Quality Foundation). *Mechanical Engineering-CIME, 114(12),* 24.

20. Cummings, T. G., & Srivastva, S. (1977). *Management of work: A sociotechnical systems approach.* San Diego, CA: University Associates.

    Frank., L. L., & Hackman, J. R. (1975). A failure of job enrichment: The case of the change that wasn't. *Journal of Applied Behavioral Science, 11,* 413–436.

    Goodman, P. S. (1979). *Assessing organizational change: The Rushton quality of work experiment.* New York: Wiley-Inter-Science.

    Manz, C. C., & Sims, H. P., Jr. (1987). Leading workers to lead themselves: The external leadership of self-managing work teams. *Administrative Science Quarterly, 32,* 106–128.

    Pasmore, W. A., & King, D. C. (1978). Understanding organizational change: A comparative study of multifaceted interventions. *Journal of Applied Behavioral Science, 14(4),* 455–468.

    Stumpf, S. A. (1977). Using integrators to manage conflict in a research organization. *Journal of Applied Behavior Science, 13(4),* 507–517.

    Trist, E. L., Susman, G. I., & Brown, G. R. (1977). An experiment in autonomous working at an American underground coal mine. *Human Relations, 30(3),* 201–236.

    Wall, T. D., Kemp, N. J., Jackson, P. R., & Clegg, C. W. (1986). Outcomes of autonomous workgroups: A long-term field experiment. *Academy of Management Journal, 29(2),* 280–304.

Chapter 19

1. Stumpf, S. A. (1977). Using integrators to manage conflict in a research organization. *Journal of Applied Behavior Science, 13(4)*, 507–517.

Chapter 20

1. McCurdy, H. G., & Lambert, W. E. (1952). The efficiency of small human groups in the solution of problems requiring genuine cooperation. *Journal of Personality, 20*, 478–494.

HOW TO GET MORE INFORMATION ABOUT STRUCTURED TEAMWORK®

Performance Resources, Inc. (PRI) is a teamwork training and consulting firm located in Austin, Texas. Its resource base includes highly experienced trainers and consultants who provide services that support organizations and teams that want to improve performance. PRI trainers and consultants are experts in Structured Teamwork and organizational breakthrough in the following types of enterprises:

- Semiconductor
- Chemical
- Aerospace
- Electronics and other high technology
- Federal, state, and local governments
- Heavy industry

The following courses are available to assist organizations in achieving breakthrough results:

1. Empowerment Overview Workshop.
2. Sponsoring High-Performing Teams.
3. Line Team Structured Teamwork Training.
4. Knowledge Team Structured Teamwork Training.
5. Coaching to Empowerment.
6. Structured Teamwork Refresher Course.

Performance Resources' consultants provide the following consulting services:

1. Organizational vision, mission, and strategic goal development.
2. Organizational teamwork readiness surveys.
3. Organizationwide assessment of current teamwork.
4. Development of teamwork road maps that are customized to your organization.
5. Cultural change activities to create a breakthrough organization.

PRI has consultants located in New York state, San Francisco, Seattle, Washington, D.C., and our headquarters in Austin, Texas. You may reach Performance Resources, Inc., at 8539 Thunderbird Road; Austin, Texas 78736; phone: (512) 288-0416; fax: (512) 288-0433.

INDEX

Other books of interest to you from Irwin Professional Publishing . . .

REWARDING AND RECOGNIZING EMPLOYEES
Ideas for Individuals, Teams, and Managers
Joan P. Klubnik

Shows everyone in the organization how to initiate and maintain a dynamic reward/recognition program that will go a long way toward making employees feel genuinely valued and appreciated. Develops team recognition, evaluates current recognition systems, and helps establish a model program to make recognition a key part of the leadership strategy.
0-7863-0297-6   150 pages

RX FOR BUSINESS
A Troubleshooting Guide for Building a High-Performance Organization
Mark Graham Brown, Darcy E. Hitchcock, Marsha L. Willard

Designed to be as simple to use as a quick-care home health reference, this book helps managers diagnose specific problems as they occur and offers helpful tips for possible solutions.
0-7863-0477-4   150 pages

REDEFINING CORPORATE SOUL
Linking Purpose & People
Allan Cox with Julie Liesse

Opens new pathways that help the reader rediscover corporate purpose, instill team values, and maximize opportunities from information technology—all to create organizational advantage.
0-7863-0555-X   160 pages